Spring Boot and Angular

Hands-on full stack web development with Java, Spring, and Angular

Devlin Basilan Duldulao

Seiji Ralph Villafranca

BIRMINGHAM—MUMBAI

Spring Boot and Angular

Group Product Manager: Pavan Ramchandani
Publishing Product Manager: Aaron Tanna
Senior Editor: Hayden Edwards
Content Development Editor: Abhishek Jadhav
Technical Editor: Saurabh Kadave
Copy Editor: Safis Editing
Project Coordinator: Sonam Pandey
Proofreader: Safis Editing
Indexer: Pratik Shirodkar
Production Designer: Aparna Bhagat
Marketing Coordinator: Anamika Singh

First published: December 2022

Production reference: 1021222

Published by Packt Publishing Ltd.
Livery Place
35 Livery Street
Birmingham
B3 2PB, UK.

ISBN 978-1-80324-321-4

www.packt.com

To my father Alberto Duldulao, I miss you, tay (dad). On the day I lost you, I lost a father,
a friend, and an idol who I looked up to. You will always be in my heart, tay. I miss you every day.
Thanks again for your love, support, and inspiration.

– Devlin Duldulao (Utoy)

To my mother Arceli Villafranca, who gave everything to me and who is the reason why I'm here.
To my sister Sheila Villafranca, who always supports me, and to my partner Shey Cadavero,
who gives me strength and inspiration every day.

– Seiji Villafranca

Contributors

About the authors

Devlin Basilan Duldulao is a full-stack engineer with over 8 years of web, mobile, and cloud development experience. He has been a recipient of Microsoft's **Most Valuable Professional (MVP)** award since 2018 and earned the title of Auth0 Ambassador for his passion for sharing best practices in application securities. Devlin has passed some prestigious exams in software and cloud development such as the MSCD, Azure Associate Developer, AWS Associate Developer, and Terraform Associate certifications.

Perhaps it was serendipity that made him venture into the coding world after a short stint in the medical field. However, once he stepped into it, he fell for it hook, line, and sinker – but in the right way, he claims. Devlin often finds himself engrossed in solving coding problems and developing apps, even to the detriment of his once-active social life.

One of the things that motivates him is ensuring the long-term quality of his code, including looking into ways to transform legacy code into more maintainable and scalable applications. Devlin enjoys tackling challenging projects or applications for high-level clients and customers, as he currently does at his company based in Norway. He also provides training and consultation for international corporations.

One of his other interests is giving talks at IT conferences worldwide and meeting unique people in the industry. Devlin is currently based in Oslo, Norway with his wife. He is a senior software engineer at Inmeta Consulting, a subsidiary of the Crayon group of companies.

Seiji Ralph Villafranca graduated cum laude with a BSc in computer science from the University of Santo Tomas in the Philippines. He has 6 years of experience in web and mobile development and has also earned the title of Auth0 Ambassador for his passion for application security. He holds several certifications in Angular development from beginner to expert level.

Seiji is also one of the community leaders of Angular Philippines, which is the largest Angular group in the Philippines; the community has led him to speak at different meetups of tech communities, workshops, and even local and international conferences. He is enthusiastic about sharing knowledge of coding and organizing events and meetups for the community, as well as writing content for students and professionals. He also has been a mentor at several hackathons, as he loves the startup community.

Seiji loves to develop new projects that are on the web or mobile and he is currently a senior software engineer at a company based in Malaysia. He is not only a coder but also a mentor, teacher, and trainer for students, professionals, and companies.

About the reviewer

Rajeshkumar Muthaiah works as Technical Lead in an international bank. He has strong experience in designing and developing high scale applications using a wide range of technologies since 2010. He works on various technologies including Java, Dart, Flutter, Angular, React, Spring, Hibernate, and Sass. Rajeshkumar has worked on various industries including Aviation, Banking, and Finance. He is very passionate about learning new technologies.

When not working on code, he likes reading books, as well as solving puzzles and traveling. He is very fond of cubes such as 5x5, megaminx, pyraminx, and so on., Currently, he lives with his wife Ranju in Singapore.

Table of Contents

Part 2: Backend Development

3

Moving into Spring Boot 35

4

Setting Up the Database and Spring Data JPA 59

5

Building APIs with Spring   79

6

Documenting APIs with the OpenAPI Specification   109

7

Adding Spring Boot Security with JWT   125

8

Logging Events in Spring Boot   167

9

Writing Tests in Spring Boot   181

Part 3: Frontend Development

10

Setting Up Our Angular Project and Architecture 209

11

Building Reactive Forms 249

12

Managing States with NgRx   275

13

Saving, Deleting, and Updating with NgRx   301

14

Adding Authentication in Angular   319

15

Writing Tests in Angular   349

Part 4: Deployment

16

Packaging Backend and Frontend with Maven   373

17

Deploying Spring Boot and the Angular App   383

Preface

Spring Boot provides JavaScript users with a platform to get an application up and running with just a few lines of code. At the same time, Angular is a component-based framework that makes building a web application's frontend easy. This book explains how Spring Boot and Angular work together to help you create full-stack applications quickly and effectively.

In this book, you will begin by exploring why Spring Boot and Angular are in-demand frameworks, before being guided by expert solutions and best practices to build your own web application. Regarding the backend, you will see how Spring Boot allows you to build applications efficiently by letting the Spring Framework and Spring Boot extension do the heavy lifting, while using Spring Data JPA and Postgres dependencies in your project to save or persist data in a database. With the frontend, you will use Angular to construct a project architecture, build Reactive forms, and add authentication to avoid malicious users stealing data from the application.

Finally, you will see how to test services with Mockito, deploy applications using continuous integration and continuous deployment, and integrate Spring Boot and Angular to create a single package so that, by the end of the book, you will be able to build your very own full-stack web application.

Who this book is for

The book is for busy Java web developers and TypeScript developers with little experience of developing Angular and Spring Boot apps who want to learn about the best practices for building full-stack web apps.

What this book covers

Chapter 1, *Spring Boot and Angular – The Big Picture*, serves as a short recap regarding Spring Boot and Angular's current state to give you a glimpse of what lies ahead in the web development of Java Spring Boot and Angular. You will also see how stable and reliable Vue.js is as an app and the team behind writing and maintaining the Vue.js framework.

Chapter 2, *Setting Up the Development Environment*, teaches you how to set up your computer's development environment to build backend and frontend web applications. We will turn to different IDEs and text editors to write the code and make sure everything has been set up before we proceed in the app development.

Chapter 3, Moving into Spring Boot, uncovers the inner workings of Spring Boot and how to start a project using Spring Initializr. This chapter will also teach you about the concept of dependency injection and the IoC container. This chapter will also tackle how Beans and annotations work.

Chapter 4, Setting Up the Database and Spring Data JPA, helps you to connect the Java Spring Boot to a database. This chapter will describe Spring Data JPA and how to add Spring Data JPA and Postgres dependencies in the project. This chapter will also show how to use a config file to connect the Java Spring Boot to a Postgres database instance.

Chapter 5, Building APIs with Spring, shows you how to start and run a Java Spring Boot application. This chapter will also show how to add models for the application and use them when writing routers and controllers. Afterward, this chapter will explain how to use Redis for caching to improve the performance of an application.

Chapter 6, Documenting APIs with OpenAPI Specification, covers the documentation part of the APIs of the Java Spring Boot application. This chapter will also show you how to include the Swagger UI in the application to provide graphical interfaces in the documentation of APIs.

Chapter 7, Adding Spring Boot Security with JWT, details what CORS is and how to add a CORS policy in the Spring Boot application. This chapter describes Spring security, authentication, and authorization. This chapter will also demonstrate how JSON web tokens work and what **Identity as a Service (IaaS)** is.

Chapter 8, Logging Events in Spring Boot, explains what logging is and what the popular packages to implement logging are. This chapter will also teach you where to save logs and what to do with logs.

Chapter 9, Writing Tests in Spring Boot, is all about writing tests for a Java Spring Boot application. This chapter describes JUnit and AssertJ. This chapter will also teach you how to write tests, how to test a repository, and how to test a service using Mockito.

Chapter 10, Setting Up Our Angular Project and Architecture, focuses on how to organize features and modules, how to structure components, and how to add Angular Material.

Chapter 11, Building Reactive Forms, demonstrates how to build Reactive forms, basic form control, and grouping form controls. This chapter will also explain how to use FormBuilder and validate form input.

Chapter 12, Managing States with NgRx, covers state management in complex applications. This chapter will also introduce NgRx and how to set it up and use it in an Angular application.

Chapter 13, Saving, Deleting, and Updating with NgRx, describes how to remove an item using NgRx, how to add an item using NgRx, and how to update an item using NgRx.

Chapter 14, Adding Authentication in Angular, explores how to add user login and logout, retrieve user profile information, protect application routes, and call an API with protected endpoints.

Chapter 15, Writing Tests in Angular, illustrates how to write basic Cypress tests and how to mock HTTP requests for testing.

Chapter 16, Packaging Backend and Frontend with Maven, exemplifies how to utilize the Maven frontend plugin for Angular and Spring Boot to integrate them into one package.

Chapter 17, Deploying Spring Boot and the Angular App, describes CI/CD and GitHub Actions. This chapter will also show you how to create a CI workflow or pipeline for a Spring Boot and Angular application.

To get the most out of this book

You should ensure that you have a basic understanding of HTML, CSS, JavaScript, TypeScript, Java, and REST API. You don't need intermediate or advanced knowledge of the requirements mentioned.

Software/hardware covered in the book	Operating system requirements
Node.js (LTS version)	Windows, macOS, or Linux
Angular	Windows, macOS, or Linux
Java 17	Windows, macOS, or Linux
Visual Studio Code	Windows, macOS, or Linux
IntelliJ IDEA	Windows, macOS, or Linux
Google Chrome	Windows, macOS, or Linux

Don't lose hope if you are facing problems when installing runtimes, SDKs, or any software tools in general when developing an application. Errors are common, but searching for error messages on Google greatly helps developers when troubleshooting certain problems.

If you are using the digital version of this book, we advise you to type the code yourself or access the code from the book's GitHub repository (a link is available in the next section). Doing so will help you avoid any potential errors related to the copying and pasting of code.

Play around with Angular on `stackblitz.com` or `codesandbox.io` to see the look and feel of Angular without installing anything on your computer.

Download the example code files

You can download the example code files for this book from GitHub at `https://github.com/PacktPublishing/Spring-Boot-and-Angular`. If there's an update to the code, it will be updated in the GitHub repository.

We also have other code bundles from our rich catalog of books and videos available at `https://github.com/PacktPublishing/`. Check them out!

Download the color images

We also provide a PDF file that has color images of the screenshots and diagrams used in this book. You can download it here: `https://packt.link/pIe6D`.

Conventions used

There are a number of text conventions used throughout this book.

`Code in text`: Indicates code words in text, database table names, folder names, filenames, file extensions, pathnames, dummy URLs, user input, and Twitter handles. Here is an example: "Spring Boot only requires `spring-boot-starter-web`, which is a Spring Starter, for our application to run."

A block of code is set as follows:

```
@Configuration
public class AppConfig
{
    @Bean
    public Student student() {
        return new Student(grades());
     }
    @Bean
    public Grades grades() {
        return new Grades();
     }
}
```

When we wish to draw your attention to a particular part of a code block, the relevant lines or items are set in bold:

```
dependencies {
    implementation 'org.springframework.boot:spring-boot-
    starter-data-jpa'
    runtimeOnly 'com.h2database:h2'
    runtimeOnly 'org.postgresql:postgresql'
}
```

Any command-line input or output is written as follows:

```
rpm -ivh jdk-17.interim.update.patch_linux-x64_bin.rpm
```

Bold: Indicates a new term, an important word, or words that you see onscreen. For instance, words in menus or dialog boxes appear in **bold**. Here is an example: "Select **Spring Initializr** and this will open a form with the same web interface."

> **Tips or important notes**
> Appear like this.

Get in touch

Feedback from our readers is always welcome.

General feedback: If you have questions about any aspect of this book, email us at customercare@ packtpub.com and mention the book title in the subject of your message.

Errata: Although we have taken every care to ensure the accuracy of our content, mistakes do happen. If you have found a mistake in this book, we would be grateful if you would report this to us. Please visit www.packtpub.com/support/errata and fill in the form.

Piracy: If you come across any illegal copies of our works in any form on the internet, we would be grateful if you would provide us with the location address or website name. Please contact us at copyright@packt.com with a link to the material.

If you are interested in becoming an author: If there is a topic that you have expertise in and you are interested in either writing or contributing to a book, please visit authors.packtpub.com.

Share Your Thoughts

Once you've read *Spring Boot and Angular*, we'd love to hear your thoughts! Scan the QR code below to go straight to the Amazon review page for this book and share your feedback.

https://www.amazon.in/review/create-review/?asin=180324321X

Your review is important to us and the tech community and will help us make sure we're delivering excellent quality content.

Download a free PDF copy of this book

Thanks for purchasing this book!

Do you like to read on the go but are unable to carry your print books everywhere?

Is your eBook purchase not compatible with the device of your choice?

Don't worry, now with every Packt book you get a DRM-free PDF version of that book at no cost.

Read anywhere, any place, on any device. Search, copy, and paste code from your favorite technical books directly into your application.

The perks don't stop there, you can get exclusive access to discounts, newsletters, and great free content in your inbox daily

Follow these simple steps to get the benefits:

1. Scan the QR code or visit the link below

https://packt.link/free-ebook/9781803243214

2. Submit your proof of purchase

3. That's it! We'll send your free PDF and other benefits to your email directly

Part 1: Overview of Spring Boot and Angular Development

This part contains a real-world scenario on how to start a web application project. The following chapters are covered in this part:

- *Chapter 1, Spring Boot and Angular – The Big Picture*
- *Chapter 2, Setting Up the Development Environment*

1

Spring Boot and Angular – The Big Picture

First of all, we would like to thank you for getting a copy of this book, which was created for developers to learn how to build a full-stack web application using the standards that are being used in the development industry. This book is tailored based on the applications we have developed from our training and workshops. So, let's begin our adventure.

This chapter will serve as a short recap regarding the Java Spring Boot and Angular foundations to give you an idea of what lies ahead in terms of conducting web development for them. You will also learn how large the community is and that the support that's available for Angular makes it reliable for developing applications.

In this chapter, we will cover the following topics:

- Introducing Spring Boot
- The advantages of using Spring Boot
- What's new in Java 17
- Introducing Angular
- The advantages of using Angular

Technical requirements

The GitHub repository for the application we will be building can be found at `https://github.com/PacktPublishing/Spring-Boot-and-Angular`.

Every chapter has a directory where the completed portion of the project is located.

> **Note**
>
> No directories will be available for *Chapter 1, Spring Boot and Angular – The Big Picture*, to *Chapter 4, Setting Up the Database and Spring Data JPA* because most of the topics we will be covering will consist of theories and some sample code. The actual project will begin in *Chapter 5, Building APIs with Spring*.

Introducing Spring Boot

Spring Boot is an open source micro framework from Pivotal. It is an enterprise-level framework for developers to create standalone applications on **Java Virtual Machines (JVMs)**. Its primary focus is to shorten your code so that it's easier for you to run your application.

The framework extends the Spring Framework, which provides you with a more opinionated way of configuring your applications. In addition, it comes with built-in autoconfiguration capabilities that configure both the Spring Framework and third-party packages based on your settings. Spring Boot uses this knowledge to avoid code errors at configuration time as it reduces boilerplate code when you're setting up our application.

Now, let's discuss the main advantages of using Spring Boot.

The advantages of using Spring Boot

The following are the four main advantages of using Spring Boot to develop applications:

- **Autoconfiguration**: When you're configuring your Spring Boot application, it downloads all the dependencies that will be needed to run your application. It will also configure your Spring Framework with the relevant third-party packages, depending on the settings you have applied. Thus, Spring Boot avoids boilerplate code and configuration errors, and you can directly start developing your Spring application.

- **Opinionated approach**: Spring Boot uses a narrow approach to installing dependencies based on your application needs. It will install all the required packages of your application and removes the idea of configuring it manually.

- **Spring starters**: You can choose a list of starter dependencies to define your application's expected needs during the initialization process. One example of a Spring Starter is Spring Web, which allows you to initialize a Spring-based web application without configuring the dependencies that are required to run the application. Instead, it will automatically install the Apache Tomcat Web Server and Spring Security for authentication features.

- **Create standalone applications**: Spring Boot can run standalone applications that have no dependencies on external web servers. For example, we can embed servers such as Tomcat and run the application.

Differences between Spring and Spring Boot

So, what is the difference between Spring and Spring Boot? And do you need to learn about the Spring Framework before working with Spring Boot? Let's start with the first question.

The following table shows the difference between the two frameworks:

spring	spring boot
The developers configure the dependencies for the project.	Using Spring Starters, Spring Boot will configure all the dependencies that will be needed to run the application.
Spring is a **Java EE framework** for building applications.	Spring Boot is commonly used to build **REST APIs**.
Spring simplifies the development of Java EE applications since modules such as Spring JDBC, Spring MVC, and Spring Security are already provided.	Spring Boot provides the configuration for the dependencies, reducing the boilerplate code for the layouts of modules. This makes it easier to run the application.
Dependency injection (**DI**) and **inversion of control** (**IOC**) are the main features of Spring for building applications.	**Spring Boot Actuator** is a feature that exposes operational information about your apps, such as metrics and traffic.

We can identify that Spring Boot is built on top of Spring and that the main difference is that Spring Boot automatically configures the dependencies we need to run a Spring application. So, to answer the question about needing to learn about the Spring Framework before working with Spring Boot, the answer is **no** – Spring Boot is just an extension of Spring, which makes configuring it faster because of its opinionated approach.

Now, let's look at the dependencies we need in Spring and Spring Boot to configure a web application.

Dependency examples for Spring and Spring Boot

In Spring, the minimum dependencies that we need for our application to run are **Spring Web** and **Spring Web MVC**:

```
<dependency>
    <groupId>org.springframework</groupId>
    <artifactId>spring-web</artifactId>
    <version>5.3.5</version>
```

```
</dependency>
<dependency>
    <groupId>org.springframework</groupId>
    <artifactId>spring-webmvc</artifactId>
<version>5.3.5</version>
</dependency>
```

Spring Boot only requires `spring-boot-starter-web`, which is a Spring Starter for our application to run. The necessary dependencies are added automatically at build time as the starter will be responsible for the configuration:

```
<dependency>
<groupId>org.springframework.boot</groupId>
<artifactId>spring-boot-starter-web</artifactId>
<version>2.4.4</version>
</dependency>
```

Another thing to consider in Spring is that we need to define some configurations, such as dispatcher servlets and mappings, for our application to run on the server:

```
public class SpringInitializer implements
WebApplicationInitializer {
@Override
public void onStartup(ServletContext container) {
AnnotationConfigWebApplicationContext context =
    new AnnotationConfigWebApplicationContext();
context.setConfigLocation("com.springexample");
container.
addListener(new          ContextLoaderListener(context));
  ServletRegistration.Dynamic dispatcher =
    container.  addServlet("dispatcher",
        new  DispatcherServlet(context));
  dispatcher.setLoadOnStartup(1);
  dispatcher.addMapping("/");
    }
}
```

After initializing the dispatcher servlets, we also need to use `@EnableWebMvc` and have a `Configuration` class with a `@Configuration` annotation where we will instantiate a view resolver for the applications.

A new `InternalResourceViewResolver()` instance will be created in the configuration class. This will be a bean for Spring. Here, all the files that are under the `/WEB-INF/view` path with a `.jsp` file extension will be resolved:

```
@EnableWebMvc
@Configuration
public class SpringWebConfig implements WebMvcConfigurer {
    @Bean
    public ViewResolver viewResolver() {
        InternalResourceViewResolver bean =
            new  InternalResourceViewResolver();
    bean.setViewClass(JstlView.class);
    bean.setPrefix("/WEB-INF/view/");
    bean.setSuffix(".jsp");
    return bean;
    }
}
```

In Spring Boot, all these configurations will be omitted because this code is already included in the Spring Starters. We only need to define some properties for our application to run using the web starter:

```
spring.mvc.view.prefix=/WEB-INF/jsp/
spring.mvc.view.suffix=.jsp
```

After defining these properties, our application will run since all the necessary configurations, such as the **Web Initializer** and **MVC Configuration**, have been included.

With that, we have discussed the advantages of Spring Boot and, at the same time, the main differences between Spring Boot and the Spring Framework and how it reduces boilerplate code at configuration time.

As you may already know, the primary language of Spring is Java, and Java 17 has now been released. In the next section, we'll learn about the new features in Java 17.

What's new in Java 17?

We have decided to discuss Java 17 in this book as this is the next **long-term support** (**LTS**) version of Java, meaning that this version will be maintained for a more extended period. It was released on September 14, 2021, and includes several new security and development features.

Let's look at some of the new features that have been included, as well as some modifications that have been applied to Java 17.

Sealed classes

Sealed classes were in the second preview stage in Java 16. Let's say, for example, that we have a class that we have created in our code. We can assume that this class can be extended with any subclasses in our application. Thus, by making our classes sealed, we can ensure that our class can't be extended by subclasses. If we want to allow some subclasses to extend our class, we can use the `permits` keyword to identify the specific classes we want to grant permission to, as shown in the following example:

```
public sealed class Animal permits Cat, Dog, Horse
```

The foreign function and memory API

A new API was introduced for accessing and using code outside the Java runtime, which it did by applying foreign functions (code outside the JVM) and safely accessing foreign memory (memory not handled by the JVM). The API allows a Java application to call native libraries without the **Java Native Interface (JNI)**.

The API aims to replace the JNI with a pure Java development model and better performance while accessing off-heap data and omitting insecure operations.

Foreign memory

One common problem in Java today is accessing off-heap data. **Off-heap data** is data that's stored in memory outside the Java runtime. We can say that this is a third-party library. Accessing this data is very critical to performance in that Java garbage collectors work only on on-heap data, which lets them avoid the unpredictability of garbage collections. The following APIs are used to handle off-heap data:

- **The ByteBuffer API**: This API allows you to create direct ByteBuffers in off-heap data so that data can be managed outside the Java runtime. However, the major drawback of ByteBuffer is that its maximum size is 2 GB and that it is not deallocated promptly, causing the application's runtime performance to slow down.

- **The Sun.misc.Unsafe API**: The Unsafe API exposes access operations that work on off-heap data. This API makes this process efficient since the **Just-in-Time (JIT)** compiler optimizes access operations. However, using the Unsafe API is discouraged as we are allowing access to any memory location.

- **The Foreign Function and Memory API**: This API solves the dilemma of accessing the memory's location and sacrificing runtime performance as it provides classes and interfaces where applications can do the following:

  - Allocate Foreign Memory

  - Manipulate and access foreign memory

  - Call Foreign Functions

Pattern matching with switch statements

Pattern matching is the idea of testing patterns and complicated expressions in switch statements. This new feature allows for more extensible and flexible usage of switch statements to accept complex expressions.

The Applet API

The Applet API is rarely used in Java as all browsers have removed support for Java browser plugins.

The experimental AOT and JIT compilers

The experimental Java-based **ahead-of-time** (**AOT**) and **JIT** compilers have been removed since their features have limited usage.

These are just some of the changes that have been applied to Java 17. Now, let's learn about Angular, one of the top JavaScript frameworks today, and the advantages of using the Angular framework to develop your frontend.

Introducing Angular

Angular is a free and open source JavaScript framework that's maintained by Google. It was built mainly for developing web applications and has expanded its capabilities to being used to create mobile and desktop applications using plugins. Angular uses component-based code, is progressive, and offers many libraries and extensions that shorten the time of developing large-scale applications.

At the time of writing, Angular is very popular for building frontend applications. It is the primary framework for developing applications for large and well-known companies such as Samsung, Upwork, PayPal, and Google. It also has a very active community and has 76,000 stars on GitHub, with around 1,500 people contributing to the framework. In addition, it has thousands of functional NPM libraries that you can use to speed up your development.

History of Angular

Before it became Angular, the first developed framework by Google was **AngularJS** or Angular Version 1. Although developers are typically confused by this, due to thinking that AngularJS and Angular are similar, AngularJS was released as an open source framework by *Miško Hevery*, a Google employee, who was developing AngularJS to develop web applications faster.

AngularJS, where you use JavaScript or Dart, became popular as its community became more extensive. At the same time, the Ionic framework was released, which allowed developers to use AngularJS to build native mobile applications.

The Great Rewrite

The fast and rapid development of JavaScript technology has affected the popularity of AngularJS, and the team came to the end of the road regarding the framework – no improvements were to be made. From 2014 to 2015, the Google team and the community decided to support mobile and large enterprise applications with the framework. Their first port of call was **The Great Rewrite** and not incrementing the design of AngularJS. The Great Rewrite is where **Angular 2.0**, or simply Angular, was released.

The problem with action

Many applications were already running on AngularJS, which meant that if a completely new version of Angular was released, support would come to an end for AngularJS users. So, another main question here was, "*How would those applications be supported after several years?*"

The other issue that emerged is that there was no direct way to migrate from AngularJS to Angular 2.0, which was difficult for developers. This was a massive step for teams – so much so that new concepts and breaking changes were introduced on every release.

The framework's comeback

Even though migrating Angular was painful, the enterprise applications that had been created by Google were supported. Around 2018, this became more stabilized as the framework had a large set of features that were ready to be used to build large applications. In addition, it didn't depend on third-party libraries to create forms and call HTTP requests because all the dependencies were already included. Google also released some documentation to help developers migrate AngularJS to the latest version of Angular.

Angular is very popular and is very effective at developing enterprise applications. Now, let's look at the advantages of Angular and why it is effective for development.

The advantages of using Angular

Angular is a component-based framework, which means that we develop parts of our applications into smaller pieces, and we can reuse these pieces throughout the application. This feature reduces boilerplate code and code errors by ensuring there's not as much repetitive code. One of the main advantages of Angular is its language. Let's take a closer look.

TypeScript-based framework

Angular is a **TypeScript language-based framework**. This language is a significant advantage since TypeScript offers features that are beneficial to development. In addition, it is a superset of JavaScript, which added new concepts that make code maintainable and effective:

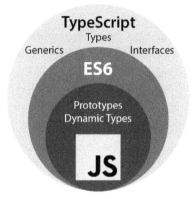

Figure 1.1 – TypeScript – a superset language

As we can see, TypeScript is built on top of ES6 and JavaScript, which is intended to add more features for development. Some of TypeScript's components include Generics, Types, and Interfaces, which we know are directly related to **object-oriented programming** (**OOP**). Now, let's look at another advantage.

Static type data

TypeScript can define static type data, which allows variables to be strictly typed. Compared to plain JavaScript, the compiler alerts you if there are any type-related mistakes – that is, which errors were caught at runtime. Thus, TypeScript can avoid mistakes in production by prompting you with these issues at compile time.

Predictability and maintainability

Since TypeScript is strictly typed, this contributes to the concept of predictability. For example, a variable is declared as a number. Therefore, it will always stay a number throughout the application, and functions will specify how to implement them as all parameters are also strictly typed. Furthermore, TypeScript is also maintainable as it gives developers the power to debug applications at compilation time.

IDE support

Since TypeScript is becoming a more widely used language, more IDEs are supporting it. IDEs offer several features such as code navigation, autocompletion, and plugins.

Microsoft Visual Studio is the primary IDE that's used for TypeScript. However, some IDEs and editors are also available for running TypeScript:

- **Atom**: A cross-platform editor
- **Eclipse**: An IDE that has a plugin for TypeScript
- **Visual Studio Code**: A lightweight cross-platform editor by Microsoft

OOP

TypeScript is an **object-oriented language**, which means it supports concepts such as classes, interfaces, and inheritance. OOP is very scalable as we develop our applications into objects, which can be an advantage if we're developing growing applications.

Early spotted bugs

Browsers do not understand TypeScript directly. Instead, they use **transpilers**, which compile the code into plain JavaScript. Here, all errors related to syntax and types are caught, allowing developers to worry about the code logic instead.

These are just the advantages of the TypeScript language. Now, let's look at the benefits of Angular itself.

Support for large enterprise applications

Angular is considered an all-in-one package framework in that most of the standard features that are needed to build an application are already included. This includes modules. For example, to use forms in an Angular application, we must import `FormsModule` and `ReactiveormsModule`. Other examples are navigation and routes. Angular provides `RouterModule` so that you can create routes within the application.

Single-page application

Angular is a **single-page application** (**SPA**), which means that when a user navigates from one page to another, the page doesn't reload as it's the data that's being fetched by the server. In addition, the client's resources are independent and are already loaded in the browser, which contributes to the loading performance of the application.

Progressive web apps (PWAs)

Progressive web apps (**PWAs**) are becoming a trend nowadays. They are a solution that allows web applications to run on mobile apps, as well as different platforms, both online and offline. It is straightforward to configure Angular as a PWA thanks to its schematics – with just a single line of code, your Angular app is configured. PWAs can also be uploaded into the Android Play Store and Microsoft Store using PWA Builder.

The following command uses the Angular CLI to convert our application into a PWA:

```
ng add @angular/pwa
```

The Angular CLI

We don't need to create or configure Angular from scratch. Instead, we can use the Angular CLI, which helps install the necessary dependencies to run our Angular application successfully. Although the schematics features are responsible for creating the required files, installing the packages, and configuring the values that we need for our application, the Angular CLI generates boilerplate code for **modules**, **components**, **services**, and **directives** for faster development.

In the following code, we're using npm to install the Angular CLI and generate our code using the ng command:

```
//command for installing angular CLI
npm install -g @angular/cli


//command for creating a new Angular App
ng new -project-name


// command for creating a new Component
ng generate component -component-name


// command for creating a new Service
ng generate service -component-name


// command for creating a new Module
ng generate module -component-name
```

Module and component-based framework

Angular is grouped into **modules**, which makes it easier to maintain the code's structure. In addition, each part of the application can be grouped by its function and placed in a single module, making it easier to navigate the application's features. It is also beneficial in unit testing as the code is tested separately, allowing for complete quality control.

Creating code as components promotes reusability and boilerplate reduction. Let's look at an example of a navigation menu:

```
<!- Example code for nav bar -->
<nav class="navbar navbar-default">
  <div class="container-fluid">
    <div class="navbar-header">
      <a class="navbar-brand" href="#">Nav bar</a>
    </div>
    <ul class="nav navbar-nav">
      <li class="active"><a href="#">Home</a></li>
      <li><a href="#">Home</a></li>
```

```
      <li><a href="#">About</a></li>
      <li><a href="#">Contact Us</a></li>
    </ul>
  </div>
</nav>
```

The navigation bar must be present on every page of our application. This process will cause redundant code, which means we will have to repeat this code over and over again. However, in Angular, it has been developed into a component, allowing us to reuse the code in different parts of the application. A specific selector is assigned to the navigation bar code and used as the HTML tag for the component, as shown in the following code:

```
<!—example selector for the navigation bar component-->
<app-navigation-bar/>
```

Cross-platform-enabled

Angular is used to build applications for the web, as well as native mobile and desktop applications. This is now possible through frameworks, such as Ionic, NativeScript, and Electron. Aside from PWAs, Ionic and NativeScript are also used to create mobile apps using Angular. On the other hand, Electron is a framework that transforms your Angular app into a desktop application using a similar code base. This feature makes Angular very flexible as a single framework can cover all the platforms for your application.

Web components

Angular supports **web components**, which are also known as **Angular elements**. Here, the idea is to break an application into smaller pieces and distribute it into an independent application or package that can be distributed and used on other applications. Angular elements cover the concepts of micro frontends. Every element has a pipeline for deployment. This component can also be used in different JavaScript frameworks, such as React and Vue.

Supports lazy loading

Loading all the JavaScript code in the client browser could introduce some issues. If the applications get more extensive, more code would be packed into one chunk. We don't want to bootstrap all of our code as this would cause our application to load slowly when it's started for the first time. We only want to load what is needed on demand. The lazy loading feature by Angular solves this. It only loads the modules, components, services, directives, and other elements of the application that are needed for a specific route. This feature reduces the loading time as the user initially opens the application.

In the following code, we've defined some routes as an array where we add new routes as an object. To enable lazy loading, we must use the `loadChildren` properties to load the modules on demand:

```
const route: Routes = [
    {
      path: "about",
  loadChildren: () =>
    import("./src/app/AboutModule").then(m =>
        m.AboutModule)
      },
    {
      path: "contact",
      loadChildren: () =>
        import("./src/app/ContactModule").then(m =>
          m.ContactModule)
      }
  ];
```

In the preceding code, as the user navigates to the `about` path, it will only load `AboutModule`, which contains the resources for that specific route. It will not load the resources under `ContactModule` unless the user navigates to the `contact` path.

Summary

In this chapter, you learned that Spring Boot is an open source framework extension for Spring and that it mainly solves the boilerplate code when you're configuring the Spring Framework. In addition, it provides **Spring Starters**, which developers can use to allow Spring Boot to configure the required dependencies automatically.

On the other hand, Angular is a component-based framework that's built with the TypeScript language to give it OOP powers. Moreover, it has cross-platform support, which allows developers to create applications on the web, mobile, and desktop. Angular is one of the top JavaScript frameworks as it is used by several large companies and is supported by Google and a large community.

In the next chapter, you will learn about the software that you must install on your computer and set up the development environment for full stack development.

2

Setting Up the Development Environment

In the previous chapter, you learned about Spring Boot in a nutshell and its advantages. We also tackled the latest features of Java 17. The same goes for Angular; you had an overview of Angular and the benefits of using it to develop frontend applications.

This chapter will teach you how to set up your computer's development environment to develop your full-stack Java and Angular application. We will tackle different IDEs and text editors to write our code and make sure everything has been configured before we start with the development.

Installing everything correctly from the beginning will help us avoid issues and write code without any interruptions.

In this chapter, we will cover the following topics:

- Installing VS Code and IntelliJ IDEA

- Installing Java 17

- Installing SDKMAN

- Setting up IntelliJ IDEA with Java 17

- Installing REST Client VS Code or JetBrains and Angular DevTools

- Installing Git version control

Technical requirements

The following are the links to the software you need to install:

- **Download VS Code (for Windows, Mac, and Linux)**: `https://code.visualstudio.com/download`

- **IntelliJ IDEA for Windows**: `https://www.jetbrains.com/idea/download/#section=windows`

- **IntelliJ IDEA for Mac**: `https://www.jetbrains.com/idea/download/#section=mac`

- **IntelliJ IDEA for Linux**: `https://www.jetbrains.com/idea/download/#section=linux`

- **Download Java 17**: `https://www.oracle.com/java/technologies/javase/jdk17-archive-downloads.html`

- **Angular DevTools**: `https://chrome.google.com/webstore/detail/angular-devtools/ienfalfjdbdpebioblfackkekamfmbnh`

- **Node.js and Node Package Manager**: `https://nodejs.org/en/`

- **PostgreSQL for Windows**: `https://www.postgresql.org/download/windows/`

- **PostgreSQL for Mac**: `https://www.postgresql.org/download/macosx/`

- **PostgreSQL for Linux**: `https://www.postgresql.org/download/linux/`

- **Git Version Control**: `https://git-scm.com/`

Installing VS Code and IntelliJ IDEA

This section will guide you through the installation and configuration of VS Code or IntelliJ IDEA. We will look at the text editor and IDE breakdown of their features and plugins that you can use throughout the development.

VS Code

Download the VS Code installer from `https://code.visualstudio.com/download`. We suggest installing VS Code regardless of your machine's OS, because VS Code is lightweight but offers many plugins for Angular development. In addition, VS Code is the most common text editor used by JavaScript developers. The editor supports TypeScript, code formatting, and code navigation and offers many extensions that you can use, especially in developing Angular applications. The following are some of the valuable extensions we can use throughout the development:

- **Code Spell Check**: This is an extension for checking the spelling of our source code, which helps us avoid issues caused by typos.

- **Prettier**: This is a code formatting tool that applies proper alignment and indentations on our file after each save.

- **Angular Snippets**: This is a prevalent extension for Angular developers as it adds snippets for Angular, TypeScript, and HTML, which saves much time in development with the use of snippets to generate codes on the fly.

- **Angular Files**: This is a valuable extension, especially when you are not familiar with the commands in the Angular CLI; this extension will add a menu where you can generate Angular components, modules, and services without using a CLI.

- **Angular2-Switcher**: This extension allows us to use shortcut keys to navigate between Angular files.

- **REST Client**: This is an extension in VS Code for testing backend APIs. Instead of using third-party applications, we can send requests on our VS Code using REST Client.

- **JSON to TS**: This extension is handy as it automatically converts JSON objects into TypeScript models in our frontend.

- **Angular Language Service**: This is one of the essential plugins for Angular development. The extension provides **Angular Code Completion**, **Angular Diagnostic Messages**, and **Go to definition** features that make development faster.

This ends VS Code installation and configuration. Your VS Code text editor is now set for Angular development.

IntelliJ IDEA

This IDE is one of the most popular IDEs when developing applications using Java. The IDE offers several features to make development easier and faster. The following is a list of the tools that IntelliJ IDEA offers:

- **Terminal**: IntelliJ IDEA comes with a built-in terminal. We can execute any commands in the terminal depending on the language we are using for the development. The terminal can be accessed by pressing *Alt + F12*.

- **Quick fixes**: IntelliJ IDEA detects syntax errors on the fly. Having this feature, IntelliJ IDEA also suggests quick fixes for developers to easily correct mistakes in the code. The quick fixes can be accessed through a small light bulb that appears when IntelliJ IDEA detects an error.

- **IntelliSense**: IntelliSense is also known as **smart code completion**. IntelliJ IDEA analyzes the fragments of code and displays suggestions to complete the code on the fly.

- **Advanced refactoring**: IntelliJ IDEA offers a wide range of refactoring options. The IDE gives the developer the capability to refactor code automatically. Refactoring can also be accessed in the refactor menu.

- **Navigation and search**: This is one of the most used features of IntelliJ IDEA and is very handy, especially with large projects. It helps developers find and navigate for a resource, and it can search all of the available controls in the IDE.

- **Detecting duplicates**: This helps developers find duplicates in code and gives suggestions to the developers.

You should go to `https://www.jetbrains.com/idea/download/` to download the installer. In addition, you can download the community version, which is the free version of Visual Studio.

After successfully downloading the IDE, run the installer, and the process is very much straightforward. It will install the IDE automatically in our terminal. After the successful installation of IntelliJ IDEA, we will install plugins/extensions that will help us throughout the development.

To install the plugins, open the IntelliJ IDEA and press *Ctrl + Alt + S*. This will open the **settings** window, then you should go to the **Plugins** menu to access the marketplace:

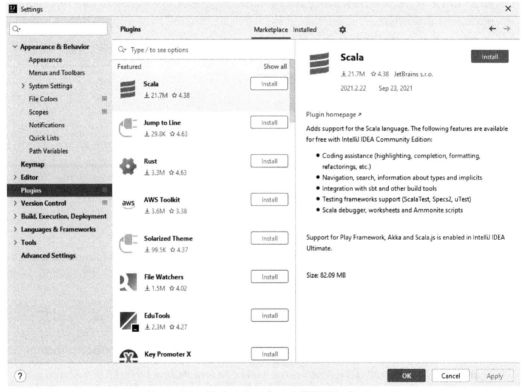

Figure 2.1 – Marketplace for IntelliJ IDEA plugins

It will list all of the available plugins we can add for our development. We will install the following plugins:

- **Lombok**: An extension that provides annotations, preventing the writing of getter and setter methods all over again; the annotation provides a fully-featured builder.

- **Maven Helper**: A tool for Maven projects that helps in analyzing conflicting dependencies. It can display the installed dependencies as a tree and allows developers to examine their relationships.

- **Junit 5 Mockito Code Generator**: An extension that helps us generate boilerplate codes that we commonly need in writing tests.

- **Eclipse Code Formatter**: A tool that integrates the code formatter of Eclipse directly to IntelliJ IDEA. This tool is very useful in solving the problem of a standard code style when developers use both Eclipse and IntelliJ IDEs.

- **Tabnine**: A tool that allows developers to complete lines of code based on a million Java programs. It helps reduce standard errors and enables developers to code faster with the help of AI.

- **Add to gitignore**: This allows developers to add specific files in `.gitignore` to be ignored directly in the IDE without having to type the path one by one.

This ends the installation and configuration of IntelliJ IDEA. Your IDE in your machine is all set.

Installing Java 17

This section will explain what Java 17 is and guide you through the installation of the kit on Windows, macOS, and Linux.

Java 17 is a **Java Development Kit** (**JDK**) required for building applications and components using the Java programming language. It is the latest **long-term support** (**LTS**) release, meaning that the vendor (Oracle) will support the version for a long time, including the patching of security issues.

Windows installation

Execute the following steps to install Java 17 on Windows:

1. Go to `https://www.oracle.com/java/technologies/downloads/#jdk17-windows`:

Product/file description	File size	Download
x64 Compressed Archive	170.64 MB	https://download.oracle.com/java/17/latest/jdk-17_windows-x64_bin.zip (sha256 🗗)
x64 Installer	151.99 MB	https://download.oracle.com/java/17/latest/jdk-17_windows-x64_bin.exe (sha256 🗗)
x64 MSI Installer	150.88 MB	https://download.oracle.com/java/17/latest/jdk-17_windows-x64_bin.msi (sha256 🗗)

Linux   macOS   **Windows**

Figure 2.2 – Java 17 installer

2. Select the installer base on your operating system and download it by clicking the link.

    After successful download, open the installer and it will prompt you with a step-by-step installation that you can follow.

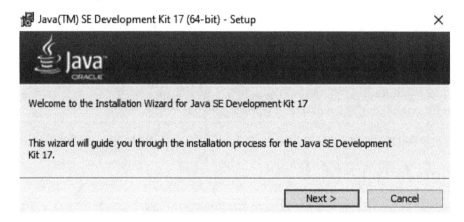

Figure 2.3 – Java 17 installation setup

3. Click **Next**, and this will ask you where to place the JDK 17 on your machine. You can choose your preferred path where to set the JDK, but the default is commonly used.

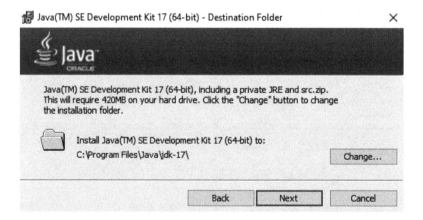

Figure 2.4 – Java 17 installation destination folder

4. Now, this will automatically install the JDK 17 on your machine after successful installation. The following files are also copied to the location:

    ```
    "C:\Program Files\Common Files\Oracle\Java\javapath\java.
    exe"
    ```

```
"C:\Program Files\Common Files\Oracle\Java\javapath\
javaw.exe"
"C:\Program Files\Common Files\Oracle\Java\javapath\
javac.exe"
"C:\Program Files\Common Files\Oracle\Java\javapath\
jshell.exe"
```

We have now successfully installed Java 17 on our Windows machine. Now, we will show you the steps for installing Java 17 on macOS.

macOS installation

There are things to consider when choosing the installer for Java 17 in macOS. First, we need to know that the installation for JDK 17 contains version notation that represents the **Feature**, **Interim**, and **Update** versions. For example, if you are installing interim 1, update 1, and patch 1, the installer name would be as follows:

- **macOS x64 systems**:

  `jdk-17.1.1.1_macos-x64_bin.dmg`

  `jdk-17.1.1.1_macos-x64_bin.tar.gz`

- **macOS aarch64 (64-bit ARM) systems**:

  `jdk-17. 1.1.1_macos-aarch64_bin.dmg`

  `jdk-17. 1.1.1_macos-aarch64_bin.tar.gz`

Execute the following steps to install Java 17 on macOS:

1. To download the installer go to `https://www.oracle.com/java/technologies/downloads/#jdk17-mac` and select the installer based on your operating system architecture. You can download either the `.dmg` or the `tar.gz` installer.

2. Double-click the `.dmg` file to start the installer. A **Finder** window will show up and it contains the name of the `.pkg` file. Double-click the `JDK 17. pkg` icon to start the installation.

3. Click **Continue** and the installation window will appear. After clicking **Install**, the following message will be displayed: **Installer is trying to install new software. Enter your password to allow this**.

4. Next, enter your administrator user name and password and click **Install software to continue**, and this will install the software automatically on your machine.

We have now successfully installed Java 17 on macOS. Now, we will show you the steps for installing Java 17 on Linux platforms.

Linux installation

When installing Java 17 on a Linux system, we also need to be aware of the version notation, as when choosing the installer for macOS. The version format represents the **Feature**, **Interim**, and **Update** versions. So, for example, if we are downloading the interim 1, update 1, and patch 2, then the installer name would be the following:

- **Linux x64 systems**: `jdk-17.1.1.2_linux-x64_bin.tar.gz`

- **Linux aarch64 systems**: `jdk-17.1.1.2_aarch64_bin.tar.gz`

You can install the JDK on a Linux platform using the archive files or **Red Hat Package Manager** (**RPM**):

- **Archive Files (.tar.gz)** will install a private version of the JDK at any location without affecting other JDK installations. The bundle is available for Linux x66 and Linux aarchx64.

- **RPM Packages (.rpm)** will execute a system-wide installation of the JDK and require users to have root access.

64-Bit on Linux platforms

To install the JDK for 64-bit Linux platforms, the `tar.gz` archive file, also known as a **tarball**, can be downloaded from the following URL: `https://www.oracle.com/java/technologies/downloads/#jdk17-linux`.

The files that we see are as follows:

- **Linux 64**: `jdk-17.interim.update.patch_linux-x64_bin.tar.gz`

- **Linux aarch64**: `jdk-17.interim.update.patch_linux-aarch64_bin.tar.gz`

After successfully downloading the tarball file, accept the license agreement and place the `.tar.gz` file in the directory where you want to install the JDK.

Unpack the file and install the downloaded JDK as follows:

```
tar zxvf jdk-17.interim.update.patch_linux-x64_bin.tar.gz
```

Or with the following code:

```
tar zxvf jdk-17.interim.update.patch_linux-aarch64_bin.tar.gz
```

After successfully installing the JDK, we can see that it is now installed in a directory called `jdk-17.interim.patch.update`.

64-Bit on RPM-based Linux platforms

We can install the JDK using RPM binary files for RPM-based Linux platforms, such as Oracle and Red Hat. Before installing the JDK, we must first make sure that we have root access. You can have root access by running the `su` command and entering the super password.

The RPM file can be downloaded from `https://www.oracle.com/java/technologies/downloads/#jdk17-linux`, and we get the following files:

- **Linux 64**: `jdk-17.interim.update.patch_linux-x64_bin.rpm`

- **Linux aarch64**: `jdk-17.interim.update.patch_linux-aarch64_bin.rpm`

Install the package using the following command:

```
rpm -ivh jdk-17.interim.update.patch_linux-x64_bin.rpm
```

Or use the following command:

```
rpm -ivh jdk-17.interim.update.patch_linux-aarch64_bin.rpm
```

After executing the command, the JDK is now successfully installed on our machine. Then, for future version upgrades, we can execute the following command:

```
rpm -Uvh jdk-17.interim.update.patch_linux-x64_bin.rpm
```

Or use the following command:

```
rpm -Uvh jdk-17.interim.update.patch_linux-aarch64_bin.rpm
```

We are done installing and configuring the JDK 17 on our machine on different operating systems. In the next section, we will install SDKMAN.

Installing SDKMAN

This section will explain what the purpose of SDKMAN is in developing Java applications. This section will also guide you through the installation of SDKMAN on Windows, macOS, and Linux.

SDKMAN (Software Development Kit Manager) is a tool for managing parallel versions of Java on our machine. We can have multiple versions of installed Java versions on our computer. You can also install Java directly using SDKMAN. It will automatically install the latest stable version or the version you specify.

SDKMAN is mainly created for Unix operating systems, but it also supports Bash and ZSH shells for other operating systems.

SDKMAN features

The following are the features of SDKMAN:

- SDKMAN makes the installation of Java easier. We will only execute a command with the version we want to install, and it will do all the work.
- SDKMAN also supports Java development packages. It can install SDKs for JVM, such as **Groovy** and **Kotlin**.
- SDKMAN can run on all Unix platforms: macOS, Cygwin, Solaris, and Linux.

SDKMAN commands

To see all the SDKs that SDKMAN supports, we can execute the following command:

```
sdk list
```

The command will list all the SDKs and the Java library managers we can download on our machine.

To install a specific SDK, for example, we want to install the latest SDK for Java, execute the following command:

```
sdk install java
```

If we want to install a specific version of the SDK, we will specify the version in the command as follows:

```
sdk install java 15-open
```

To switch between versions when multiple versions are installed on our computer, we will execute the following command:

```
sdk default java 15-open
```

Installation on macOS and Linux

It only takes a few commands to install SDKMAN on macOS and Linux. For us to install SDKMAN, we will execute the following command:

```
curl -s https://get.sdkman.io | bash
```

After following all the instructions on installing SDKMAN, open a new terminal and execute the following command:

```
source "$HOME/.sdkman/bin/sdkman-init.sh"
```

The command will successfully install the manager in your terminal. To check whether the installation is successful, we can execute the following command:

```
sdk version
```

This will display the current SDKMAN version installed on your machine.

Installation on Windows

We need several steps to install SDKMAN on Windows since SDKMAN requires Bash tools. In this case, the first thing we need is a **Git Bash Environment** (**MinGW**):

1. First, we will install 7-Zip, and after successful installation, we will execute the following command to make a symbolic link in the Git Bash environment, having 7-Zip as the zip command:

    ```
    ln -s /c/Program\ Files/7-Zip/7z.exe /c/Program\ Files/
    Git/mingw64/bin/zip.exe
    ```

    Now we can use the commands we use in Linux to install the SDKMAN.

2. To install SDKMAN, we will execute the following command:

    ```
    export SDKMAN_DIR="/c/sdkman" && curl -s "https://get.
    sdkman.io" | bash
    ```

3. After the installation, restart the Git Bash shell to run the SDKMAN commands. We can execute the following command to verify that our installation is successful:

    ```
    sdk version
    ```

    It will prompt the current version of SDKMAN installed in our terminal.

We are done installing and configuring SDKMAN on our machine on different operating systems. In the next section, we will configure IntelliJ IDEA with the installed Java 17.

Setting up IntelliJ IDEA with Java 17

We have installed our IDE (IntelliJ IDEA) and Java 17 on our machine in the previous sections. Now, we will guide you on how to configure Java 17 on new and existing projects.

Using Java 17 on new projects

We only need the following few steps to use Java 17 on our new Java project:

1. Open your IntelliJ IDEA terminal and select **File | New | New Project**.

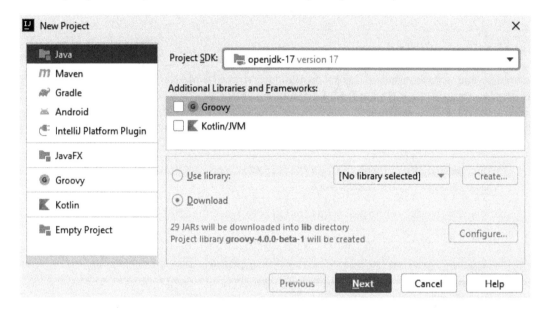

Figure 2.5 – Creating a new project in IntelliJ IDEA

We will see the preceding modal and select the type of project we need to develop. We can also see that we can choose the SDK version we need for our project.

2. We will use Java 17, so we need to select **OpenJDK-17**.

3. Click **Next** and configure your project name and directory. This will set up your Java application with the chosen SDK version.

We have now successfully configured our new project with JDK 17. Now we want to configure existing projects with JDK 17.

Using Java 17 on existing projects

Upon upgrading our project from an older version to Java 17, we need to follow several steps for our applications to work. First, remember that this upgrading to Java 17 step is only the general configuration in upgrading. It depends on the current version of the project. Also, some code and dependencies are being used on your project that are already deprecated.

We only need a few steps to use Java 17 on our existing Java project:

1. Open your IntelliJ IDEA IDE and open your existing project.

2. Choose **File** in the menu and select **Project Structure**. We will see a modal where we can configure our **Project Settings**.

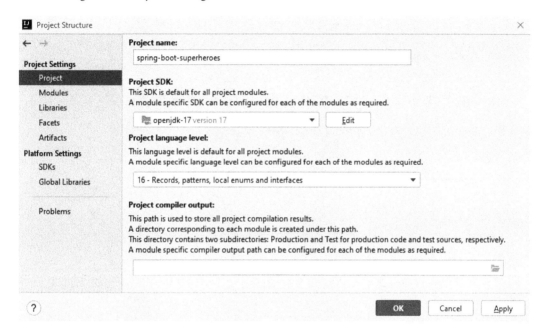

Figure 2.6 – IntelliJ IDEA project settings

3. Under the **Project SDK** field, we will choose **openjdk-17** to use Java 17 in our project. We can also select **Project language level** to use some of the new features of Java 17, such as **sealed classes** and **pattern matching for switch**. Remember, when changing **Project language level**, make sure that the same level is also set for the modules under the **Modules** tab.

We are now done configuring our project with Java 17. In the next section, we will install helpful tools for our development in Java and Angular, such as REST Client and Angular DevTools.

Installing REST Client VS Code or JetBrains and Angular DevTools

In this section, we will guide you through the installation of **REST Client** and **Angular DevTools**. REST Client is an essential tool in RESTful APIs. It is a tool for sending HTTP requests to the API you develop to debug the flow of your code on the endpoint as well as its response. There are several third-party platforms for API testing, such as Postman, but REST Client can be directly installed in your IDE.

Angular DevTools, on the other hand, is a Chrome extension for Angular that provides debugging and profiling capabilities for Angular applications. The extension supports **Angular version 9** and later, and it is also Ivy enabled.

Installing REST Client in VS Code

We only need to follow these steps to install REST Client in VS Code:

1. First, open VS Code Editor and go to the **Extensions** tab.

2. Search for `REST client`.

3. Select **REST Client** developed **by Huachao Mao** and install the extension.

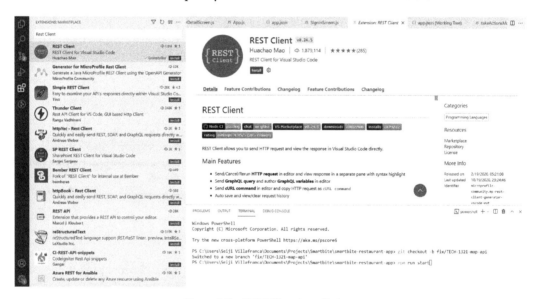

Figure 2.7 – REST Client installation

After installation, we can use the extension by creating HTTP files in our project and writing the endpoints with the HTTP requests. The following is an example format of using REST Client:

```
GET https://test.com/users/1 HTTP/1.1
###


GET https://test.com /blogs/1 HTTP/1.1
###


POST https://test.com/rate HTTP/1.1
content-type: application/json
```

```
{
    "name": "sample",
    "rate": 5:
}
```

We have now successfully installed REST Client in our VS Code and can test RESTful APIs. Now, we will show you how to install Angular DevTools, which will be important for debugging Angular applications.

Installing Angular DevTools

Angular DevTools is a Chrome extension. To install the extension, you can directly install it from `https://chrome.google.com/webstore/detail/angular-devtools/ienfalfjdbdpebioblfackkekamfmbnh` and follow these steps:

1. Click **Add to chrome** and we can directly use Angular DevTools on our browser. Remember that we can only use Angular DevTools on Angular applications running in **development mode**.

2. We will see in our developer tools that a new tab named **Angular** was added.

3. Run your Angular project and select the **Angular** tab.

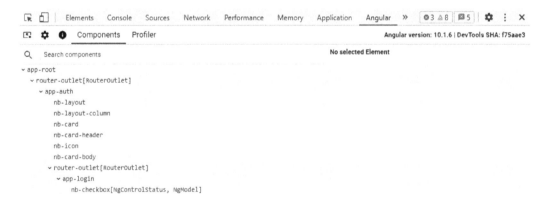

Figure 2.8 – Angular DevTools installation

Angular DevTools will have two tabs: the **Components** tab, which will display your application structure, and the **Profiler** tab, which is used to identify application performance and bottlenecks.

We have successfully installed Angular DevTools. Last but not least, we will install Git version control, which will be useful for code versioning and team collaboration.

Installing Git version control

Installing **Git**, a distributed version control system, will be the last thing we need in development. Git is important for developers as it is used to save your project's different versions and stages of your repository. Git also helps you revert your repository's recent working version if you made changes in your code that broke your app and you can't fix them anymore.

Go to `http://git-scm.com/` and click the **Download** button on the screen to download and install Git.

Now you have learned from this final section about Git version control, where to get it, what it does, and why it is crucial. Let's summarize everything.

Summary

With this, we have reached the end of this chapter. Let's have a recap of the valuable things you have learned. You have learned how to install VS Code, its features, and the essential extensions we can use in Angular development.

You have also learned how to install IntelliJ IDEA, its features, and the plugins that we will use in Java development. You have also learned how to install Java 17 and configure it with new and existing projects in IntelliJ IDEA.

SDKMAN is a development kit manager and it gives us the capability to switch JDK versions and install Java development packages directly. REST Client is a tool for testing RESTful APIs without downloading any third-party tools on our machine.

Angular DevTools is a Chrome extension for Angular that provides debugging and profiling capabilities for Angular applications. And last but not least, Git version control is a tool for creating histories of your code where you can quickly revert or create a new version of your application.

In the next chapter, we will be focusing on Spring Boot and its features.

Part 2: Backend Development

This part contains a real-world scenario of developing a Java Spring Boot 2.5 application. The following chapters are covered in this part:

- *Chapter 3, Moving into Spring Boot*
- *Chapter 4, Setting Up the Database and Spring Data JPA*
- *Chapter 5, Building APIs with Spring*
- *Chapter 6, Documenting APIs with OpenAPI Specification*
- *Chapter 7, Adding Spring Boot Security with JWT*
- *Chapter 8, Logging Events in Spring Boot*
- *Chapter 9, Writing Tests in Spring Boot*

3

Moving into Spring Boot

In the previous chapter, you learned how to set up your development environment for developing your REST APIs using Java and your Angular application. We also installed SDKMAN! to manage multiple versions of Java, a REST client to test APIs without the use of third-party tools, Angular DevTools to debug your Angular application, and Git for code versioning and collaboration.

This chapter will now teach you the concepts of Spring Boot. We will deep-dive into Spring Boot's fundamentals and the essential things we need to learn to develop our backend application. We will also learn how to create a Spring Boot project using Spring Initializr.

In this chapter, we will cover the following topics:

- Understanding Spring Boot
- Using Spring Initializr
- Dependency injection
- Beans and annotations

Technical requirements

Here is what you need to complete this chapter:

- **For building the backend**: JetBrains' IntelliJ IDEA and the Java 17 SDK
- **For generating the Java project**: Spring Initializr

> Note
>
> There will be no directories of repositories for chapters 1 to 4 because most topics here are only theory and feature some sample code. The actual application project will begin in *Chapter 5, Building APIs with Spring*.

Understanding Spring Boot

We have already discussed an overview of Spring in *Chapter 1, Spring Boot and Angular – The Big Picture*. In this section, we will have a deeper understanding of the essential concepts of Spring Boot in building your backend application, but first, let's recap what Spring Boot is and its significant advantages.

Spring Boot is an open source micro-framework from Pivotal. It is an enterprise-level framework for developers to create standalone applications on **Java Virtual Machines** (**JVMs**). Its primary focus is to shorten your code length to make it easier for you to run your application.

The framework extends the Spring Framework, which allows a more opinionated way to configure your applications. In addition, it comes with built-in autoconfiguration capabilities that configure both Spring Framework and third-party packages based on your settings.

Here are the significant advantages of Spring Boot:

- **Auto-configuration**: When configuring your Spring Boot application, it downloads all the dependencies needed to run your application.

- **Opinionated approach**: Spring Boot uses a narrow approach to installing dependencies based on your application's needs. Manual configuration is removed as it adds the packages you need for your application.

- **Spring starters**: We can choose a list of starter dependencies to define your application's expected needs during the initialization process. One example is Spring Web, which allows us to initialize a Spring-based web application.

Now, we know what Spring Boot is and its advantages. Let's now discuss the architecture of Sprint Boot.

Spring Boot architecture

Spring Boot consists of different layers and classes to process the data and logic in your backend. The four layers and their use are as follows:

1. **Presentation/display layer**: The presentation layer is responsible for interpreting JSON parameters as objects. This layer is the upper layer that is also responsible for handling authentication and HTTP requests. After accomplishing JSON translation and authentication, we will now move to the business layer.

2. **Business layer**: The business layer, as the name suggests, handles all the business logic in the application. It is composed of service classes that perform authorization and additional validation.

3. **Persistence layer**: The persistence layer is mainly responsible for storage logic that converts objects from and to database rows to insert data.

4. **Database layer**: The database layer performs **Create, Read, Update, and Delete** (**CRUD**) operations. The layer can consist of multiple databases.

The Spring Boot architecture depends on the Spring Framework. The framework uses all of its features, such as Spring **Model-View-Controller (MVC)**, Spring Data, and Spring Core. The only difference is that Spring Boot does not require **Data Access Object (DAO)** and `DAOimpl` classes.

Now, let's discuss the Spring Boot Flow architecture, where we will see how data is processed inside an application.

Spring Boot flow architecture

The Spring Boot flow architecture will explain how the HTTP requests are processed and how layers communicate. The flow is composed of controllers, service layers, databases, and models. To have a better understanding, let's look at the following diagram.

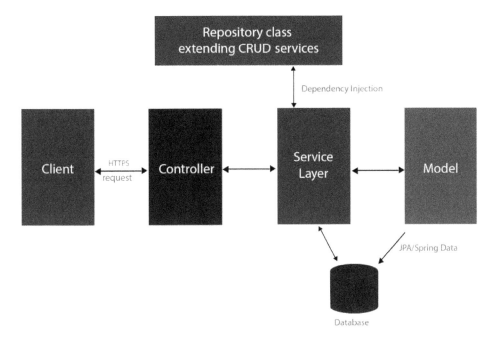

Figure 3.1 – Spring Boot flow architecture

In the Spring Boot flow architecture, the first thing that occurs is the client sends a request (an HTTPS request) to the controller. The controller maps the request and decides what to do with it. Next, it calls the service layer, where all business logic is performed, and gets additional dependencies required for operations from repository classes. The service layer is also responsible for performing logic on the data represented as a model and will be used by JPA to be inserted into the database.

We have learned the flow of the Spring Boot architecture. Now, we will discuss **Representational State Transfer (REST)** and its concepts.

Understanding REST

Before we start building our backend application, we must first know the concept of REST, as this is the primary architectural approach that we will apply for our backend to be consumable with client applications.

REST is a web service the primary goal of which is to make web services more effective. It allows direct access to applications through a **Uniform Resource Identifier (URI)** and can provide the resource in the XML or JSON format, making it more flexible.

The URI is where communication happens between two applications. Think of it as a bridge where the backend and frontend communicate. The client (frontend) requests a resource and returns a response represented by the XML or JSON format. Requesting a resource is used with the following HTTP methods:

- GET: This is used to get and read a resource.
- POST: This creates a new resource.
- PUT: This updates an existing resource.
- DELETE: This deletes a resource.

Let's have a simple real-world example (a blog application) where we use HTTP methods to access a resource with the provided endpoints:

- GET /user/{id}/blogs: This gets the list of blogs of a specific user.
- POST /user/{id}/blog: This creates a blog for a specific user.
- PATCH /user/{id}/blog/{blog_id}: This updates an existing blog for a specific user.
- DELETE /user/{id}/blog/{blog_id}: This deletes an existing blog for a specific user.

In the preceding example, we request a resource using HTTP methods and endpoints. The endpoint returns an object in the form of XML or JSON in the response body. REST also supports the standard status code that will define whether our request is successful or not. The list of commonly used status codes is as follows:

- 200: Success status for the request
- 201: Indicates that an object was successfully created
- 400: Indicates a bad request – usually happens when the request body is invalid
- 401: Unauthorized access to the resource
- 404: Indicates that the resource is not found
- 500: Indicates an internal server error

The status codes are a helpful indication of what the client application will do after the HTTP call, providing an overview of how we can use REST in client and server communication.

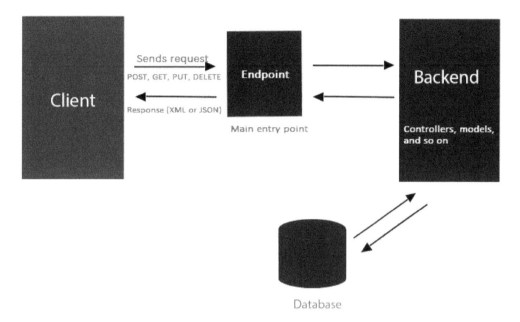

Figure 3.2 – Communication between client and server applications

We learned about the concept and architecture of Spring Boot in this section. We also now know the ideas of REST and how it works to provide backend solutions. In the next section, we will generate our new Spring Boot project using Spring Initializr.

Using Spring Initializr

This section will explain what **Spring Initializr** is and how to configure and start our project. Spring Initializr is a web application that can generate a Spring Boot project on the fly. Spring Initializr will configure the build file with the required dependencies to run our project, focusing only on the code in the application. Spring Initializr makes it easier to set up our project, with the help of the **Spring Boot CLI** on the side, helping us configure our application. Spring Initializr generates a more traditional Java structure.

There are several ways to use Spring Initializr:

- Via a web-based interface
- Via Intellij IDEA

We will discuss these different ways to generate our Spring Boot application.

Web-based interface

The first way to use Spring Initializr is using a web-based interface. The application can be accessed through `https://start.spring.io`. You will see the following form once you open the link:

Figure 3.3 – Spring Initializr

The form will ask you for some basic information about your project. The first question is, *what is your choice between Maven and Gradle to build your project?* The app will also need information such as what language you will use, the artifact name, project name, and package name to be used, and what JDK version will be used when building the application.

Now, on the right side of the interface, you will see the **Add Dependencies** button. The **Add Dependencies** feature is one of the most important features of Spring Initializr, as this will allow us to choose the dependencies depending on the needs of our project. For example, we need to have a relational database with JPA access; we should add the Spring Data JPA.

Therefore, we added **Lombok**, **Spring Web**, **Spring Data JPA**, **PostgreSQL Driver**, and **Spring Data Reactive Redis** in the following example. We will also discuss each dependency as we go through building our example application.

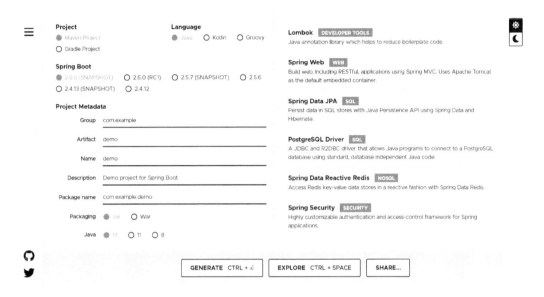

Figure 3.4 – Generating Spring Boot with the dependencies

We can see in the preceding example that we have already added the dependencies we need in our project. The last would be generating our application by clicking the **Generate** button; this will download a zip file that will contain our application. Before generating our project, we can click the **Explore** button to check our project structure and verify the configuration.

After successfully downloading the generated Spring Boot application, we will extract the file, and we can now open the Spring Boot project with the IDE of our choice. Finally, we are ready to write our code, but first, let's check out the project structure generated by Spring Initializr.

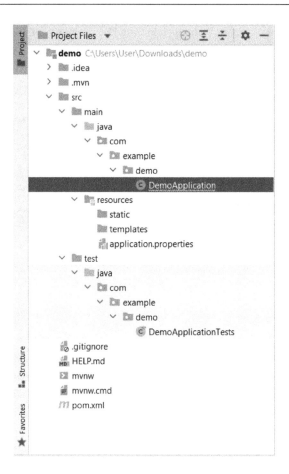

Figure 3.5 – A generated Spring Boot application

We can see from the generated project that there is not much application code included. However, the project consists of the following:

- `DemoApplication.java`: A class with the `main()` function for the application bootstrap
- `DemoApplicationTests.java`: An empty JUnit test class for unit testing
- `Pom.xml`: A Maven build specification that contains the dependencies needed for the application
- `Application.properties`: A properties file that is used to add configuration properties

We can see on the generated project that empty directories are included, such as the `static` folder; this is significant, as this is used for placing static content such as CSS and JavaScript files.

We have successfully generated our Spring Boot project using the web interface. Now, we will use Spring Initializr directly in IntelliJ IDEA.

Via IntelliJ IDEA

Another way of generating our Spring Boot project is by using Spring Initializr directly in IntelliJ IDEA; note that this is only available in the Ultimate edition of IntelliJ. If you are using the Community edition, you can install Spring Assistant at the following link: `https://plugins.jetbrains.com/plugin/10229-spring-assistant`. This will add a Spring Assistant option to generate your Spring Boot projects.

Execute the following steps:

1. Select **New Project** upon opening IntelliJ IDEA to start generating the project, which will open a new modal.

2. Select **Spring Initializr**, which will open a form with the same web interface as Spring Initializr.

3. It will ask for details such as the project name, the language that will be used, the artifact name, and the SDK version that will be used to build the project:

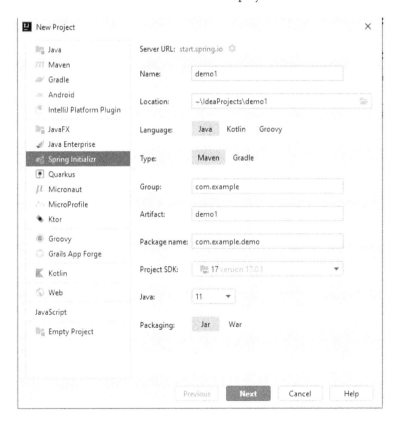

Figure 3.6 – The form for using Spring Initializr with IntelliJ IDEA

We can see in the preceding figure that we have populated all the required details for our project.

4. Clicking the **Next** button will redirect us to the **Dependencies** selection. We will choose the dependencies we need for the Spring Boot development, which are the same as what we entered in the Sprint Initializr interface.

5. After successfully checking the dependencies, click **Finish**, and our Spring Boot application is configured. Finally, we are ready to write our code.

We have successfully generated our Spring Boot application through the Spring Initializr web interface and built-in IntelliJ IDEA. In the next section, we will learn one of the most important and commonly used concepts in Spring Boot – dependency injection.

Dependency injection

We have successfully generated our own Spring Boot project, and now, we will start learning the concepts of Spring, and one of the most important concepts we need to understand is **dependency injection**. As we develop our backend using Spring Boot, we will mainly use dependency injection throughout our development, as this makes our Java program modular and enables easier switching of implementations.

Dependency injection is an essential feature of **object-oriented programming languages**, but first, let's discuss the concept of inversion of control, which is what dependency injection is trying to achieve.

Inversion of control

Inversion of Control (**IoC**) is the design pattern used for object-oriented programming languages. IoC is the concept of inverting the flow of your program, and it is used for decoupling the components in your application, making your piece of code reusable and modular. Hence, the IoC design pattern will provide us with a way to inject a custom class into other classes of our application.

The injected class will be instantiated in different parts of our application. Instead of letting our class decide its implementations or making its code fixes, we allow the injection of dependencies to change the class's flow, performance, and code depending on the case. Thus, IoC mainly offers flexibility and modularity, but it also provides several other advantages in designing your applications:

- Having control of an object's life cycle, we can define some objects as a singleton, and some objects can have their instance.

- It makes the application more maintainable as your code reduces because of reusable components.

- Testing components is more manageable, as we can isolate components and mock their dependencies, not covering other code that will not be included in unit testing.

We have learned about the IoC pattern and how it is advantageous for developing our application. Now, we will use dependency injection, which allows us to achieve this pattern.

The basics of dependency injection

We have already discussed how IoC works, and it is achieved by allowing an implementation to be decided by giving dependencies to the object. So, this idea is mainly **dependency injection**. We allow objects or classes to accept other dependencies that can provide implementations of different classes without writing them again, making our code flexible and reusable. Dependency injection can be achieved in different ways, and here are the following implementations.

Constructor-based dependency injection

Constructor-based dependency injection can be achieved by creating an object class with a constructor, with arguments of a specific type representing the dependency we can set.

Let's have a look at the following code example:

```
package com.springexample;

/* Class for Student */
public class Student {
   private Grades grades;

   public Student(grades: Grades) {
      this.grades = grades;
   }
   public void retrieveGrades() {
      grades.getGrades();
   }
}
```

In the preceding example, the Student class has a constructor, public Student() {}, which accepts a parameter of type Grades. The constructor allows us to inject a Grades object in Student, allowing all implementations of the Grades object to be accessible in the Student object. Now, we have accessed the getGrades() method in our Student. To use the Student object, we will execute the following example:

```
package com.springexample;
import org.springframework.context.ApplicationContext;
import org.springframework.context.support.
ClassPathXmlApplicationContext;
```

```
public class Main {
   public static void main(String[] args) {
      ApplicationContext context =
        new ClassPathXmlApplicationContext("Beans.xml");

      Student student =
        (Student) context.getBean("student");
      student.retrieveGrades();
   }
}
```

We can see in the preceding example that we have instantiated a new student in our main class by getting the bean of our Beans.xml file. The Beans.xml file is our main configuration file for our construction-based injection, which is where we will define our beans together with their dependencies.

Let's examine the following example of what Beans.xml looks like:

```
<?xml version = "1.0" encoding = "UTF-8"?>

<beans xmlns =
   "http://www.springframework.org/schema/beans"
   xmlns:xsi = "http://www.w3.org/2001/XMLSchema-instance"
   xsi:schemaLocation =
      "http://www.springframework.org/schema/beans
      http://www.springframework.org/schema/beans/
      spring-beans-3.0.xsd">

   <!-- Definition for student bean -->
   <bean id = "student"
     class = "com.springexample.Student">
     <constructor-arg ref = "grades"/>
   </bean>

   <!-- Definition for grades bean -->
   <bean id = "grades"
     class ="com.springexample.Grades"></bean>

</beans>
```

In the preceding example, we have defined the `Student` and `Grades` object as beans. The only difference is that the `Student` object has a `constructor-arg` that references grades; this indicates that we are injecting the `Grades` object into our `Student` object.

We have already achieved constructor-based dependency by using the `Beans.xml` configuration. We can also use annotations directly in our code to configure our beans and their dependencies.

Let's look at the following example of how to configure beans and dependencies with annotations:

```
@Configuration
public class AppConfig
{
    @Bean
    public Student student() {
        return new Student(grades());
    }

    @Bean
    public Grades grades() {
        return new Grades();
    }
}
```

We can see in the preceding example that instead of using XML, we have used annotations to identify our beans and configuration. For example, the `@Configuration` annotation indicates that the `AppConfig` class is the source of the bean definitions, and the `@Bean` annotation defines the bean in our application. We will discuss annotations and beans intensely as we go throughout this chapter.

We have successfully learned how to implement constructor-based dependency injection by using `Bean.xml` and annotations. Now, let's move on to the implementation of setter-based dependency injection.

Setter-based dependency injection

The injection of dependencies can be achieved when the container calls the setter methods of our class. So, instead of creating a constructor for the class, we will create a function that will set the object's dependency.

Let's look at a basic code example:

```
package com.springexample;

/* Class for Student */
public class Student {
    private Grades grades;

    public void setGrades(grades: Grades) {
        this.grades = grades;
    }
    public Grades getGrades() {
        return grades;
    }
    public void retrieveGrades() {
        grades.getGrades();
    }
}
```

In the preceding example, we can see that we have created a setter method named `setGrades()`, which accepts a `Grades` object, and its primary function is to set a value for the `grades` dependency.

Instead of using the constructor with arguments, we use setters to inject our dependencies into our object.

To use the `Student` object, let's see the following example:

```
package com.springexample;
import org.springframework.context.ApplicationContext;
import org.springframework.context.support.
ClassPathXmlApplicationContext;

public class Main {
    public static void main(String[] args) {
        ApplicationContext context = new
            ClassPathXmlApplicationContext("Beans.xml");

        Student student =
            (Student) context.getBean("student");
```

```
        student.retrieveGrades();
    }
}
```

We can see in the preceding example that it's the same as how we used setter-based objects and constructor-based objects. The difference here is how we configure our beans in Bean.xml.

Let's see the Beans.xml example for setter-based dependency injection:

```xml
<?xml version = "1.0" encoding = "UTF-8"?>

<beans xmlns =
    "http://www.springframework.org/schema/beans"
    xmlns:xsi = "http://www.w3.org/2001/XMLSchema-instance"
    xsi:schemaLocation =
      "http://www.springframework.org/schema/beans
       http://www.springframework.org/schema/beans/
       spring-beans-3.0.xsd">

    <!-- Definition for student bean -->
    <bean id = "student"
      class =   "com.springexample.Student">
      <property name="grades" ref = "grades"/>
    </bean>

    <!-- Definition for grades bean -->
    <bean id = "grades"
      class ="com.springexample.Grades"></bean>

</beans>
```

We configured the beans in our Beans.xml, Student, and the Grades object in the preceding example. The only difference here is when we declare dependencies. We use the property tag instead of constructor-arg to define our dependencies.

We have successfully created our object with setter-based dependency injection, and now, we will discuss field-based dependency injection.

Field-based dependency injection

As the name suggests, **field-based dependency injection** is a concept where we inject the object's dependencies directly into the fields. We will not create a constructor or a setter method to inject our dependencies, but we will use the @Autowired annotation for injection.

Let's see the following example of injecting dependencies into a field:

```
package com.springexample;


/* Class for Student */
public class Student {
    @Autowired
    private Grades grades;
}
```

In the preceding example code, we can see that we didn't create a constructor or a setter method to inject our dependency. Instead, we only used the @Autowired annotation to inject the Grades object.

The field-based injection may be clean at first glance, having only annotations in our code and fewer methods, but many things happen behind our @Autowired dependency. For example, it uses reflection to inject dependencies that are costlier than a constructor and setter-based injection; it also violates the **single responsibility principle**. We can add more dependencies directly in the fields without warning.

We have learned the basics of dependency injection and the different ways to implement it in our Java application. Now, we will discuss the concept and importance of annotations and beans in Spring.

Annotation and beans

Annotation and beans are essential parts of developing your Spring applications. They are considered the building blocks of Spring and make our code less boilerplate and maintainable.

Spring annotations are used to define the different types of beans. They are simply a form of metadata that marks our code to provide information. Conversely, **beans** are objects that are instantiated and created and can be injected with other beans. We will discuss more as we go through this section.

Types of annotations

Annotations in Spring are categorized into different types depending on their functionality. The following are annotations grouped into their respective categories.

Core annotations

Core annotations are used to leverage the Spring DI engine in our applications. They can be found in the org.springframework.beans.factory.annotation and org.springframework.context.annotation packages. The following is a list of core annotations:

- @Required: This is applied in the setter methods of a bean and implies that the bean must be injected with the dependency at configuration. Otherwise, it will throw BeanInitializationException. Let's look at the following example of how to use the @Required annotation:

```
public class Car
{
private String brand;
@Required
    public void setBrand(String brand)
    {
       this.brand = brand;
}
    public Integer getBrand()
    {
       return brand;
    }
}
```

In the preceding example, we can see that the setBrand() method was annotated with @Required; this indicates that the brand must be populated on initialization.

- @Autowired: We have encountered the @Autowired annotation several times in DI, and this is mainly used to inject dependencies without the use of constructors and setter methods. Let's look at the following example of how to use the @Autowired annotation:

```
package com.springexample;

public class Car {
    @Autowired
    private Brand brand;
}
```

We can see in the preceding example that @Autowired is applied directly in the field. This is because the annotations use reflection to inject dependencies, with more processes involved than constructors and setter methods.

- @ComponentScan: The annotation is a class-level annotation to indicate the packages we want to be scanned for beans. @ComponentScan can accept arguments about what specific packages are to be scanned, and not providing any will allow the current packages and all sub-packages. Let's look at the following example of how to use @ComponentScan:

```
@Configuration
@ComponentScan
public class SpringApp
  {
    private static ApplicationContext
      applicationContext;
    @Bean
    public SpringBean springBean()
    {
       return new SpringBean();
    }
    public static void main(String[] args) {
      applicationContext = new
        AnnotationConfigApplicationContext(
          SpringComponentScanApp.class);
    }
  }
```

We can see in the preceding example that the @ComponentScan app is applied to the Spring App class, and it is usually implemented together with the @Configuration annotation. Let's say that SpringApp is found under the com.example.spring.app package; this will scan the package and its sub-packages if there are existing beans.

- @ComponentScan: The annotation is also a class-level annotation to indicate that a class is the source of bean definitions that the Spring container will process at runtime. Let's look at the following example of how to use the @ComponentScan annotation:

```
@Configuration
public class SpringApp {

    @Bean(name="demoBean")
    public DemoBean service()
    {

    }
}
```

We can see in the preceding example that the @Configuration annotation is applied to the SpringApp class, which indicates that SpringApp will be the source of beans.

- @Bean: The annotation is a method-level annotation, and it is used to tell a method to produce a bean. Let's look at the following example of how to use the @Bean annotation:

```
@Configuration
public class AppConfig {
    @Bean
    public BeanExample beanExample() {
        return new BeanExampleImlp();
    }
}
```

In the preceding example, the @Bean annotation is applied to the beanExample method. Once JavaConfig encounters the method, it will be executed and register the return value as a bean in BeanFactory, and the name will be the same as the method name when none is specified.

The @Bean annotation can also be configured in Spring XML, and the equivalent configuration is the following:

```
<beans>
    <bean name="transferService"
      class="com.acme.TransferServiceImpl"/>
</beans>
```

Stereotype annotations

Stereotype annotations are mainly used to create Spring beans on the fly in an application context. The following is a list of stereotype annotations:

- @Component: This is the primary stereotype annotation. As with the @Bean annotation, the @Component annotation is used to define a bean or a Spring component. The difference between the two is that @Component is applied at the class level while @Bean is applied at the method level.

  The other difference is that the @Component class cannot also be used to create a bean if the class is outside the Spring container, whereas we can create a bean using @Bean even if the class is found outside the Spring container. Let's look at the following example of how to use the @Component annotation:

```
@Component
public class Car
```

```
{
. . . . . . .
}
```

We can see in the preceding example that @Component is applied to the Car class. This means that this will create a car bean at runtime. We also need to remember that @Component cannot be used with the @Configuration annotation.

- @Service: This annotation, used for the service layer, indicates that a class is used to execute business logic, perform calculations, and call external APIs. @Service is a kind of @Component annotation.

- @Repository: This annotation is used for classes that directly access a database. This is an indication of a class that executes the role of a data access object.

- @Controller: The annotations used for Spring controller classes. It is also a type of @Component annotation, used for Spring MVC and the methods annotated with @RequestMapping, which is used for REST.

Spring Boot annotations

These annotations are created explicitly for Spring Boot, and this is mostly the combination of several annotations. The following is a list of Spring Boot annotations:

- @EnableAutoConfiguration: This annotation is used to auto-configure the bean present in the classpath and then to configure it to run the methods. The annotation is now rarely used, as @SpringBootApplication has already been released in Spring 1.2.0.

- @SpringBootApplication: The annotation is the combination of @EnableAutoConfiguration, @ComponentsScan, and @Configuration.

REST annotations

These are specialized annotations used to create endpoints, specify the HTTP requests, and serialize return objects. The following list shows the different REST annotations:

- @RequestMapping: This is used to create endpoints and map web requests. The annotations can be used in a class or a method.

- @GetMapping: This maps the HTTP GET requests and is used for fetching data, and it is the equivalent of @RequestMapping(method = RequestMethod.GET).

- @PostMapping: This maps the HTTP POST requests and is used for creating data, and it is the equivalent of @RequestMapping(method = RequestMethod.POST).

- @PostMapping: This maps the HTTP PUT requests and is used for updating data, and it is the equivalent of @RequestMapping(method = RequestMethod.PUT).

- `@DeleteMapping`: This maps the HTTP PUT requests and is used for deleting data, and it is the equivalent of `@RequestMapping(method = RequestMethod.DELETE)`.

- `@DeleteMapping`: This maps the HTTP PATCH requests and is used for partial updates on data, and it is the equivalent of `@RequestMapping(method = RequestMethod.PATCH)`.

- `@RequestBody`: This is used to bind HTTP requests with an object in a method parameter. The Spring framework binds the HTTP request body of the parameter with the `@RequestBody` annotation.

- `@ResponseBody`: This attaches the method's return value to the response body. The annotation indicates that the return object should be serialized into a JSON or XML format.

- `@PathVariable`: This is used to get the values from the URI. It is allowed to define multiple `@PathVariable` instances in a method.

- `@RequestParam`: This is used to get the query parameters from the URL.

- `@RequestHeader`: This is used to extract the details about the incoming HTTP request headers. We use this annotation in the parameters of a method.

- `@RestController`: This is a combination of the `@Controller` and `@ResponseBody` annotations. The importance of this annotation is that it prevents annotating each method with `@ResponseBody`.

We have learned about the different types of annotations and their uses in Spring. Now, we will discuss and understand more in the next section the actual definition and importance of beans in Spring applications.

Understanding beans

We have already encountered beans several times in the previous section. We have learned how to create and initialize beans using `@Bean` and `@Component` annotations, but the main question is, *what is the primary use of a bean in Spring applications?*

A **bean** is the central concept of the Spring Framework we need to understand. It is essential to learn its purpose and functionality to use the Spring Framework effectively.

To define a bean in Spring, it is an object that forms the backbone of your application managed by the Spring IoC container. These are the objects that we mainly use for data and to inject dependencies to create multiple implementations. For better understanding, let's have some examples of beans.

Let's assume we have a domain class named `Car`:

```
public class Car
{
```

```
    private Brand brand;
    public Car (Brand brand)
    {
    this.brand = brand;
    }
}
```

We can see in the example that the car needs a `Brand` dependency. The `Brand` class has the following code:

```
public class Brand
{
    private String name;
    private int year;
    public Address(String name, int year)
    {
        this.name = name;
        this.year = year;
    }
}
```

The typical approach is to create a new instance of the `Brand` class and pass it as a parameter upon creating a new `Car` class. This approach will work fine, but this can cause issues when we have many classes. So, a better process is that instead of constructing dependencies by themselves, the objects can retrieve their dependencies from an IoC container in the form of beans.

So, what we only need to do is configure the beans and dependencies using annotations or XML to identify the dependencies required for a specific object. Let's convert the previous example into a bean:

```
@Component
public class Car
{
    . . . .
}
```

We will annotate the `Car` class with the `@Component` annotation to identify the class as Bean:

```
@Configuration
@ComponentScan(basePackageClasses = Car.class)
public class Config
```

```
{
  @Bean
  public Brand getBrand() {
    return new Brand("Toyota", 2021);
  }
}
```

The next thing we need to do is create a configuration class. In the preceding example, we have annotated the class with @Configuration and @ComponentScan to identify that this is our configuration class; this will produce a Bean of type Brand, having configured the Brand class as a Bean. We will only need to pull the beans in the application context, and the dependencies are already injected:

```
ApplicationContext context = new
AnnotationConfigApplicationContext(Config.class);
Car car = context.getBean("car", Car.class);
// execute function
car.getName()
car.getYear()
```

In the preceding example code, we can see that we have extracted the Car bean in the application context. Therefore, we can automatically use the getter methods of the Brand dependency; this means that the IoC container manages the beans and their dependencies.

Summary

With this, we have reached the end of this chapter. Let's have a recap of the valuable things you have learned. You have learned the fundamentals of Spring Boot, its architecture, and the basics of REST. You have also learned how to use Spring Initializr to create your own Spring Boot project.

Dependency injection allows objects or classes to accept other dependencies that can implement different classes without writing them again. Annotations define the different types of beans; they are simply a form of metadata that marks our code to provide information.

And finally, beans are objects that form the backbone of an application managed by the Spring IoC container.

In the next chapter, we will be learning how to set up a database and use Spring Data JPA.

4
Setting Up the Database and Spring Data JPA

In the previous chapter, you learned about Spring Boot's fundamentals to develop our backend application, such as dependency injection, beans, and annotations. In addition, we now know how to create a Spring Boot project using Spring Initializr.

This chapter will teach you how to connect your Spring Boot application to a database by adding a PSQL container and PostgreSQL dependencies and accessing data using the **Java Persistence API** (**JPA**).

In this chapter, we will cover the following topics:

- Connecting to database using a PSQL container
- Spring Data JPA
- Adding Spring Data JPA and PostgreSQL dependencies
- Connecting to a database

Technical requirements

Here is what you need to complete this chapter:

- **PostgreSQL**: `https://www.postgresql.org/download/windows/`
- **pgAdmin**: `https://www.pgadmin.org/download/`
- **Docker**: `https://docs.docker.com/get-docker/`

Connecting to a database using a PSQL container

This section will teach us how to set up and configure our PostgreSQL in our terminal by using the conventional method, using the installer, or through a Docker container. But first, let's discuss what PostgreSQL is and what its advantages are.

PostgreSQL

PostgreSQL is an open source object-relational database system that uses the SQL language to store and handle complicated and large workloads. PostgreSQL also supports both *SQL (relational)* and *JSON (non-relational)* querying. It is commonly used as primary data storage for geospatial and analytics applications because of its flexibility and rich features. Its community has improved and continuously backed it for more than 20 years to add more features and reliability to the database system.

PostgreSQL's flexibility means that it is widely used in developing applications. Here are some of the everyday use cases:

- **Scientific data**: Research projects can be demanding in storing data, which requires effective and efficient handling. PostgreSQL provides analytical features and a powerful SQL engine that can process a large amount of data.

- **Financial industry**: PostgreSQL is used in financial companies because of its analytical capabilities and easy integration with mathematical software such as MATLAB and R.

- **Web applications**: PostgreSQL is also used widely in web applications because apps nowadays require processing thousands of pieces of data. It is compatible with modern web frameworks such as Node.js, Hibernate PHP, and Django.

- **Government GIS data**: PostgreSQL offers extensions such as PostGIS that provide functions to process geometric data.

The features of PostgreSQL

Here's a list of some of the features that PostgreSQL offers:

- **Compatibility with multiple data types**: PostgreSQL is compatible with several data types:

  - **Structured**: Arrays, date and time, **Universally Unique Identifiers** (**UUIDs**), and range

  - **Customizations**: Custom types, and composite

  - **Primitives**: String, integer, numeric, and Boolean

  - **Geometry**: Polygon, circle, line, and point

  - **Document**: XML, JSON/JSONB, and key-value

- **Supports different features of SQL**: It offers the various features of SQL, such as the following:

  - Multiple indexing, such as B-tree and expressions

  - SQL subselects

  - Complex SQL queries

  - **Multi-Version Concurrency Control (MVCC)**:

    - Table partitioning

- **Data integrity compatibility**: It also offers data integrity, which includes the following:

  - Primary keys

  - Foreign keys

  - Explicit locks

  - Advisory locks

  - UNIQUE

  - NOT NULL

- **Secure database**: It adheres to standard security protocols, which includes the following:

  - Authentications such as **Lightweight Directory Access Protocol** (**LDAP**), SCRAM-SHA-256, and the **Security Support Provider Interface** (**SSPI**)

  - Supports column and row-level security

- **Highly extensible**: It offers several features, making it modifiable, such as the following:

  - JSON/SQL path expressions

  - Stored procedures and functions

  - Compatibility with foreign data wrappers

Now that we have an overview of the features and use cases of PostgreSQL, let's move on to installing it on our terminal.

Installing PostgreSQL

There are two ways for us to set up our PostgreSQL in our development terminal. The two approaches are as follows:

- **Conventional method**: Download the installer directly from the PostgreSQL website.

- **PostgreSQL on a Docker container**: Connect our application directly to a container.

The conventional method – installation on Windows, macOS, and Linux

PostgreSQL was mainly developed for Unix-like platforms. However, it was created to be portable and can be installed on Windows and macOS platforms.

The first step we need to take is to download the PostgreSQL installer through this URL: `https://www.enterprisedb.com/downloads/postgres-postgresql-downloads`.

Figure 4.1 – PostgreSQL installation

The steps for the three operating systems are the same, and we only need to configure some settings:

1. Click the latest version (**14.1**) and download the installer, depending on your operating system.

2. After a successful download, open the installer, click **Next**, and specify the path where PostgreSQL will be installed:

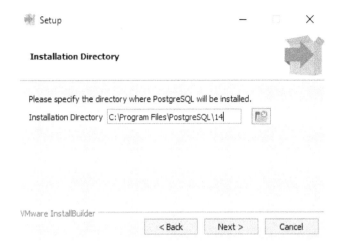

Figure 4.2 – The PostgreSQL installer (specify the path to install)

In the preceding example, we have chosen the default installation path. Click **Next** again, which will ask us what components we want to install. The components that we select are as follows:

- **PostgreSQL Server**: Installs the server where our database will run

- **pgAdmin 4**: A GUI management tool for interacting with the database

- **Stack Builder**: A GUI that allows us to download and install drivers that are compatible with PostgreSQL

- **Command Line Tools**: Provides interaction with PostgreSQL using command-line tools:

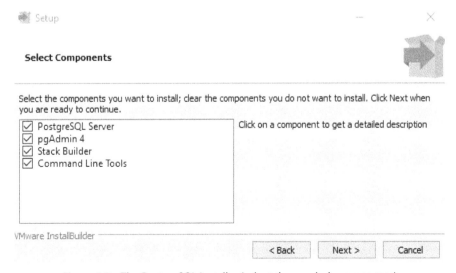

Figure 4.3 – The PostgreSQL installer (select the needed components)

We have checked all the components in the preceding example, as we will need all of them throughout our development.

3. Click **Next** again, and you will be asked to specify the directory to store the data:

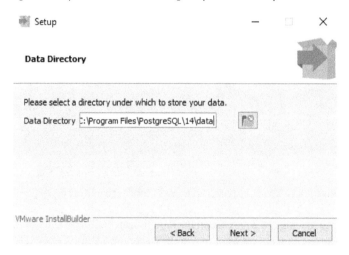

Figure 4.4 – The PostgreSQL installer (select the directory for the data)

In the preceding example, we can see that the default path is the same as where PostgreSQL is installed, and it has created a new folder named data. It is recommended that you use the default path.

4. Click **Next**, which will let you configure the password for the super user (postgres).

5. Click **Next**, which will allow you to set the port to be used for the postgres database.

6. Click **Next** again, and you will now be asked what locale should be used for the database cluster:

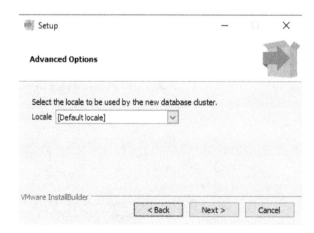

Figure 4.5 – The PostgreSQL installer (select a locale for the database cluster)

In the preceding example, we have selected [**Default locale**] as our locale for the database.

7. Click **Next** again, which will display all of the settings we have configured; make sure all the details are correct before proceeding.

8. After reviewing, click **Next**, which will now install PostgreSQL in our terminal.

    After installation, we can verify whether PostgreSQL is installed successfully by checking the currently installed version.

9. To do this, open **SQL Shell (psql)** and enter the information of our databases, such as `Server`, `Port`, `Database`, `Username`, and `Password`.

10. Since we have used the default settings, we can press *Enter* until password confirmation. After successful validation of our password, execute the `select version()` command to display the currently installed PostgreSQL:

```
Server [localhost]:
Database [postgres]:
Port [5432]:
Username [postgres]:
Password for user postgres:
psql (13.4)
WARNING: Console code page (437) differs from Windows code page (1252)
         8-bit characters might not work correctly. See psql reference
         page "Notes for Windows users" for details.
Type "help" for help.

postgres=# select version();
                              version
------------------------------------------------------------------
 PostgreSQL 13.4, compiled by Visual C++ build 1914, 64-bit
(1 row)


postgres=#
```

Figure 4.6 – The PostgreSQL installer (displaying the version of PostgreSQL)

In the preceding example, we can see that we have successfully installed **PostgreSQL** version **13.4** on our terminal.

Now, let's learn how to install and configure PostgreSQL using Docker.

PostgreSQL on a Docker container

We have installed PostgreSQL on our terminal using the conventional installer; now, we will learn to configure PostgreSQL using Docker. This method will help us skip the complex steps in configuring PostgreSQL for us to start with development and provide a GUI for database management:

1. The first step you need to do is install Docker on your terminal. You can install Docker at the following link: `https://docs.docker.com/get-docker/`. For documentation on the system requirements and installation steps for Docker, you can refer to this link: `https://docs.dockerocker.com/desktop/windows/install/`.

2. After successful installation of Docker, open Docker Desktop and start Docker on your Terminal. Then, open your command line and execute the following command:

   ```
   Docker run --name postgresql-container -p 5434:5434 -e
   POSTGRES_PASSWORD=pass -d postgres
   ```

   The preceding command will pull the PSQL from `Docker-hub`. The `postgresql-container` part in the command can be replaced, as this is a container name that we can define. The `POSTGRES_PASSWORD` parameter is the password for the `postgres` admin, which we can also configure.

3. After executing the command, we can verify the newly created container by executing the `Docker ps -a` command or viewing Docker Desktop to check the list of containers running:

```
C:\Users\Seiji Villafranca>docker ps -a
CONTAINER ID   IMAGE      COMMAND             CREATED          STATUS             PORTS
      NAMES
fccc91ee479f   postgres   "docker-entrypoint.s…"   About a minute ago   Up About a minute   5432/tcp, 0.0.0.0:5434->5434
/tcp   postgresql-container

C:\Users\Seiji Villafranca>
```

Figure 4.7 – The PostgreSQL installation using Docker

In the preceding example, we have executed the `Docker ps -a` command, and we can see that our PostgreSQL image has been pulled:

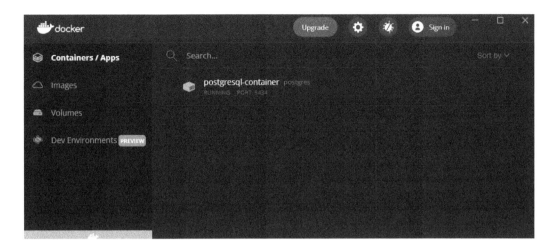

Figure 4.8 – The PostgreSQL installation using Docker (viewing the container in Docker Desktop)

4. We can also view the pulled `postgresql-container` in Docker Desktop and verify its status in our terminal.

We have successfully configured our PostgreSQL with Docker. We can connect this to our `pgAdmin` by creating a new server with our terminal IP address and port.

We have configured the PostgreSQL database in our terminal. Now, we will learn about Spring Data JPA and its importance in developing Spring applications.

Spring Data JPA

Spring Data JPA (Java Persistence API) is a widely used specification for managing relational data in Java applications. It helps develop Spring, as it reduces boilerplate code by not implementing read and write operations. It also handles the complex process involved in JDBC-based accessing of database and object-relational mappings.

Before discussing Spring Data JPA, let's discuss its clear advantages and why it is commonly used in Spring development.

The advantages of Spring Data JPA

The following are the advantages of Spring Data JPA:

- **No-code repositories**: Spring Data JPA promotes *no-code* repositories, which means that we don't have to write the repository pattern, which creates a lot of repetitive code. It provides a set of interfaces that we can use to extend our classes to apply data-specific implementations.

For example, we have a `BlogRepository` class in our application; when we extend it with the `CrudRepository<Blog, Long>` interface, it will have methods that have the following functionalities:

- Persisting, updating, and deleting one or multiple blog entities

- Finding one or multiple blogs by their primary keys

- Counting all blogs

- Validating whether a single blog exists

Extending the repository with the interface provided by Spring Data JPA includes all data-related methods, which allows us to focus more on business logic.

- **Boilerplate reduction**: Spring Data JPA offers built-in implementations for methods. As stated in the first advantage, we only need to focus on business logic and no longer need to code read and write operations, as written under the interfaces. This also prevents human errors, as all implementations are already registered for us.

- **Generated queries**: Spring Data JPA also can create queries based on method names. For example, if we wanted to query a single blog by an author, the only step we need to take is to create a method on our interface with a name that starts with `findBy`, and Spring will parse the name and create a query:

```
public interface BlogRepository
extends    CrudRepository<Blog, Long> {
Blog findByAuthor(String author);
}
```

In the preceding example, we have created a `findByAuthor()` method, which will allow Spring to generate a query and set the parameters as bind parameter values. It will execute the query once we call the method.

Repositories provided by Spring Data JPA

Spring Data JPA provides repositories that provide different methods for data-related implementations. The repositories are the following:

- `CrudRepository`: The interface repository, which provides the basic operations to **Create**, **Read**, **Update**, and **Delete (CRUD)**.

- `PagingAndSortingRepository`: Extends `CrudRepostiory` and adds a method named `findAll`, which can sort results and be retrieved in a paginated manner.

- `JpaRepository`: Adds specific JPA methods and has all the functions of `CrudRepository` and `PagingAndSortingRepository`. It also adds methods such as `flush()`, which flushes the persistence context, and `deleteInBatch()`, which deletes records in a batch.

We have learned about the different repositories we can use with Spring Data JPA. We will now take a look at Spring Data JPA on Spring Boot.

Spring Data JPA on Spring Boot

For us to implement Spring Data JPA in our application, we need the following components:

- Entity: This is a simple class that defines our model. It will be used as a JPA entity, generated with a primary key.

  For example, we will create an entity for Villain by making a plain class and adding @Entity annotations to indicate the Villain class as a JPA entity. The entity will be used as the type for extending our repository:

  ```
  @Entity
  public class Villain {

    @Id
    @GeneratedValue(strategy = GenerationType.AUTO,
                    generator   = "UUID")
    @Column(nullable = false, updatable = false)
    private UUID id;

    @NotNull(message = "First Name is required")
    private String firstName;

    private String lastName;
    private String house;
    private String knownAs;
  }
  ```

  We can see in the preceding example that our Villain class is annotated with @Entity, indicating it as a JPA entity. We have also defined an id field of the UUID type and annotated it with @Id to indicate that this is the primary key, and @GeneratedValue, where we specified that this is automatically generated using strategy = GenerationType.The AUTO and the ID generated should be of the UUID type, using generator = "UUID".

- Repository: This is an interface that we need to extend with JPA repositories for the entities to have built-in operations.

  In the previous example, we have a Villain entity. To implement the CRUD operations, we will create a VillainRepository interface and extend it with CrudRepository, with a type of Villain and UUID:

  ```
  @Repository
  public interface VillainRepository extends
  CrudRepository<Villain, UUID> {


      // custom composite repository here
  }
  ```

- Service: This is where we will use our created repository. We can use the @Autowired annotation to inject the repository and call the JPA and custom-defined methods:

  ```
  @Service
  public class VillainService {
  private final VillainRepository villainRepository;

  @Autowired
  public VillainService (VillainRepository
  villainRepository) {
    this. villainRepository = villainRepository;
  }

    public Iterable<Villain> findAllVillains () {
      return villainRepository.findAll ();
    }

    public Villain findVillainById (UUID id) {
      return findOrThrow (id);
    }
  ```

In the preceding example, we can see that we have injected VillainRepository in VillainService using the @Autowired annotation.

Let's continue with the following methods using the same file:

```
public void removeVillainById(UUID id) {
    villainRepository.deleteById(id);
}

public Villain addVillain(Villain villain) {
    return villainRepository.save(villain);
}

public void updateVillain(UUID id, Villain villain) {
    findOrThrow(id);
    villainRepository.save(villain);
}

private Villain findOrThrow(final UUID id) {
    return villainRepository
        .findById(id)
        .orElseThrow(
            () -> new NotFoundException("Villain by id " +
                id + " was not found")
        );
}
}
```

We have also created methods by using the built-in JPA implementation, such as `save()`, `deleteById()`, `findAll()`, and `findById()`, which are found in the `CrudRepository` interface. The service can now be injected into our controllers or other services to use the methods.

We've now learned about Spring Data JPA, its advantages, and an overview of implementation on Spring JPA. In the next section, we will learn how to add Spring Data JPA and PostgreSQL dependencies to our Spring Boot application.

Adding Spring Data JPA and PostgreSQL dependencies

This section will add Spring Data JPA, PostgreSQL, and other valuable dependencies to our application. We will add the dependencies with Spring Initializr and an existing Spring Boot project.

Adding with Spring Initializr

Adding dependencies after creating a Spring Boot application using Spring Initializr is simple. We only need to select the dependencies on Initializr before generating our project:

1. The first thing to do is to go to `https://start.spring.io/` or to your IntelliJ IDEA (for Ultimate users) to open Spring Initializr (for a recap of the *Using Spring Initializr* section, refer to *Chapter 3, Moving into Spring Boot*).

2. Choose your project if it will use Maven or Gradle and set the required configurations, which are **Group**, **Artifact, Name, Description**, **Package name**, **Packaging**, and the **Java** version of the project.

3. Next, click **Add Dependencies** at the top right and select the following dependencies:

   • **Spring Data JPA**: This dependency is for adding Spring Data JPA used for built-in data store-related implementation.

   • **H2 Database**: This is an in-memory database that supports the JDBC API and R2DBC access, which is commonly used for unit testing

   • **PostgreSQL Driver**: This is a JDBC and R2DBC driver that will allow the connection of Java applications to the PostgreSQL database:

Figure 4.9 – Adding dependencies in Spring Initializr

After successfully adding the dependencies, we can see that our dependencies are already listed.

4. Click on **GENERATE**, which will download our already generated project.

5. Extract the ZIP file and open the project on your IDE. If you developed your project using Maven, open pom.xml in the src folder, or if you are using Gradle, open build.gradle, which is also found in the src folder:

Figure 4.10 – The Spring Boot application (a view of pom.xml)

In the preceding example, we can see that the Spring Boot application is generated with Maven, and we can see that our pom.xml file has included the dependencies we added in Spring Initializr:

Figure 4.11 – The Spring Boot application (a view of build.gradle)

Now, in the preceding example, where the Spring Boot application is generated with Gradle, we can see the list of dependencies is already added under the `build.gradle` file.

We will now add the dependencies to an existing Spring Boot application.

Adding an existing project

In the previous example, we added the dependencies to generate our Spring Boot application using Spring Initializr. Now, we will add our dependencies to an existing application. It is simple to add a dependency to an existing Spring app; we only need to modify the `pom.xml` (Maven) or `build.gradle` (Gradle) files.

To install Spring Data JPA, the H2 database, and PostgreSQL Driver using Maven, we will add the dependencies in the form of XML, as follows:

```
<dependencies>
    <dependency>
        <groupId>org.springframework.boot</groupId>
        <artifactId>spring-boot-starter-data-jpa</artifactId>
    </dependency>

    <dependency>
        <groupId>com.h2database</groupId>
        <artifactId>h2</artifactId>
```

```
        <scope>runtime</scope>
    </dependency>

    <dependency>
        <groupId>org.postgresql</groupId>
        <artifactId>postgresql</artifactId>
        <scope>runtime</scope>
    </dependency>

    <dependency>
        <groupId>org.springframework.boot</groupId>
        <artifactId>spring-boot-starter-test</artifactId>
        <scope>test</scope>
    </dependency>
</dependencies>
```

And for a Spring application using Gradle, we will add the dependencies as follows:

```
dependencies {
    implementation 'org.springframework.boot:spring-boot-
    starter-data-jpa'
    runtimeOnly 'com.h2database:h2'
    runtimeOnly 'org.postgresql:postgresql'

}
```

IntelliJ will automatically recognize the added dependencies and install them for the project, and we can successfully build and run the Spring Boot application on the fly.

We have learned how to add Spring Data JPA and PostgreSQL Driver to our Spring Boot application. In the next section, we will learn how to connect our Spring Boot application to our PostgreSQL database.

Connecting to a database

We have already configured our PostgreSQL database and initialized our Spring Boot application with the needed dependencies. Now, we will learn how to connect our PostgreSQL to our application. There are two ways we can connect to our database – the first is through Spring JDBC, and the other is Spring Data JPA. Spring Data JPA is the most convenient way to connect to our database, but we will demonstrate both methods in this section.

Configuring the database properties

The first thing we need to do is configure the database properties in our Spring Boot application. We need to specify the server URL of the database, the admin username, and the password by adding the following source code to the `application.properties` file:

```
spring.datasource.url=jdbc:postgresql://localhost:5432/springDB
spring.datasource.username=postgres
spring.datasource.password=password
```

In the preceding example, we can see that we have configured the basic connection settings for our PostgreSQL. `springDB` on the URL will be the name of the database in PostgreSQL, which should already exist on our server.

Connecting using Spring JDBC

The first method to connect to the database is by using Spring JDBC. We will add an additional dependency to our application for us to use this method.

To add JDBC, we will add the following code to our `pom.xml` (Maven) or `build.gradle` (Gradle) files:

```
<dependency>
    <groupId>org.springframework.boot</groupId>
    <artifactId>spring-boot-starter-jdbc</artifactId>
</dependency>
```

After successfully adding the JDBC dependency, we can now use `JdbcTemplate` to execute queries on our application:

```
import org.springframework.beans.factory.annotation.Autowired;
import org.springframework.boot.SpringApplication;
import org.springframework.boot.autoconfigure.
SpringBootApplication;
import org.springframework.jdbc.core.JdbcTemplate;

@SpringBootApplication
public class AwesomeJavaProject  {
    @Autowired
    private JdbcTemplate jdbcTemplate;
    public static void main(String[] args) {
```

```
        SpringApplication.run(AwesomeJavaProject .class,
                                args);
    }
    @Override
    public void run(String... args) throws Exception {
        String sql = "INSERT INTO blog (title, author,
           body) VALUES ("+ "'Awesome Java Project',
                        'Seiji Villafranca', 'This is an
                           awesome blog for java')";
        int rows = jdbcTemplate.update(sql);
    }

}
```

In the preceding example, we can execute database statements such as INSERT in our application and call the update() method to modify data in the database.

Connecting using Spring Data JPA

The second method is by using the Spring Data JPA plugin. The first step we need to take is to add additional details to the application.properties file:

```
spring.jpa.hibernate.ddl-auto=update
spring.jpa.show-sql=true
spring.jpa.properties.hibernate.dialect=org.hibernate.dialect.
PostgreSQLDialect
spring.jpa.properties.hibernate.format_sql=true
```

After adding the new settings, we can now create Entity and Repository for a specific table in our application – for example, we have a Blog table:

```
package net.codejava;
import javax.persistence.*;
@Entity
@Table(name = "blog")
public class Blog {
    @Id
    @GeneratedValue(strategy = GenerationType.IDENTITY)
```

```
    private Integer id;

    private String title;
    private String body;
    private String author;

}
```

In the preceding example, we have created a `Blog` class and annotated it with `@Entity` and `@Table` to indicate that this is an object connected to our database table:

```
package net.codejava;
import org.springframework.data.JPA.repository.JpaRepository;

public interface BlogRepository extends JpaRepository<Blog,
Integer> {
}
```

After creating our entity, we have made the repository for the blog, which can be extended by the repositories provided by JPA. `BlogRepository` can now be injected into our services or controllers to read, add, modify, or delete data on our database.

Summary

That brings you to the end of this chapter. Let's have a recap of the valuable things you have learned. You learned how to set up PostgreSQL on your local machine using the installer or Docker container.

You have also learned about the concepts and advantages of Spring Data JPA in Spring Boot and how to add it to your application, which is helpful in creating services with CRUD capabilities with less boilerplate code.

Last but not least, you learned how to connect your Spring Boot application with the PostgreSQL database using JDBC and Spring Data JPA.

In the next chapter, we will be learning how to start our server, how to add controllers, models, and services in our code, and about Redis for caching.

5

Building APIs with Spring

In the previous chapter, you learned about the concepts and advantages of PostgreSQL and set it up on your local machine using the installer or the Docker container. You know how to configure **Spring Data Java Persistence API** (**Spring Data JPA**) on our project and use its provided repositories to perform **Create, Read, Update**, and **Delete** (**CRUD**) operations on our database with less boilerplate code. Lastly, you have also learned to connect your application with PostgreSQL using the **Java Database Connectivity** (**JDBC**) driver and Spring Data JPA.

This chapter will create your Spring Boot **application programming interface** (**API**) project; we will focus on coding, making our models, and adding controllers and services to develop our endpoints. We will also add **Remote Dictionary Server** (**Redis**) for caching to help improve our application performance.

In this chapter, we will cover the following topics:

- Starting the server
- Adding models
- Writing services
- Adding controllers
- Adding Redis for caching

Technical requirements

There are no technical requirements for this chapter.

The link to the finished version of this chapter can be found here:

```
https://github.com/PacktPublishing/Spring-Boot-and-Angular/tree/
main/Chapter-05/superheroes
```

Starting the server

In this section, we will now attempt to run our Spring Boot application on our server but first, let's have a recap of the previous chapter: we learned how to configure Spring Data JPA and connect our application to our PostgreSQL database, and—most importantly—we have installed all of the needed dependencies in our application. These are all prerequisites before running the Spring Boot application.

In the following examples, we will be using an application named `spring-boot-superheroes`. We will generate a new Spring Boot application using **Spring Initializr** with the same dependencies. Throughout developing our application, we will also show you several ways to write the different parts of your API, such as how to write models, services, and controllers. These are the most common ways used now in the industry. Still, first things first: let's proceed with running our Spring Boot application.

We assume that you have already generated your Spring Boot application with the needed dependencies. However, if you have missed this part or are unsure whether all dependencies are included on your generated project, let's list again all the dependencies we installed in the previous chapter, as follows:

- **Spring Data JPA**: Dependency for adding Spring Data JPA used for built-in data store-related implementation.

- **PostgreSQL Driver**: A JDBC and **Reactive Relational Database Connectivity** (**R2DBC**) driver that will allow the connection of Java applications to the PostgreSQL database.

- **H2 Database**: An in-memory database that supports JDBC API and R2DBC access; this is commonly used for unit testing.

If you have successfully initialized your application with the listed dependencies, open your project in your preferred **integrated development environment** (**IDE**); we will be using IntelliJ for Spring Boot in the following examples. Then, proceed as follows:

1. Expand the project folder; we will see several folders inside, as indicated in the following screenshot:

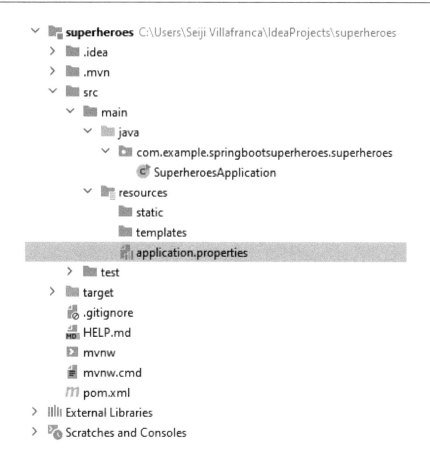

Figure 5.1 – Project structure of the Spring Boot application

We can see the files and folders in our Spring Boot application in the preceding screenshot. We can find our main class, named `SuperHeroesApplication`, under `src/main/java`. This main class will be used in running our application on the server.

`application.properties` is also an important file that we need to configure, as this is where all the properties are placed that are necessary for connecting to our database.

2.   Open the `application.properties` file, and we should set the following configuration:

```
spring.main.allow-bean-definition-overriding=true
spring.datasource.url=jdbc:postgresql://localhost:5432/
{{databasename}}
spring.datasource.username=postgres
spring.datasource.password=pass
spring.jpa.hibernate.ddl-auto=update
```

```
spring.jpa.show-sql=true
spring.jpa.properties.hibernate.dialect=org.hibernate.
dialect.PostgreSQLDialect
spring.jpa.properties.hibernate.format_sql=true
```

This configuration will allow us to connect to our **PostgreSQL database** on our local machine. Remember that the database should exist on our PostgreSQL servers; otherwise, our application will not run successfully. If you haven't created your database, open **pgAdmin** and enter your master password; on the left panel, expand the **Servers** section.

3. You will see the PostgreSQL instance on your local machine. Right-click on the instance, select **Connect Server**, and enter the password for the `postgres` user. This will now access the databases on our server, as illustrated in the following screenshot:

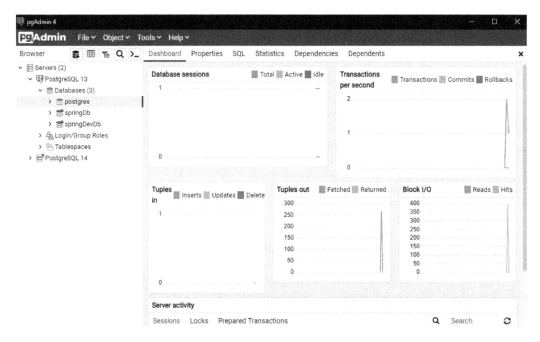

Figure 5.2 – Accessing PostgreSQL server using pgAdmin

4. After successfully accessing the server, right-click on **Database**, select **Create**, and click on **Database**; this will open the following modal:

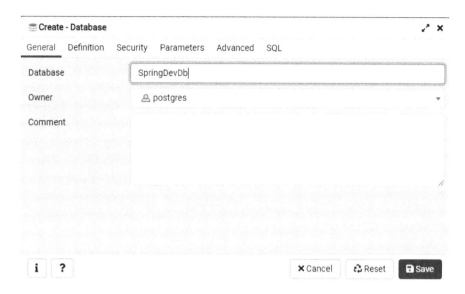

Figure 5.3 – Creating a database

In the preceding screenshot, we named our database `SpringDevDB` and set the `postgres` user value in the **Owner** field. Click **Save**, and our database is all set in our server.

5. Our Spring Boot application is now ready to run on our server; in your IntelliJ IDE, click on **Add Configuration**, found on the upper-right side of the panel. This will open the modal where we will configure our entry point to run our application, as illustrated in the following screenshot:

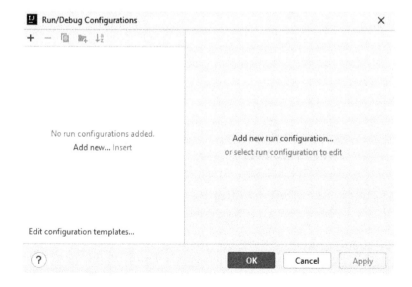

Figure 5.4 – Adding configuration for Spring Boot

6.   Click on **Add new run configuration…** shown in the preceding screenshot and select **Application**. Under the **Main class** field, type the main class, which is SuperheroesApplication, and this will automatically fill the program arguments with the correct fully qualified name of the class, as illustrated in the following screenshot:

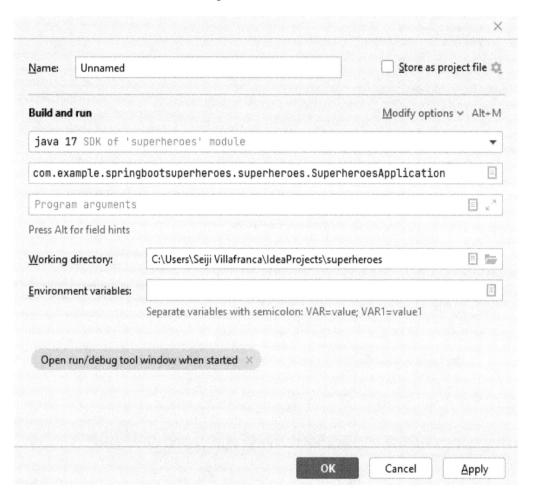

Figure 5.5 – Configuration for application

Click on **Apply** and then click **OK** to save the configuration changes.

7.   In the upper-right panel of the IDE, select the created configuration and run the project by clicking on the green play icon. The application will run on the installed Tomcat server on the default port 8080; we can also use the terminal to check whether the Spring Boot project has successfully started on the server. You can see the process running in the following screenshot:

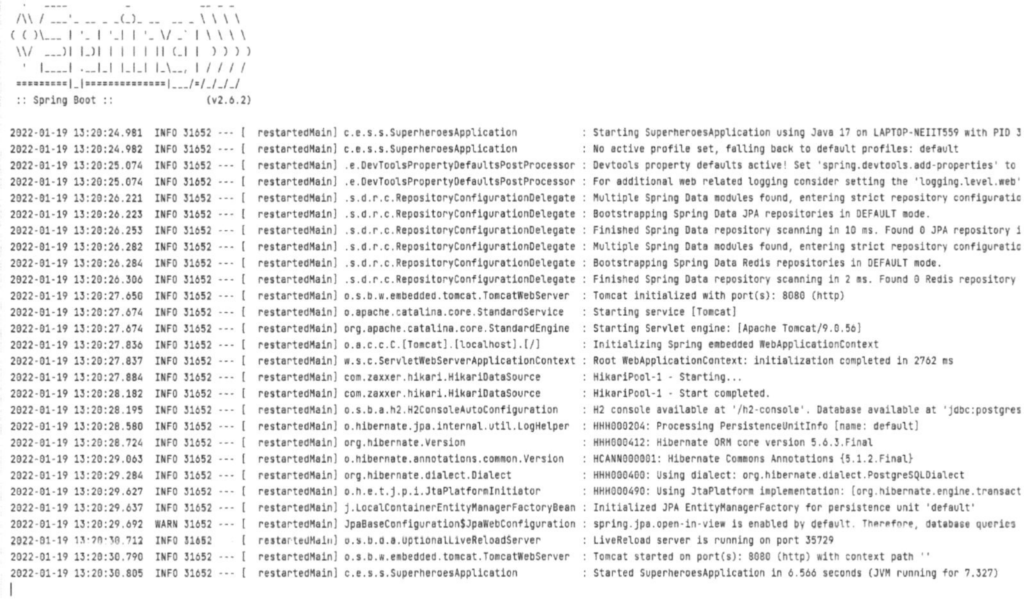

Figure 5.6 – Spring Boot logs

In the preceding screenshot, we can see that our application has started successfully; we are also connected to our PostgreSQL database, and we can now start writing our code.

We will now try to create our application models in the next section.

Adding models

In this section, we will now write code for our application, and the first thing we will create is models. In simple terms, models are the object of our application; the models will serve as our entities and will define our tables in the database.

Once we create models and run the application, this will also generate tables in our database automatically with the help of annotations, which will also be discussed throughout this example.

Creating models with DTOs and Lombok

We will first show you how to write models using Lombok and **data transfer objects** (**DTOs**). First, we will discuss DTOs.

DTOs

DTOs are responsible for carrying data between processes to reduce the number of method calls. DTOs are **plain old Java objects** (**POJOs**) that commonly consist of data accessors.

DTOs are very useful for creating representations of our entities to have views for clients without affecting the pattern and design. Let's have an example use case for DTOs. You can see this here:

```
public class Blog {
private String id;
private String title;
private String description;
private String author;
public Blog(String title, String description,
            String author) {
    this.name = title;
    this.description = description
    this.author = author
}
```

In the preceding code, we have created an example domain model that will represent entities in our database. There are instances where we would not want to include some information on sending data to the client, which is where DTOs would enter the scene. We will create two DTOs for the blog model used for getting and creating data, as follows:

```
Public class BlogDTO {
    private String title;
    private String description;
}
```

In the preceding example DTO, we have created a `BlogDTO` class that will be used for retrieving data; our objective is to hide the author's name, thus not including it as a field in the DTO. The code is illustrated in the following snippet:

```
Public class BlogCreationDTO {
    private String title;
    private String description;
    private String author;
}
```

The next DTO we have created is `BlogCreationDTO`, which will create a new blog. We can see that all fields necessary to create a new blog are included.

The created DTOs will be used for our controllers in the following sections.

Lombok

Lombok is a third-party library used to reduce boilerplate code using annotations. Lombok allows us to avoid repetitive code, especially in creating models such as getter and setter methods.

Let's have a comparison between a model without Lombok and a model using Lombok, as follows:

```
public class Blog {
    private String title;
    private String description;
    private String author;
    public Blog() {}
    public Blog(String title, String description,
                String author) {
    super()
      this.name = title;
      this.description = description
      this.author = author
}
    public String getAuthor() {return author;}
    public void setAuthor(String author) {
    this.author = author; }
    public String getTitle() {return title;}
    public void setTitle(String title) {
    this.title = title; }
    public String getDescription() {return description;}
    public void setDescription(String description) {
    this.description = description; }

    @Override public String toString()
    {return "Blog ["
            + "author=" + author + ", title=" + title
            + ", " + " description =" + description + "]";
    }
}
```

In the preceding code example, we have created a blog model without using Lombok; we can see that we have created a getter and setter method for each field, and we have also created constructors with and without arguments. The code in this example is still manageable.

Still, if our model is required to contain more fields, we need to create setters and getters for the new fields, creating more boilerplate code inside our model and sacrificing the maintainability of our code.

The class and annotations should be as shown in the following code block:

```
@Data
@AllArgsConstructor
@NoArgsConstructor
public class Blog {
    private String title;
    private String description;
    private String author;
}
```

In the preceding screenshot, we have used Lombok to create our blog model, and we can see that a considerable amount of code has been omitted from the model. The @Data annotation generates setter and getter methods, a toString() method, and a constructor with required arguments.

@AllArgsConstructor and @NoArgsConstructor are accountable for the constructor with all and no arguments.

The advantage of using Lombok is evident in the previous examples; it makes code easier to read and less error-prone, promotes easy cleanup and maintainability, and gives effortless logging and debugging.

Model application

Now that we have learned about the importance of DTO and Lombok, let's go back to our Spring Boot application. Under the java folder, right-click on the package and select **Package**. This will display a small window that will allow you to enter a new package.

In this example, we will create a new package named antiHero. After completing the new package, we will create two new packages under antiHero, calling them dto and entity. You can see the packages in the following screenshot:

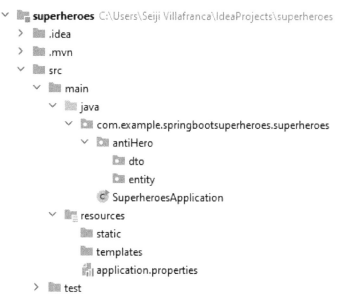

Figure 5.7 – Project structure after the creation of packages

Our project structure should now look just as it is presented in the preceding screenshot. Let's first create our entity; right-click on the entity package we have created, and then click on **New | JPA | Entity**. This will open a model for creating a new entity. We will name our entity `AntiHeroEntity` and click on the **OK** button. The process is illustrated in the following screenshot:

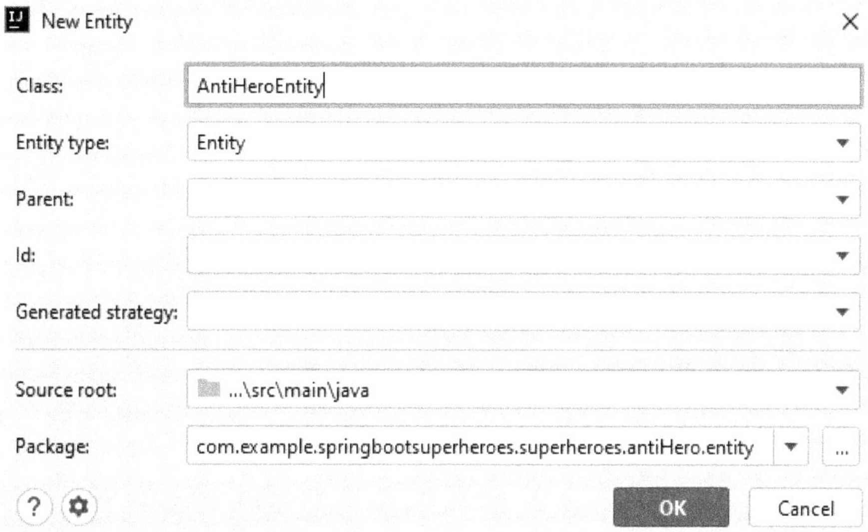

Figure 5.8 – Creating an entity

We will see a newly generated class under the `entity` package, and it will have the following code:

```
package com.example.springbootsuperheroes.superheroes.antiHero.
entity;

import javax. persistence.Entity;
import javax.persistence.Table;

@Entity
@Table(name = "anti_hero_entity")
public class AntiHeroEntity {


}
```

An entity was automatically generated with the `@Entity` and `@Table` annotations that will be used to identify this model as an object in the database. The current code will have some issues, stating that the entity does not have a **primary key (PK)**; in this case, we will add the following to our model:

- `@Data`: Lombok annotations that will set the getter and setter methods, the `toString()` method, and `@RequiredArgsConstructor`.

- `@AllArgsConstructor`: Lombok annotations for generating a constructor for the model with all fields as arguments.

- `@NoArgsConstructor`: Lombok annotations for generating a constructor for the model with no arguments.

- `@Id`: Found under `javax.persistence.*`, this will determine the model's PK.

- `@GeneratedValue`: Used on the PK to determine which generation type will be used.

- `@NotNull`: Found under `javax.validation.constraints` and validates that a specific field cannot be null.

The dependency should be installed by adding the following code to `pom.xml`:

```
<dependency>
    <groupId>org.springframework.boot</groupId>
    <artifactId>spring-boot-starter-validation</artifactId>
</dependency>
```

After adding the dependency to `pom.xml`, right-click on your project and select **Maven | Reload project** to install the new dependency.

After successfully adding the Lombok annotations, PK, validations, and fields to our model, we will have the following code:

```
package com.example.springbootsuperheroes
.superheroes.antiHero.entity;
…


import java.text.SimpleDateFormat;
import java.util.Date;
import java.util.UUID;
import javax.persistence.*;
import javax.validation.constraints.NotNull;
import lombok.AllArgsConstructor;
import lombok.Data;
import lombok.NoArgsConstructor;
…
```

After adding all the preceding packages, we can now start writing our class and the annotations, like so:

```
@Data
@Entity
@Table
@AllArgsConstructor
@NoArgsConstructor
public class AntiHeroEntity {

    @Id
    @GeneratedValue(strategy = GenerationType.AUTO,
                    generator = "UUID")
    @Column(nullable = false, updatable = false)
    private UUID id;

    @NotNull(message = "First Name is required")
    private String firstName;

    private String lastName;
    private String house;
```

```
    private String knownAs;
    private String createdAt =
      new SimpleDateFormat("dd-MM-yyyy HH:mm:ss z")
          .format(new Date());
}
```

In the preceding code block, we can see that we have added a PK of the UUID type; this will be automatically generated once we insert new anti-hero data into our database. The type is defined using the @GeneratedValue annotation, where we have also indicated that the strategy will be using an auto generator. We have also added several fields that will be used to store the anti-hero information.

We have successfully created our entity; now, we will create a DTO for the anti-hero entity. Right-click on the dto package, select **New** | **Java class**, and we will name the new class AntiHeroDto. After successfully creating the DTO, we will place the following code into it:

```
package com.example.superheroes.antiHero.dto;

import java.util.UUID;
import javax.validation.constraints.NotNull;
import lombok.Getter;
import lombok.Setter;

@Getter
@Setter
public class AntiHeroDto {

  private UUID id;

  @NotNull(message = "First Name is required")
  private String firstName;

  private String lastName;
  private String house;
  private String knownAs;
}
```

In the preceding code example, we have added fields that we only want to display as we send the anti-hero data to the client; in this case, we have removed the createdAt field in our DTO. We have also added @Getter and @Setter annotations to generate getter and setter methods for our DTO, and lastly, we have also added @NotNull validation to match our constraint with the entity.

We have successfully created our DTO and models with Lombok in our application. In the next section, we will make our services responsible for the CRUD functionalities of our Spring Boot application.

Writing services

In this section, we will now write the services for our application, but first, let's discuss the primary purpose of services in Spring Boot. Services are classes where we place all of our business logic; this is where we will write our CRUD functionalities with the help of JPA repositories. In this case, we will not only make our service class but will also create our JPA repository.

JPA repository

As discussed in *Chapter 4*, *Setting Up the Database and Spring Data JPA*, the JPA repository is a widely used specification for managing relational data in Java applications. It helps develop Spring by reducing boilerplate code by not implementing read and write operations.

It is simple to create a JPA repository in Spring Boot; having said that, the JPA library provides classes such as `CrudRepository` that we can use to extend our classes. Let's make one in our Spring Boot application example. Proceed as follows:

1. Right-click on our `antiHero` package, select **New**, and click on the **Package** option.

2. Create a new package named `repository`.

3. After creating the new package, right-click on the `repository` package, select **New**, and click on the **Class** option.

4. As the small modal pops up, switch to the **Interface** option and name the interface `AntiHeroRepository`. The following code will be generated:

```
package com.example.springbootsuperheroes.superheroes.
antiHero.repository;

import com.example.springbootsuperheroes.superheroes.
antiHero.entity.AntiHeroEntity;
import org.springframework.data.repository.
CrudRepository;

import java.util.UUID;

public interface AntiHeroRepository {
}
```

We have created our interface, but this is just a simple interface. We will extend our interface with the CrudRepository class to convert it to a JPA repository, as follows:

```
public interface AntiHeroRepository extends
CrudRepository<AntiHeroEntity, UUID> {
}
```

AntiHeroRepository, as we have already extended it with CrudRepository<Type, ID>, will have methods that have the following functionalities:

- Persisting, updating, and deleting one of the blog entities
- Finding one or multiple blogs by their PKs
- Counting all blogs
- Validating whether a single blog exists

We have successfully created our JPA repository; our next step is to do our service. Our goal is to create a service that will have the capability to get an entire list, get a single database in a PK, insert new data, update selected data, and delete data. We can achieve this through the following methods provided by the JPA repository:

- findAll(): Gets all the existing data in a specific entity
- findById(Id): Finds a particular database by PK
- save(): Inserts new data in the table
- save(data): Updates existing data in the table
- deleteById(id): Deletes specific data in the table by PK

Now that we have successfully identified the methods we need for our service, let's next create our service. Right-click on the antiHero package and create a new package named service; after creating the new package, create a new class under the service package called AntiHeroService, and we will place the following methods inside the service:

```
public class AntiHeroService {

    private final AntiHeroRepository repo;

    public Iterable<AntiHeroEntity> findAllAntiHeroes() {
        return repo.findAll();
    }
}
```

```
public AntiHeroEntity findAntiHeroById(UUID id) {
    return findById(id);
}

public void removeAntiHeroById(UUID id) {
    repo.deleteById(id);
}

public AntiHeroEntity addAntiHero(
  AntiHeroEntity antiHero) {
    return repo.save(antiHero);
}

public void updateAntiHero(UUID id,
  AntiHeroEntity antiHero) {
    repo.save(antiHero);
}
}
```

Let's discuss the preceding code; we have added several methods to our service, and these are explained in more detail here:

- `Iterable<AntiHeroEntity> findAllAntiHeroes()`: This method calls `findAll()` from `AntiHeroRepository`, which returns an `Iterable` instance of `AntiHeroEntity`.

- `AntiHeroEntity findAntiHeroById(UUID id)`: This method calls `findById(id)` from `AntiHeroRepository`, which returns a single `AntiHeroEntity` instance based on the `Id` value.

- `removeAntiHeroById(UUID id)`: This method calls `deleteById(id)` from `AntiHeroRepository`, which deletes a single `AntiHeroEntity` instance based on the `Id` value.

- `void AntiHeroEntity addAntiHero(AntiHeroEntity antiHero)`: This method calls `save()` from `AntiHeroRepository` and inserts a new `AntiHeroEntity` instance in the database.

- `void updateAntiHero(UUID id, AntiHeroEntity antiHero)`: This method calls `save(antiHero)` from `AntiHeroRepository`, which updates a specific `AntiHeroEntity` instance in the database.

After successfully adding the method for our service, we will add @AllArgsConstructor and @Service annotations to AntiHeroService. @AllArgsConstructor is an annotation from Lombok that will generate a constructor that requires one argument of each field; in our example, this will produce the following code:

```
public AntiHeroService(AntiHeroRepository repo) {
   this.repo = repo;
}
```

This will now allow the wiring of our AntiHeroRepository dependency on our service.

The @Service annotation, on the other hand, is functional when we want Spring Context to autodetect classes based on their classification.

We have now successfully created our service with CRUD methods, but what if something went wrong as we call our service? For example, the **identifier (ID)** of the anti-hero we have passed may not exist. We would want to catch the error and return an understandable message to the user. Now, we will create runtime exception handling for our service.

Runtime exceptions

Runtime exceptions are also known as unchecked exceptions. These are programming errors and will happen upon the current execution of our application. This should be prevented directly by the developers.

Some known runtime exceptions are listed here:

- IndexOutOfBoundsException: This exception occurs when we access an index of an array string or an iterable that is out of range, as illustrated in the following code snippet:

```
String[] array = new String[100];
String name = array[200]; // throws index out of bounds
as array variable only has a length of 100
```

- IllegalArgumentException: This exception occurs when a method has been passed by an illegal argument, as illustrated in the following code snippet:

```
public class Hero {
    int number;
    public void givePositiveNumber(int number) {
        if(number < 0)   throw new
          IllegalArgumentException(
            Integer.toString(number));
        else { m = number; }
```

```
    }
    public static void main(String[] args) {
        Hero h = new Hero();
        // throws illegal argument exception as -1 is a
        // negative number
        h.givePositiveNumber(-1);
    }
        }
```

- NullPointerException: This exception occurs when a variable is accessed that does not point to any object or is simply null, as illustrated in the following code snippet:

```
public void doAction(ExampleObject obj) {    obj.
doActionOnMethod();
}
// call doAction()
// throws null pointer exception as we are accessing a
// method on a null object
doAction(null)
```

These are just common runtime exceptions that we use in our application; we can also create runtime exceptions using the RunTimeException class. In this example, let's create a NotFoundException runtime exception that we will use to get a non-existent ID. Proceed as follows:

1. Under the main package, create a new package named exception; after successfully creating the package, create a class named NotFoundException. We will extend our created class with the RunTimeException class and will add the following code:

```
public class NotFoundException extends RuntimeException {

    public NotFoundException(String message) {
        super(message);
    }

    public NotFoundException(String message,
                                Throwable cause) {
        super(message, cause);
    }
```

```
        public NotFoundException(Throwable cause) {
            super(cause);
        }
    }
```

In the preceding code snippet, we have declared several methods with `NotFoundException` with different arguments; having successfully created our custom exception, we can now use it on our service.

2. Go back to `AntiHeroService`, and we will add the following method:

```
private AntiHeroEntity findOrThrow(final UUID id) {
    return repo
            .findById(id)
            .orElseThrow(
                () -> new NotFoundException("Anti-hero
                    by id " + id + " was not found")
            );
}
```

In the preceding code example, we have created a new method named `findOrThrow()`; this is also calling the `findById()` method. The only difference is that it checks whether the given ID exists on the database; otherwise, it will throw something based on our code. In this case, we would want to throw a `NotFoundException` runtime exception.

3. After this, we can use it now on `findAntiHeroById()` by replacing `findById()` with the `findOrThrow()` method and also add it to the `updateAntiHero()` and `deleteAntiHero()` methods to check whether the data exists before updating or deleting it. The code to accomplish this is illustrated here:

```
public AntiHeroEntity findAntiHeroById(UUID id) {
    return findOrThrow(id);
}

public void updateAntiHero(UUID id,
                           AntiHeroEntity antiHero) {
    findOrThrow(id);
    repo.save(antiHero);
}
```

We have now successfully created our service for our application. The next section will discuss how to make controllers and define endpoints in our code.

Adding controllers

This section will now discuss the use of controllers and how to create them in our application. **Controllers** are responsible for intercepting incoming requests and converting the payload of the request for the internal structure of the data; this is also where we will define our endpoint paths that will be available for access for our frontend applications.

In creating controllers, we will use several annotations, as described here:

- @RestController: This is a specialized form of the @Controller annotation; compared to using the @Controller annotation, it already includes both the @Controller and @ResponseBody annotation, not needing to specify the @ResponseBody annotation on each method.

- @RequestMapping: This is an annotation used to map **HyperText Transfer Protocol (HTTP)** requests to the methods of **REpresentational State Transfer** (REST) controllers. It is also where we define a base path for the controller.

- @GetMapping: This maps HTTP GET requests on a method; the annotation is a shortcut for @RequestMapping(method = RequestMethod.GET).

- @PutMapping: This maps HTTP PUT requests on a method; the annotation is a shortcut for @RequestMapping(method = RequestMethod.PUT).

- @PostMapping: This maps HTTP POST requests on a method; the annotation is a shortcut for @RequestMapping(method = RequestMethod.POST).

- @DeleteMapping: This maps HTTP DELETE requests on a method; the annotation is a shortcut for @RequestMapping(method = RequestMethod.DELETE).

- @PathVariable: This annotation is used to get the value of endpoint parameters.

- @Valid: This annotation is used to check the validity of an object; it is commonly used on the request body to check whether a passed request is a valid object.

We have successfully identified the annotations we will use for our controller. We can now create our controller. Under the antiHero package, create a new package named controller, and after completing the controller package, create a new class called AntiHeroController.

In the AntiHeroController class, we will use the @AllArgsConstructor, @RestController, and @RequestMapping annotations, as follows:

```
@AllArgsConstructor
@RestController
@RequestMapping("api/v1/anti-heroes")
public class AntiHeroController {

}
```

Our controller is now configured; the next step is to place our dependencies inside our controller. We have used the @AllArgsContructor annotation. We don't need to create a constructor method with the parameters; we only need to define dependencies.

First, we will determine the AntiHeroService class where all our CRUD logic is baked. The next one is ModelMapper; this is important, seeing as we need to convert our entity into a DTO when we use it as a response, and vice versa if we want to read an object from a request body. ModelMapper will easily map the values of an entity to a DTO object with the same property.

To install the dependency, we just need to add the following code to our pom.xml file:

```
<!--Dto mapper-->
<dependency>
    <groupId>org.modelmapper</groupId>
    <artifactId>modelmapper</artifactId>
    <version>2.3.9</version>
</dependency>
```

After successfully adding the ModelMapper dependency, we need to define our ModelMapper dependency as a Bean in our configuration to use it on our application. To achieve this, we will create a new package named config under the main package, and we will create a new class called ModelMapperConfig. After creating a new class, we will add a new method annotated with @Bean and return a new instance of ModelMapper. The code is illustrated in the following snippet:

```
@Configuration
public class ModelMapperConfig {

    @Bean
    public ModelMapper modelMapper() {
        return new ModelMapper();
    }
}
```

Our configuration is all done, and now, we can add AntiHeroService and ModelMapper to our controller, as follows:

```
@AllArgsConstructor
@RestController
@RequestMapping("api/v1/anti-heroes")
public class AntiHeroController {
    private final AntiHeroService service;
```

```
    private final ModelMapper mapper;


}
```

We now have our controllers with the needed dependencies. Now, let's create two functions that will convert our entity into a DTO, or vice versa. As mentioned a while ago, we will be using the ModelMapper dependency to make these methods, and in this case, we will add the following code:

```
private AntiHeroDto convertToDto(AntiHeroEntity entity) {
  return mapper.map(entity, AntiHeroDto.class);
}


private AntiHeroEntity convertToEntity(AntiHeroDto dto) {
  return mapper.map(dto, AntiHeroEntity.class);
}
```

We have created two functions in the preceding code example. First, we created the convertToDto() method, which will convert the given AntiHeroEntity instance into an AntiHeroDto instance, for which we have used the map() method from ModelMapper to map the entity's values. The second function is the convertToEntity() method, which converts the DTO into an entity.

Now, we can create mappings for our CRUD methods. Let's first start a method that will return a specific entity base on the id value; we will use the @GetMapping annotation to identify that this will use a GET request, and we will add /{id} as a parameter to indicate that we can pass the entity ID as a dynamic parameter in the endpoint.

In creating the method, we will use the @PathVariable annotation to get the value of /{id} in the endpoint and define it as a UUID type. Lastly, we will call the service.findAntiHeroById() function under AntiHeroService and pass the retrieved ID to get the entity in the database, and we will use the convertToDto() function to convert it to a DTO. The code is illustrated in the following snippet:

```
@GetMapping("/{id}")
public AntiHeroDto getAntiHeroById(@PathVariable("id") UUID id)
{
  return convertToDto(service.findAntiHeroById(id));
}
```

Now, to create the create mapping, we will use the @PostMapping annotation to identify that this will use a POST request, we will use the @RequestBody annotation to get the object on the request body, and we can also use the @Valid annotation to check whether the object is a valid entity.

In creating the function, we will call the `convertToEntity()` method to convert the object into an entity, and we will call the `service.addAntiHero()` method to insert the converted entity into the database. The code is illustrated in the following snippet:

```
@PostMapping
public AntiHeroDto postAntiHero(@Valid @RequestBody AntiHeroDto
antiHeroDto) {
   var entity = convertToEntity(antiHeroDto);
   var antiHero = service.addAntiHero(entity);


   return convertToDto(antiHero);
}
```

The next thing we need to create is the PUT mapping. We will use the `@PutMapping` annotation to identify that this will use a PUT request, the same as how we created the GET mapping. We will add `/{id}` as a parameter, and we will also use the `@RequestBody` annotation to get the object on the request body and the `@PathVariable` annotation to get the value of id in the parameter.

In implementing the function, we will also call the `convertToEntity()` method and call the `service.updateAntiHero(id, entity)` method to update the specific entity with the DTO values. The code is illustrated in the following snippet:

```
@PutMapping("/{id}")
public void putAntiHero(
   @PathVariable("id") UUID id,
   @Valid @RequestBody AntiHeroDto antiHeroDto
) {
   if (!id.equals(antiHeroDto.getId())) throw new
     ResponseStatusException(
     HttpStatus.BAD_REQUEST,
     "id does not match."
   );

   var antiHeroEntity = convertToEntity(antiHeroDto);
   service.updateAntiHero(id, antiHeroEntity);
}
```

Next, we'll create DELETE mapping. We will use the `@DeleteMapping` annotation to identify that this will use a DELETE request. We will also add `/{id}` as a parameter to receive the ID of the entity we need to delete, and we will add the `@PathVariable` annotation to get the value of id.

To implement the method, we simply call the `service.removeAntiHeroById()` method to delete the specific entity in the database, as follows:

```
@DeleteMapping("/{id}")
public void deleteAntiHeroById(@PathVariable("id") UUID id) {
  service.removeAntiHeroById(id);
}
```

And lastly, we need to create a method that will return all the entities in the database. One way we can implement this is using `StreamSupport` to convert our retrieved list into a stream and convert each object into a DTO, but first, we will create a method that returns a type of `List<AntiHeroDto>` with the `@GetMapping` annotation. After completing the method, we will now call the `service.findAllAntiHeroes()` method to get the entities in the database. Since this returns to an `Iterable` instance, we will convert it into a stream and transform it into a list using `Collectors.toList()`. The code is illustrated in the following snippet:

```
var antiHeroList = StreamSupport
  .stream(service.findAllAntiHeroes().spliterator(),
          false)
  .collect(Collectors.toList());
```

After successfully retrieving and converting the data into a list, we want each object converted into a DTO. We can achieve this by converting the list into a stream. Call the `convertToDto()` method and convert it to a list again, as follows:

```
antiHeroList
  .stream()
  .map(this::convertToDto)
  .collect(Collectors.toList());
```

We will return the converted list in response, and our method will now look like this:

```
@GetMapping
public List<AntiHeroDto> getAntiHeroes() {
  var antiHeroList = StreamSupport
    .stream(service.findAllAntiHeroes().spliterator(),
            false)
    .collect(Collectors.toList());

  return antiHeroList
    .stream()
```

```
      .map(this::convertToDto)
      .collect(Collectors.toList());
 }
```

We have successfully created mappings on our controller, and our code should look like this:

```
@AllArgsConstructor
@RestController
@RequestMapping("api/v1/anti-heroes")
public class AntiHeroController {
    private final AntiHeroService service;
    private final ModelMapper mapper;

    ...

    public AntiHeroDto getAntiHeroById(
      @PathVariable("id") UUID id) {
        return convertToDto(service.findAntiHeroById(id));
    }

    @DeleteMapping("/{id}")
    public void deleteAntiHeroById(
      @PathVariable("id") UUID id) {
        service.removeAntiHeroById(id);
    }

    @PostMapping
    public AntiHeroDto postAntiHero(
        @Valid @RequestBody AntiHeroDto antiHeroDto) {
        var entity = convertToEntity(antiHeroDto);
        var antiHero = service.addAntiHero(entity);
    ...

        return mapper.map(dto, AntiHeroEntity.class);
    }

 }
```

We have completed our Spring Boot application, we have created our models and DTO that defines the structure of our object, we have built services that are responsible for the business logic, and we have created controllers that map the HTTP requests in our applications, so our endpoint will work as expected.

Still, we can improve our backend in terms of performance, and we can do this with caching mechanisms. In the next section, we will discuss the concepts and application of Redis.

Adding Redis for caching

In this section, we will now discuss Redis, which can improve the performance of our REST applications. Redis is an open source, in-memory, key-value data store that allows data to reside in memory to enable low latency and faster data access. Compared to traditional databases, Redis doesn't require disk access, having all data cached in the memory, which gives a quicker response.

It is now widely used, especially for large applications that receive millions of requests. It is compatible with different data structures such as strings, lists, sets, hashes, bitmaps, and geospatial and is compatible with **Publish/Subscribe** (**Pub/Sub**), used for real-time chat applications.

Installing the Redis server

Before using Redis on our Spring Boot application, we will need to install the Redis server in our terminal. Let's discuss how to install Redis on different operating systems.

macOS

Redis is simple to install in a macOS system; we can use Homebrew to install Redis and execute the following command:

```
brew install redis
```

After successful installation, we can set the Redis server to start automatically with the following command:

```
brew services start redis
```

And we have successfully installed and run our Redis server on macOS.

Ubuntu Linux

For installing Redis on Ubuntu OS, we will execute the following command:

```
sudo apt-get install redis-server
```

This will automatically install and start the Redis server on port 6739, and we have successfully installed and run our Redis server on Linux.

Windows

For installing Redis on Windows, we can install the different versions from the following link: `https://github.com/microsoftarchive/redis/releases`, download the `.zip` or `.msi` file, and extract to your chosen directory. Run the `Redis-server.exe` file to start the Redis server on port `6739`.

Thus, we have successfully installed and run our Redis server on Windows. We can now use Redis on our Spring Boot application.

Configuring Redis on Spring Boot

We have successfully configured and started the Redis server on our local machine; our next step is to use Redis in our developed Spring Boot project. We'll now follow these steps:

1. The first thing we need to do is include the Redis dependency; to achieve this, we need to add the following code to our `pom.xml` file:

    ```
    <!-- Redis -->
    <dependency>
        <groupId>org.springframework.data</groupId>
        <artifactId>spring-data-redis</artifactId>
        <version>2.4.5</version>
    </dependency>
    <dependency>
        <groupId>redis.clients</groupId>
        <artifactId>jedis</artifactId>
        <version>3.5.1</version>
        <type>jar</type>
    </dependency>
    ```

    After successfully adding the Redis dependency, we will add our **Redis configuration** that will define the connection properties for the Redis server, under the `config` package.

2. Create a class named `RedisConfig`. We will use the `@Configuration` annotation to identify whether this class has Bean definition methods that will be bootstrapped on the execution of the application. We will also add the following method to our class:

    ```
    @Bean
    JedisConnectionFactory jedisConnectionFactory() {
      RedisStandaloneConfiguration
        redisStandaloneConfiguration =
    ```

```
        new RedisStandaloneConfiguration();

    return new JedisConnectionFactory(
        redisStandaloneConfiguration);
    }
```

`jedisConnectionFactory()` is the method used to identify the connection properties for our Redis server; this uses default values since we have not specified connection properties.

Still, if our Redis server is hosted on a different server, hosted on a different port, or has a username and password, we can use the following methods:

* `redisStandaloneConfiguration.setHostName("host")`: This sets the host **Uniform Resource Locator (URL)** where the Redis server is running.
* `redisStandaloneConfiguration.setPort("port")`: This sets the port where the application will connect.
* `redisStandaloneConfiguration.setUsername("username")`: This sets the username for the Redis server.
* `redisStandaloneConfiguration.setPassword("password")`: This sets the password for the Redis server.

The next step is to use the connection factory to create a Redis template; this is used for Redis data interactions. It allows the automatic serialization and deserialization between objects and binary data stored in the Redis server.

3. We will create a method that will also use the `@Bean` annotation; we will create a new Redis template and set the connection factory with the following code:

```
RedisTemplate<UUID, Object> template = new
RedisTemplate<>();
template.setConnectionFactory(jedisConnectionFactory());
```

After successfully creating the template instance with the connection factory, we can also define serializers depending on the data structures. If we want to use the default serializer, which is `JdkSerializationRedisSerializer`, we will just return a template instance.

4. In the following code snippet, we have used different serializers for different data structures:

```
@Bean
    public RedisTemplate<UUID, Object> redisTemplate() {
        RedisTemplate<UUID, Object> template =
            new RedisTemplate<>();
        template.setConnectionFactory(
```

```
                    jedisConnectionFactory());
            template.setKeySerializer(
              new StringRedisSerializer());
            template.setHashKeySerializer(
              new StringRedisSerializer());
            template.setHashKeySerializer(
              new JdkSerializationRedisSerializer());
            template.setValueSerializer(
              new JdkSerializationRedisSerializer());
            template.setEnableTransactionSupport(true);
            template.afterPropertiesSet();

            return template;
        }
    }
```

5. The last thing we need to do is add the `@RedishHash` annotation to our entity. This serves as a mark for objects as an aggregate root to be stored on the Redis hash; in our example, we will use it on `AntiHeroEntity`, as follows:

```
@RedishHash("AntiHero")
public class AntiHeroEntity {
  ...
}
```

And this will successfully use the Redis server to cache data on our Spring Boot application as operations are executed.

Summary

With this, we have reached the end of this chapter. Let's have a recap of the valuable things you have learned. You have learned how to start the Spring Boot application on a Tomcat server using IntelliJ. You have also known how to create a complete Spring Boot application step by step by creating entities, using Lombok and DTOs, writing services with CRUD logic with the help of JPA repositories, and creating controllers using HTTP annotations and `ModelMapper` for converting entities to DTO, and vice versa.

Lastly, you have also learned how to configure a Redis server and use it on a Spring Boot application.

The skills you have learned here will make your code readable and concise because of the Lombok and JPA repositories.

In the next chapter, we will be learning how to create documentation for our APIs using `springdoc-openapi` and Swagger UI.

6

Documenting APIs with the OpenAPI Specification

In the previous chapter, we learned how to develop our Spring Boot application. First, we configured our application to run on the server using IntelliJ. Then, we developed the different parts of the REST application, such as the models and entities, which serve as the objects; the services, which hold the business logic and call the JPA repository to perform CRUD operations in the database; and the controllers, which define the endpoints. We also learned how to apply Redis, which adds a caching mechanism to improve the performance of our REST APIs.

This chapter will focus on creating the documentation for our Spring Boot project. We will focus on configuring `springdoc-openapi` and Swagger UI and generating documentation on the fly for the endpoints that we have developed.

In this chapter, we will cover the following topics:

- Setting up `springdoc-openapi`
- Setting up Swagger UI

Technical requirements

The following link will take you to the finished version of this chapter: `https://github.com/PacktPublishing/Spring-Boot-and-Angular/tree/main/Chapter-06/superheroes`.

Setting up springdoc-openapi

In this section, we will configure `springdoc-openapi` in our Spring Boot application. Since we developed our REST APIs in the previous chapter, the next thing we need to do is create documentation for our endpoints. This is an essential part, especially in the development industry, as this will tell the developers what endpoints can be implemented, what the required requests and their formats are, and what response body to expect when calling the endpoint. This also reduces errors and conflicts regarding the API integration as the available endpoints are transparent. However, the major drawback of creating documentation manually is that it is tedious and error-prone. This is where `springdoc-openapi` comes into the picture.

First, let's discuss what `springdoc-openapi` is. `springdoc-openapi` is a library that automates the generation of API documentation in Spring Boot projects. This automation is possible as the library uses annotations, class structures, and Spring configurations to identify the available APIs.

`springdoc-openapi` can generate the necessary documentation in JSON/YAML and HTML APIs that can be viewed with a newly generated URL on our application. It also supports several frameworks and protocols, including the following:

- `spring-boot`
- JSR-303, specifically for `@NotNull`, `@Min`, `@Max`, and `@Size`
- `swagger-ui`
- OAuth 2

Now, let's discuss the properties and plugins of `springdoc-openapi`.

The properties of springdoc-openapi

We can modify the behavior and settings of `.springdoc-openapi` based on our preference. It has different properties, as we can set their values under the `application.properties` file.

Here are some of the commonly used properties in `springdoc-openapi`:

- `springdoc.swagger-ui.path`: The default value is `/swagger-ui.html`. It defines the path to access the HTML documentation.
- `springdoc.swagger-UI.enabled`: The default value is `true`. It enables or disables the `swagger-UI` endpoint.
- `springdoc.swagger-ui.configUrl`: The default value is `/v3/api-docs/swagger-config`. It is a URL that retrieves an external configuration document.
- `springdoc.swagger-ui.layout`: The default value is `BaseLayout`. It's the top-level layout used by Swagger UI to display the documentation.
- `springdoc.swagger-ui.tryItOutEnabled`: The default value is `false`. It enables or disables the **Try it out** section, where the user can test the endpoints.
- `springdoc.swagger-ui.filter`: The default value is `false`. It enables or disables filtering and adds a textbox to place the filter criteria. It can be a Boolean or a string; this will act as the filter expression.

- `springdoc.swagger-ui.operationsSorter`: This applies a sort to the operations list of the API. The value can be `'alpha'` (sort by paths alphanumerically), `'method'` (sort by HTTP method), or a function that will identify the sorting criteria.

- `springdoc.swagger-ui.tagsSorter`: This applies a sort to the operations list of the API. The value can be `'alpha'` (sort by paths alphanumerically) or a function that will identify the sorting criteria.

The plugins of springdoc-openapi

`springdoc-openapi` also has plugins that we can use to generate the documentation. Let's take a look.

springdoc-openapi-maven-plugin

`springdoc-openapi-maven-plugin` generates a JSON and YAML OpenAPI description during build time. The plugin also works in the integration phase. To enable the plugin, we need to add the following declaration to the `<plugin>` section of the `pom.xml` file:

```
<plugin>
    <groupId>org.springframework.boot</groupId>
    <artifactId>spring-boot-maven-plugin</artifactId>
    <version>${spring-boot-maven-plugin.version}</version>
    <configuration>
        <jvmArguments>
          -Dspring.application.admin.enabled=true

        </jvmArguments>
    </configuration>
    <executions>
        <execution>
            <goals>
                <goal>start</goal>
                <goal>stop</goal>
            </goals>
        </execution>
    </executions>
</plugin>
```

We just added the `spring-boot-maven-plugin` plugin. Copy the preceding code and paste it into your `.pom` file.

Now, let's add version 1.4 of `springdoc-openapi-maven-plugin` just below the `spring-boot-maven-plugin` plugin code block:

```
<plugin>
    <groupId>org.springdoc</groupId>
    <artifactId>springdoc-openapi-maven-plugin</artifactId>
    <version>1.4</version>
    <executions>
        <execution>
            <id>integration-test</id>
            <goals>
                <goal>generate</goal>
            </goals>
        </execution>
    </executions>
</plugin>
```

We can also customize the behavior of `openapi-maven-plugin` by specifying the following properties:

- `attachArtifact`: The default value is `false`. It deploys the API documentation to the repository.

- `apiDocsUrl`: The default value is `http://localhost:8080/v3/api-docs`. This is the local URL to the generated JSON or YAML description.

- `outputDir`: The default value is `project.build.directory`. This is where the OpenAPI description is generated.

- `outputFileName`: The default value is `openapi.json`. This specifies the filename when the OpenAPI description is generated.

- `skip`: This skips execution if it is set to `true`.

- `headers`: The default value is `empty`. It specifies the list of headers to send in the request.

The following code example shows how to use these properties:

```
<plugin>
 <groupId>org.springdoc</groupId>
 <artifactId>springdoc-openapi-maven-plugin</artifactId>
 <version>${version}</version>
 <executions>
  <execution>
```

```
   <id>integration-test</id>
   <goals>
    <goal>generate</goal>
   </goals>
  </execution>
 </executions>
 <configuration>
  <apiDocsUrl>
    http://localhost:8080/v3/api-docs</apiDocsUrl>
  <outputFileName>openapi.json</outputFileName>
  <outputDir>/home/springdoc/output-folder</outputDir>
  <skip>false</skip>
  <headers>
    <header1-key>header1-value</header1-key>
  </headers>
 </configuration>
</plugin>
```

In the preceding example XML code, we have added several properties to apply custom configuration for OpenAPI. We have manually set the output filename, directory, and headers for generating the API documentation.

springdoc-openapi-gradle-plugin

`springdoc-openapi-gradle-plugin` generates the OpenAPI specification for a Spring Boot application from a Gradle build. To enable the plugin, we must place the following code in our `plugins` section:

```
plugins {
        id "org.springframework.boot" version "${version}"
        id "org.springdoc.openapi-gradle-plugin"
            version "${version}"
}
```

Once the plugins and dependencies have been added, the following tasks will be created:

- `generateOpenApiDocs`: The job that will be run to generate the OpenAPI documentation. `generateOpenApiDocs` makes a REST call to the application's documentation URL to store the OpenAPI docs in JSON format.

- `forkedSpringBootRun`: The Spring Boot application runs in the background using this task.

We can also customize the behavior of `openapi-graven-plugin` by specifying the following properties:

- `apiDocsUrl`: The URL where the Open API documentation can be downloaded
- `outputDir`: The directory where the documentation is generated
- `outputFileName`: The name of the generated output file
- `waitTimeInSeconds`: The time to wait in seconds for the Spring Boot application to start before calling the REST APIs to generate the OpenAPI documentation
- `forkProperties`: A system property that's required for running your Spring Boot application
- `groupedApiMappings`: A set of URLs from where the OpenAPI documentation can be downloaded

To use these properties, we must specify them using `generateOpenApiDocs`:

```
openApi {
    apiDocsUrl.set("https://localhost:4000/api/docs")
    outputDir.set(file("$buildDir/docs"))
    outputFileName.set("swagger-test.json")
    waitTimeInSeconds.set310)
    forkProperties.set("-Dspring.profiles.active=special")
    groupedApiMappings.set(
        ["https://localhost:8000/v3/api-docs/group-1" to
         "swagger-group-1.json",
         "https://localhost:8000/v3/api-docs/group-2" to
         "swagger-group-2.json"])
}
```

With that, we have learned about the properties and plugins that we can use in OpenAPI docs. Now, let's configure the plugin for our Spring Boot application.

Configuring springdoc-openapi

Now, we will install and configure `springdoc-openapi` in our Spring Boot application. First, we must add the dependency to the previous project we made. Go to the `pom.xml` file and add the following XML code:

```
<dependency>
    <groupId>org.springdoc</groupId>
```

```
<artifactId>springdoc-openapi-ui</
artifactId>            <version>1.6.4</version>
</dependency>
```

After successfully installing the OpenAPI dependency, we can run our Spring Boot project. Once the server has started, we can go to `http://localhost:8080/v3/api-docs/` to access the OpenAPI documentation in JSON format. You will see that all of your endpoints and their associated HTTP requests are displayed as JSON objects. The following is a snippet of the generated JSON documentation for our project:

```
{
  "servers": [
    {
      "url": "http://localhost:8080/",
      "description": "Generated server url"
    }
  ],
  "paths": {
    "/api/v1/anti-heroes/{id}": {
      "get": {
        "tags": [
          "anti-hero-controller"
        ],
        "operationId": "getAntiHeroById",
        "parameters": [
          {
            "name": "id",
            "in": "path",
            "required": true,
            "schema": {
              "type": "string",
              "format": "uuid"
            }
          }
        ],
        "responses": {
          "200": {
            "description": "OK",
```

```
            "content": {
              "*/*": {
                "schema": {
                  "$ref": "#/components/schemas/AntiHeroDto" ……
    // other created paths UPDATE DELETE and CREATE Inputs
```

Here, we can see that the generated JSON object displays the available endpoints in our project. It is shown together with the operation ID, which is the default name of the method; it also specifies the parameters with the types required and the possible responses of the endpoint.

We have used the default URL where OpenAPI can be accessed. We can change the URL using the application's `springdoc.api-docs.path property.properties` file. For example, we have set it to `springdoc.api-docs.path=rest-docs`, which means we can now access the JSON document using `http://localhost:8080/rest-docs/`.

We can also access the YAML version of the documentation by accessing `http://localhost:8080/v3/api-docs.yaml`.

With that, we have successfully generated the documentation for our endpoints using `springdoc-openapi`. In the next section, we will learn how to configure, access, and use Swagger UI.

Setting up Swagger UI

Swagger UI is a documentation tool that allows users to call the available APIs in your project directly from a browser. This is a more interactive tool that enables a more detailed and practical use of the APIs. Swagger UI is also open source, enabling more communities to support the tool.

Installing and using Swagger UI

Swagger UI is already included under the `springdoc-openapi-ui` dependency. We have already included the OpenAPI extension code by adding the following code:

```
<dependency>
    <groupId>org.springdoc</groupId>
    <artifactId>springdoc-openapi-ui</artifactId>
    <version>1.6.4</version>
</dependency>
```

The OpenAPI dependency includes the Swagger UI extension; we can access the UI with the following URL: `http://localhost:8080/swagger-ui.html`. This will open the Swagger UI's **OpenAPI definition** page:

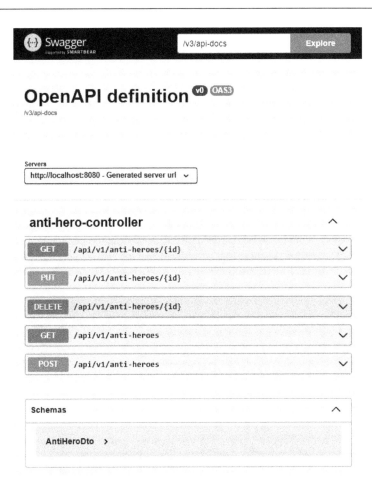

Figure 6.1 – The Swagger UI's OpenAPI definition page

Here, we can see that our Swagger UI has been accessed successfully. Our created endpoints in the Spring Boot project are also displayed, together with their HTTP methods. Let's discuss the different parts of the Swagger UI documentation.

The first thing we can see in Swagger UI is that it contains text input, alongside the **Explore** button. This is where Swagger UI gets the list of endpoints it will render. In the preceding example, we can see that the default value is v3/api-docs. This means that the JSON documentation we have generated using the OpenAPI library is being used by Swagger to get the available endpoints.

We can change this and access the URL that contains the OpenAPI documentation in JSON or YAML format. The next component we will see is the list of available endpoints in our project. In the preceding example, the five endpoints we have developed are listed in Swagger UI. This is not a list as the Swagger UI tool is interactive, allowing us to try the available endpoints.

Let's have a look at the following example:

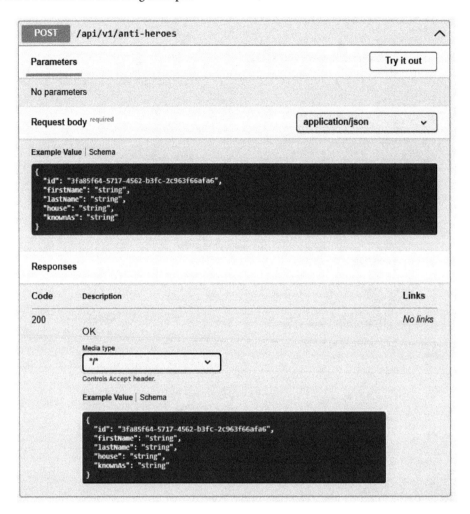

Figure 6.2 – POST request for anti-heroes

We can expand the /api/v1/anti-heroes endpoint to create a new Anti-Hero object in our database since this is using the POST HTTP method. The schema of the object we need to pass in our request body is specified. It defines both the names and the types of properties. In this case, the Anti-Hero entity has the following schema:

```
{
    "id": "3fa85f64-5717-4562-b3fc-2c963f66afa6",
    "firstName": "string",
```

```
    "lastName": "string",
    "house": "string",
    "knownAs": "string"
}
```

The possible responses are also specified in the example endpoint. The possible response has a status of 200, which specifies success. It will also return the newly created entity in the database.

We want to test the endpoint and insert some example data into the database. To do this, we must click the **Try it out** button, which can be found at the top right, and click the **Execute** button to call the endpoint. Once the API call is successful, we will see the following output:

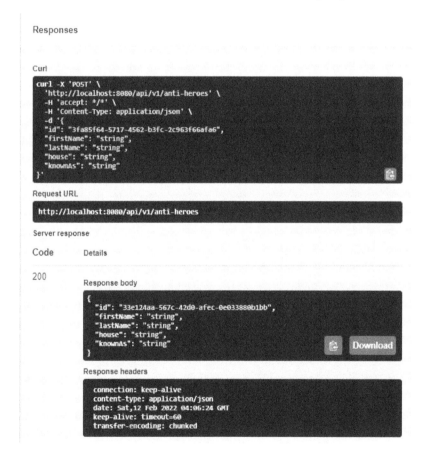

Figure 6.3 – Response from the POST request

Here, we can see that the API returned successfully as it returned a **Code** of **200** and the newly created entity in the database.

We can check whether our endpoint has successfully inserted the data into our table by accessing pgAdmin, as shown in the following screenshot:

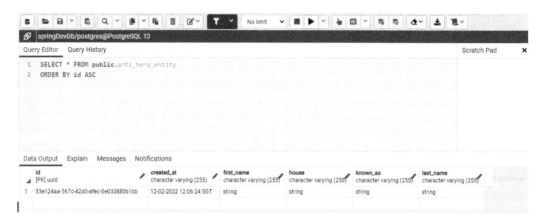

Figure 6.4 – Verifying whether data has been inserted from the POST request

In the preceding example, we can see that our data has been inserted successfully into our table. Now, we can test the other available endpoints by getting, updating, or deleting the data we have created in the database.

We have successfully navigated through the Swagger UI tool and interacted with the available endpoints, but we can also modify Swagger UI based on our preferences and requirements by using properties, similar to what we can do with the OpenAPI documentation. We can also modify the URL to access Swagger UI; for example, we can place `springdoc.swagger-ui.path=/{custom-path}.html` in the `application.properties` file.

The other behavior we can also modify is the sorting behavior of our endpoints. We can change how the endpoints are arranged in the list in terms of `alpha` (arranged alphanumerically) or `method` (arranged by methods), or we can use a custom function to change the sorting method. For this, we can place `springdoc.swagger-ui.operationsSorter=(sort behavior)` in the `application.properties` file.

In this example, we will use `springdoc.swagger-ui.operationsSorter=method`. We will see the following output:

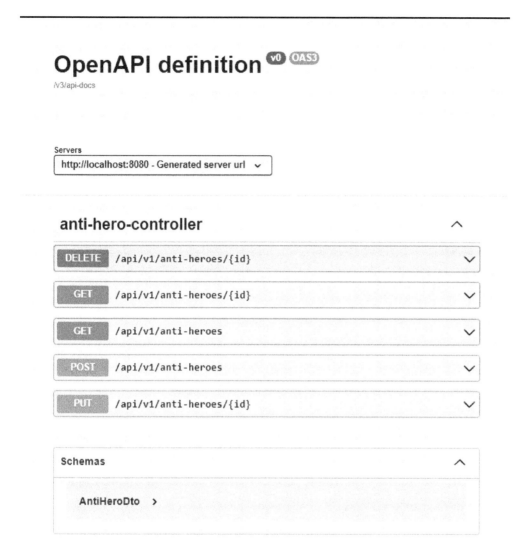

Figure 6.5 – Endpoints arranged by methods

As we can see, our endpoints are now arranged by the HTTP methods.

Displaying pagination information in Swagger UI

Swagger UI can also be integrated with endpoints that use pagination. We can specify the page number, the size of the list on each page, and the sorting expression. For us to integrate the pagination parameters in Swagger UI, we need to add the `springdoc-open-data-rest` dependency.

To add the library, we must add the following code to our pom.xml file:

```
<dependency>
    <groupId>org.springdoc</groupId>
    <artifactId>springdoc-openapi-data-rest</artifactId>
        <version>1.6.4</version>
</dependency>
```

After successfully adding the library, let's modify our getAntiHeroes method under AntiHeroesController so that we have a working pagination feature:

```
.... import org.springframework.data.domain.Pageable;


@GetMapping
public List<AntiHeroDto> getAntiHeroes(Pageable pageable) {
    int toSkip = pageable.getPageSize() *
                 pageable.getPageNumber();



    var antiHeroList = StreamSupport
             .stream(service.findAllAntiHeroes().spliterator(),
false)
             .skip(toSkip).limit(pageable.getPageSize())
             .collect(Collectors.toList());



    return antiHeroList
             .stream()
             .map(this::convertToDto)
             .collect(Collectors.toList());
}
```

Now, let's expand api/v1/anti-heroes, which uses the GET method:

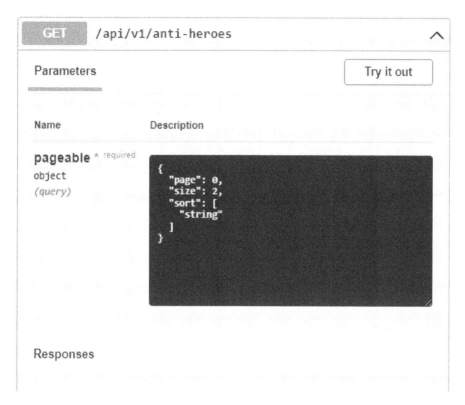

Figure 6.6 – GET method for anti-heroes

Here, we can see that the **Parameters** section has a **pageable** property and that we can specify the page we want to retrieve, the size of each page, and the sorting expression. Now, we can execute it to retrieve the data from the database.

Summary

With this, we have reached the end of this chapter. Let's recap the valuable things you have learned.

First, you learned about the available features and properties of `springdoc-openapi` and how to configure and use the OpenAPI specification to generate the JSON and YAML documentation for our API calls. You also learned how to access Swagger UI, an interactive documentation tool for calling APIs directly in a browser. We simulated this to send test calls and modify certain behaviors, such as the domain URL and the sorting order. This newly acquired knowledge for generating documentation for APIs is very useful in real-world applications. This knowledge is used by developers to easily identify the available APIs that can be consumed, as well as their parameters and object responses.

In the next chapter, we will learn about the concept of **Cross-Origin Resource Sharing** (**CORS**), Spring Security, and **JSON Web Tokens** (**JWTs**).

7

Adding Spring Boot Security with JWT

In the previous chapter, we learned mainly how to generate automated documentation for our created APIs in our Spring Boot project. We learned how to add and use the features and properties of `springdoc-openapi`, configure the plugin on the project, and access the generated JSON and YAML documentation. We also learned how to implement the Swagger UI to make our documentation interactive and allow us to test endpoints directly on the browser.

This chapter will now focus on the security side of our application. We will discuss the concept of **Cross-Origin Resource Sharing** (**CORS**) and how it can secure our application. We will also be discussing the features and implementation of Spring Security in Spring Boot, the concept of **JSON Web Token** (**JWT**), and **Identity as a Service** (**IDaaS**).

In this chapter, we will cover the following topics:

- Understanding CORS

- Adding a CORS policy

- Understanding Spring Security

- Authentication and authorization in Spring Boot

- IDaaS

Technical requirements

The link to the finished version of this chapter's code is here: `https://github.com/PacktPublishing/Spring-Boot-and-Angular/tree/main/Chapter-07/superheroes`.

Understanding CORS

We might have already encountered the term CORS several times when creating our applications as developers. Still, we may ask questions such as what does CORS do? Or what is the advantage of implementing CORS in our application? With these questions in mind, we will dive deeply, in this section, into the concepts and features of CORS and understand how it is used to secure our applications.

CORS is a header-based mechanism that allows a server to define a set of domains, schemes, or ports permitted to access the application's resources. CORS is commonly used in REST APIs. Different frontend applications can access the APIs under our backend applications, especially in complex architectures. We don't want our APIs to be accessed by unknown applications, and CORS is responsible for securing this part.

Let's see a simple example of a cross-origin request. Say we have a frontend application with a domain of `https://domain-one.com` and a backend application served with a domain of `https://domain-two.com`. We can see that our application is served with different domains, and once the frontend application sends a request to the backend, this is considered a cross-origin request.

We should never forget that browsers restrict cross-origin requests by default, and same-origin requests are the only ones allowed for requesting resources unless the origin requesting the resources includes the proper CORS headers and is permitted on the backend application. This is just a simple example of how CORS works. Let's look at a more detailed overview of the concept of CORS.

How CORS works

CORS is a header-based mechanism, which means that the first step to achieving cross-origin sharing is to add new HTTP headers that will describe the list of origins that are permitted to access resources. These headers can be described as our key to communication. The HTTP headers are divided into two categories, which are as follows:

- Request headers
- Response headers

Request headers

Request headers are the headers required for the client to make use of the CORS mechanism. They are as follows:

- `Origin`: This indicates the origin of the requesting client or simply the host of your frontend application.

- `Access-Control-Request-Method`: This header is used on a preflight request to indicate the HTTP method used to make the request.

- `Access-Control-Request-Headers`: This header is used on a preflight request to indicate the list of HTTP headers used for the request.

Let's see an example of what a request would look like using the request headers:

```
curl -i -X OPTIONS localhost:8080/api/v1 \
-H 'Access-Control-Request-Method: GET' \
-H 'Access-Control-Request-Headers: Content-Type, Accept' \
-H 'Origin: http://localhost:4200
```

Response headers

Response headers are the headers that the servers send back with the response. They are as follows:

- `Access-Control-Allow-Origin`: This is a header used to specify the origin of accessing the resource on the server.

- `Access-Control-Expose-headers`: This header indicates the headers that the browser can access.

- `Access-Control-Max-Age`: This is a header that indicates the information of preflight request expiration.

- `Access-Control-Allow-Credentials`: This is a header that indicates that a browser can access the response when the request has valid credentials.

- `Access-Control-Allow-Headers`: This header indicates the list of headers allowed to be used in a request.

- `Access-Control-Allow-Methods`: This is a header that indicates the list of request methods that are allowed to be used in the server.

Let's see an example of what response we would like with the given headers:

```
HTTP/1.1 204 No Content
Access-Control-Allow-Origin: *
Access-Control-Allow-Methods: GET,HEAD,PUT,PATCH,POST,DELETE
Vary: Access-Control-Request-Headers
Access-Control-Allow-Headers: Content-Type, Accept
Content-Length: 0
Date: Sun, 16 Nov 2022 3:41:08 GMT+8
Connection: keep-alive
```

These are the standard headers that we will use to allow the CORS mechanism, but there are several different scenarios in which cross-origin sharing works.

Simple requests

These are requests that don't trigger CORS preflight requests and, having no initial request, will be sent to the server for validation. To consider a request to be simple, it should satisfy the following conditions:

- Uses the `POST` and `GET` methods.

- Contains headers that can be manually set, such as `Accept`, `Accept-Language`, `Content-Language`, and `Content-Type`.

- `Content-Type` should have one of the following types: `text/plain`, `multipart/form-data`, or `application/x-www-form-urlencoded`.

- No `ReadableStream` object is used in the request.

Let's see an example of a simple request:

```
GET /content/test-data/ HTTP/1.1
Host: example.host
User-Agent: Mozilla/5.0 (X11; Linux x86_64) AppleWebKit/537.36
(KHTML, like Gecko) Chrome/77.0.3865.90 Safari/537.36
Accept: text/html,application/xhtml+xml,application/
xml;q=0.9,*/*;q=0.8
Accept-Language: en-us,en;q=0.5
Accept-Encoding: gzip,deflate
Connection: keep-alive
Origin: https://frontend.com
```

This request will perform a simple exchange between the client and the server. In response, the server returns the header with `Access-Control-Allow-Origin: *`, which means that the resource or endpoint can be accessed by any origin.

Preflight requests

The browser sends a test or first HTTP request using the `OPTIONS` method to validate that the request is permitted or safe. Preflight requests will always occur on cross-origin requests as preflight requests check whether a different origin is allowed or permitted to access the resource.

Let's see an example of a preflight request:

```
OPTIONS /content/test-data/ HTTP/1.1
Host: example.host
User-Agent: Mozilla/5.0 (X11; Linux x86_64) AppleWebKit/537.36
(KHTML, like Gecko) Chrome/77.0.3865.90 Safari/537.36
```

```
Accept: text/html,application/xhtml+xml,application/
xml;q=0.9,*/*;q=0.8
Accept-Language: en-us,en;q=0.5
Accept-Encoding: gzip,deflate
Connection: keep-alive
Origin: https://frontend.com
Access-Control-Request-Method: POST
Access-Control-Request-Headers: X-PINGOTHER, Content-Type
```

The preceding example shows that the preflight request uses the OPTIONS request method to execute the preflight request. The OPTIONS method is used to identify more information from the servers to know whether the actual request is permitted.

We can also see that Access-Control-Request-Method and Access-Control-Request-Headers are identified. This indicates the request headers and request method to be used in the actual request.

Here is the header info:

```
HTTP/1.1 204 No Content
Date: Sun, 16 Nov 2022 3:41:08 GMT+8
Server: Apache/2
Access-Control-Allow-Origin: https://frontend.com
Access-Control-Allow-Methods: POST, GET, OPTIONS
Access-Control-Allow-Headers: X-PINGOTHER, Content-Type
Access-Control-Max-Age: 86400
Vary: Accept-Encoding, Origin
Keep-Alive: timeout=2, max=100
Connection: Keep-Alive
```

Now, in the preceding example, this is an example response returned after the preflight request. Access-Control-Allow-Origin indicates that access to resources is only allowed on the specified domain (https://frontend.com in the example). Access-Control-Allow-Methods confirms that POST and GET are valid methods. Access-Control-Allow-Headers ensures that X-PINGOTHER and Content-Type are proper headers for the actual request.

We have learned the basic concepts of CORS; now, we will implement CORS in our Spring Boot application in the next section.

Adding a CORS policy

We have learned how CORS works and the advantage it brings to the security of our applications. Now, we will configure and implement a CORS policy in our Spring Boot project.

There are several ways to configure CORS on our project. We will discuss them one by one.

CORS applications for each method

We can enable CORS on a single endpoint; this means that we can specify different permitted origins for other endpoints. Let's have a look at the following example:

```
@CrossOrigin
@GetMapping
public List<AntiHeroDto> getAntiHeroes(Pageable pageable) {
  ..code implementation
}
```

In our Spring Boot project, we have the getAntiHeroes() method. To enable CORS on a specific method, we will use the @CrossOrigin annotation. We can see that we have not configured any other settings, and this applies the following:

- All origins are permitted.
- HTTP methods that are allowed are the ones configured for the method (in this method, the allowed HTTP method is GET).
- The time of the preflight response is cached at 30 minutes.

We can also specify the configuration of the CORS policy by adding the values of the origin, methods, allowedHeaders, exposedHeaders, allowedCredentials, and maxAge:

```
@CrossOrigin(origin = "origin.example")
@GetMapping
public List<AntiHeroDto> getAntiHeroes(Pageable pageable) {
  ..code implementation
}
```

CORS applications at the controller level

In the previous configuration, we were adding CORS to each method. Now, we will add the CORS policy at the controller level. Let's have a look at the following example:

```
@CrossOrigin
@AllArgsConstructor
```

```
@RestController
@RequestMapping("api/v1/anti-heroes")
public class AntiHeroController {
.. methods
}
```

We can see that @CrossOrigin is added at the class level. This means that the CORS policy will be added to all the methods under AntiHeroController.

CORS application at the controller and method levels

We can combine the application of CORS at both the controller and method levels in our application. Let's have a look at the following example:

```
@CrossOrigin(allowedHeaders = "Content-type")
@AllArgsConstructor
@RestController
@RequestMapping("api/v1/anti-heroes")
public class AntiHeroController {
    private final AntiHeroService service;
    private final ModelMapper mapper;

    @CrossOrigin(origins = "http://localhost:4200")
    @GetMapping
    public List<AntiHeroDto> getAntiHeroes(Pageable    pageable)
{
… code implementation
    }
```

We can see in our example that we have applied the @CrossOrigin annotation at both the controller and method levels, @CrossOrigin(allowedHeaders = "Content-type") will be used on all the methods under AntiHeroController, and @CrossOrigin(origins = http:// localhost:4200) will be applied only on the getAntiHeroes() method, thus other methods will allow all origins.

Global CORS configuration

The last way we can implement a CORS policy is by using **global configuration**, which means that our CORS policy applies to all the existing methods in our project. There are several ways to implement global CORS configuration, and we will see how to implement CORS by using `CorsFilter`:

1. The first step is to add a configuration class for our CORS policy. To accomplish this, go to the `config` folder of our project and create a new class named `CorsConfig`. We will add the `@Configuration` annotation to identify this class as a configuration upon starting the application, and we should have the following code:

    ```
    @Configuration
    public class CorsConfig {


    }
    ```

2. The next step is to create our `CorsFilter` `Bean`. We will just create a new method with `@Bean` that returns a `CorsFilter` object:

    ```
    @Bean
    CorsFilter corsFilter() {
    CorsConfiguration corsConfiguration =
      new CorsConfiguration();
    }
    ```

3. Under the `corsFilter()` method, we will place all of our CORS settings. We will instantiate a `CorsConfiguration` object that we will use to set the attributes by calling several methods. The methods that we will use are as follows:

    *   The `setAllowCredentials()` method indicates whether the browser should send credentials such as cookies with cross-origin requests. This means that we want to set this option to `true` if we retrieve cookies and **Cross-Site Request Forgery (CSRF)** tokens:

        ```
        corsConfiguration.setAllowCredentials(true);
        ```

    *   The `setAllowedOrigins()` method allows us to set the permitted origins that can access our endpoints. These are the domains for the trusted frontend applications. In the following example, we have set `http://localhost:4200`, which will be the development server of our frontend application:

        ```
        corsConfiguration.setAllowedOrigins(Arrays.
        asList("http://localhost:4200"));
        ```

- The `setAllowedHeaders()` method allows us to configure the list of headers permitted in the HTTP requests. In the preceding example, we have set several headers that can be used in the requests:

```
corsConfiguration.setAllowedHeaders(
        Arrays.asList(
                "Origin",
                "Access-Control-Allow-Origin",
                "Content-Type",
                "Accept",
                "Authorization",
                "Origin, Accept",
                "X-Requested-With",
                "Access-Control-Request-Method",
                "Access-Control-Request-Headers"
        )
);
```

- The `setExposedHeaders()` method allows us to specify the list of response headers from the server. We can use this method to limit the headers on the response for security measures:

```
corsConfiguration.setExposedHeaders(
        Arrays.asList(
                "Origin",
                "Content-Type",
                "Accept",
                "Authorization",
                "Access-Control-Allow-Origin",
                "Access-Control-Allow-Origin",
                "Access-Control-Allow-Credentials"
        )
);
```

- The `setAllowedMethods()` method will allow us to add the HTTP request methods that are authorized to be used to access the endpoints. In the following example, we have configured GET, POST, PUT, DELETE, and OPTIONS as the allowed methods since we are only building a simple **Create, Read, Update, and Delete (CRUD)** application:

```
corsConfiguration.setAllowedMethods(
        Arrays.asList("GET", "POST", "PUT", "DELETE",
```

```
                           "OPTIONS")
    );
```

4. The last step we need to do is register the CORS configuration. We will instantiate a new urlBasedCorsConfigurarationSource() and use the registerCorsConfiguration() method for the registration. The first parameter is "/**", which indicates that the configuration applies to all the methods found in the application, and the second parameter is corsConfiguration, which is the configuration we have created:

```
var urlBasedCorsConfigurationSource =
  new UrlBasedCorsConfigurationSource();

urlBasedCorsConfigurationSource.registerCorsConfiguration(
        "/**",
        corsConfiguration
);
return new CorsFilter(urlBasedCorsConfigurationSource);
```

5. After the registration, we will use the configuration source as a parameter for CorsFilter, and this is how our corsFilter() method would look after successfully configuring the CORS settings:

```
@Bean
CorsFilter corsFilter() {
    CorsConfiguration corsConfiguration =
      new CorsConfiguration();
    corsConfiguration.setAllowCredentials(true);
    corsConfiguration.setAllowedOrigins(
      Arrays.asList("http://localhost:4200"));

    corsConfiguration.setAllowedHeaders(
      Arrays.asList("Origin",
        "Access-Control-Allow-Origin",
        "Content-Type","Accept","Authorization",
        "Origin, Accept","X-Requested-With",
        "Access-Control-Request-Method",
        "Access-Control-Request-Headers"));
```

```
      corsConfiguration.setExposedHeaders(
        Arrays.asList( "Origin","Content-Type",
        "Accept","Authorization",
        "Access-Control-Allow-Origin",
        "Access-Control-Allow-Origin",
        "Access-Control-Allow-Credentials"));
      corsConfiguration.setAllowedMethods(
         Arrays.asList("GET", "POST", "PUT", "DELETE",
                        "OPTIONS")
      );

      var urlBasedCorsConfigurationSource =
        new UrlBasedCorsConfigurationSource();
      urlBasedCorsConfigurationSource
        .registerCorsConfiguration(
              "/**",
              corsConfiguration
      );

      return new CorsFilter(
        urlBasedCorsConfigurationSource);
    }
```

Having started our application, we will now apply the CORS configuration to all the methods in our project. We have successfully implemented a CORS policy in our application, but this is just part of how we secure our application.

In the next section, we will discuss the concept of Spring Security and how to implement it in a Spring Boot project.

Understanding Spring Security

Spring Security is an application-level security framework widely used in Spring Boot applications. It is a flexible authentication framework that provides most of the standard security requirements for Java applications. Spring Security is popular owing to the fact that it allows developers to integrate different authorization and authentication providers on the fly with the other modules available.

As we're using Spring Security in our application, we do not need to code security-related tasks from scratch as Spring Security has these features under the hood.

Let's discuss the concepts of Spring Security further.

Features of Spring Security

Spring Security mainly focuses on integrating authentication and authorization into applications. To compare the two, **authentication** refers to validating that a user can access your application and identifying who the user is. This mainly refers to the login page itself. On the other hand, **authorization** is used for more complex applications; this relates to the operations or actions that a specific user can do inside your applications.

Authorization can be accomplished by integrating roles to implement user access controls. Spring Security also provides different password encoders – one-way transformation passwords – which are as follows:

- `BCryptPasswordEncoder`
- `Argon2PasswordEncoder`
- `Pbkdf2PasswordEncoder`
- `SCryptPasswordEncoder`

The preceding list is of the most commonly used password encoders and can be accessed directly when using Spring Security. It also provides different features that will help you to meet security requirements, which are as follows:

- **Lightweight Directory Access Protocol** (**LDAP**): A protocol for containing and accessing distributed directory information services over an internet protocol.

- **Remember me**: This feature provides a capability to remember a user from a single machine to prevent logging in again.

- **Single Sign-On** (**SSO**): This feature allows users to access multiple applications with a single account, centralizing user information.

- **Software localization**: This feature gives the capability to develop a user interface with our preferred language.

- **HTTP authorization**: This feature provides authorization.

- **Basic access authentication**: This feature provides the base authentication process, which requires a username and password for requests.

- **Digest access authentication**: This feature provides more secure authentication that confirms the user's identity before accessing resources.

- **Web form authentication**: A form will be generated that will authenticate the user credentials directly from the web browser.

Spring Security offers a wide range of features for the application. In this case, the design of Spring Security is divided into separate **Java Archive** (**JAR**) files based on its functionality, only requiring the installation of the needed part for our development.

The following is a list of JAR files that are included in the Spring Security module:

- `spring-security-core`: The standard requirement for an application to use Spring Security. `Spring-security-core` consists of the core authentication classes and interfaces.

- `spring-security-web`: This JAR file is used for web authentication and URL-based access control. It is found under `org.springframework.security.web`.

- `spring-security-config`: This JAR file is used for implementing Spring Security configuration, using XML and Java. All classes and interfaces are found under `org.springframework.security.config`.

- `spring-security-ldap`: This JAR file is required for implementing LDAP in our application. All classes and interfaces are found under `org.springframework.security.ldap`.

- `spring-security-oauth2-core`: This JAR file is used to implement the OAuth 2.0 authorization framework and OpenID Connect Core. The classes are located under `org.springframework.security.oauth2.core`.

- `spring-security-oauth2-client`: This JAR file provides the OAuth login and OpenID client support. All classes and interfaces are located under `org.springframework.security.oauth2.client`.

- `spring-security-openid`: This JAR file is used for OpenID web authentication support to validate users with an external OpenID server.

- `spring-security-test`: This JAR file is used to support testing for the Spring Security application.

- `spring-security-cas`: This JAR file implements web authentication with a CAS SSO server. All classes and interfaces are found under `org.springframewok.security.cas`.

- `spring-security-acl`: This JAR file is used to integrate security into the application's domain object. We can access the classes and interfaces under `org.springframework.security.acls`.

We have now learned about the different features and modules that Spring Security offers. In the next section, we will learn how to implement authentication and authorization using Spring Security in our Spring Boot application.

Authentication and authorization in Spring Boot

We have already discussed the concepts of Spring Security in the previous section; now, we will learn how to integrate Spring Security into our Spring Boot application. As we move on to the examples, we will be using all the modules and features of Spring Boot Security.

Authentication and authorization are the most common concepts that we come across when we implement security in our applications. These are the two validations we apply for our application to be secure.

Configuring Spring Boot and implementing authentication

We will first implement authentication in our application. We first need to add the Spring Boot Security dependency to our project. To add the dependency, we will add the following to pom.xml:

```
<dependency>
    <groupId>org.springframework.boot</groupId>
    <artifactId>spring-boot-starter-security</artifactId>
</dependency>
```

Reload the project to install the new dependency and run the server. Let's try to visit localhost:8080 to open the Spring Boot application project in the browser. As we can see, a login page is now applied to our project as we've installed Spring Boot Security:

Figure 7.1 – Login page integrated from Spring Boot Security

To create credentials for the login, we can configure the username and password under the application.properties file by placing the following setting:

```
spring.security.user.name=admin
spring.security.user.password=test
```

In the preceding example, we have used `admin` as the username and `test` as the password for our Spring Boot Security login, which will allow us to log in successfully to our application.

We have now successfully set up Spring Boot Security for our project, and this automatically applies authentication to our endpoints. The next step we need to do is add a configuration for our security; we would want to override the default configuration and implement a customized login endpoint for our application to give access to our other endpoints provided.

To start with the configuration, let's first create a new class named `SecurityConfig` under the config file. We will extend our new `SecurityConfig` class with `WebSecurityConfigurerAdapter`. This adapter allows us to override and customize the configuration of `WebSecurity` and `HttpSecurity`, and after extending the class, we will override the first two methods:

```
@Override
protected void configure(AuthenticationManagerBuilder auth)
throws Exception {
    //We will place the customized userdetailsservice here in
the following steps
}


@Bean(name = BeanIds.AUTHENTICATION_MANAGER)
@Override
public AuthenticationManager authenticationManagerBean() throws
Exception {
    return super.authenticationManagerBean();
}
```

The first method that we will override on `WebSecurityConifigurerAdapter` is the `configure(AuthenticationManagerBuilder auth)` method, which accepts `AuthenticationManagerBuilder`, which is used to build LDAP authentication, JDBC-based authentication, adding a custom `UserDetailsService`, and adding `AuthenticationProviders`. In this case, we will use this to access `userDetailsServiceMethod()` to customize our authentication. We will do that in the following steps as we have not yet created our modified `UseDetailsService`.

The second method is `authenticationManagerBean()`; we override this method to expose `AuthenticationManager` as a bean in our application, which we will later use in `AuthenticateController`. The next step is to implement the configuration we want for our HTTP requests. To achieve this, we will override the `configure(HttpSecurity http)` method.

`HttpSecurity` allows us to call methods that will implement configuration for web-based security requests for the HTTP requests. By default, the security configuration will be applied to all HTTP requests, but we can also set only specific requests by using the `requestMatcher()` methods. `HttpSecurity` is the same as the Spring Security XML configuration.

Let's discuss the standard methods under `HttpSecurity`:

- `csrf()`: Enables the **CSRF** protections. This is enabled by default.

- `disable()`: Disables the initial configurations; a new version can be applied after calling the method.

- `antMatcher("/**")`: By default, our configuration will be applied to all HTTP requests. We can use the `antMatcher()` method to specify the URL patterns where we want to apply the configuration.

- `antMatchers("/**")`: Similar to the `antMatcher()` method, but accepts a list of patterns where we want to apply the configuration.

- `permitAll()`: Specifies that access to any URL endpoints are allowed by anyone.

- `anyRequest()`: Applies to any type of HTTP request.

- `authenticated()`: Specifies that any URL endpoints are allowed by any authenticated user.

- `exceptionHandling()`: Exception handling configuration.

- `sessionManagement()`: This method is commonly used to manage how many allowed sessions for a user can be active; for example, we configure `sessionManagement()`. `maximumSessions(1).expiredUrl("/login?expired")`, which indicates that when the user is logged in to another terminal and attempts to log in to another instance, it will automatically log them out of the other instance.

- `sessionCreationPolicy()`: Allows us to create a policy for when a session should get created; the possible values are ALWAYS, IF_REQUIRED, NEVER, and STATELESS.

In our code, let's configure a basic configuration for our security. Let's place the following code inside the `configure(HttpSecurity http)` method:

```
@Override
protected void configure(HttpSecurity http) throws Exception {
    http
        // first chain
        .csrf()
        .disable()
        // second chain
        .antMatcher("/**")
```

```
    .authorizeRequests()
    // third chain
    .antMatchers("/**")
    .permitAll()
    // fourth chain
    .and()
    .sessionManagement()
    .sessionCreationPolicy(
      SessionCreationPolicy.STATELESS);
}
```

In the preceding example configuration, we have implemented several configurations for our application. You can notice that we have divided the methods into chains. This is to show the methods are related to each other.

The first chain, with `.csrf().disable()`, disables the use of CSRF protection. This is just an example, and disabling CSRF is not recommended when building your application. The second chain, with `.antMatcher("/**").authorizedRequests()`, states that any requests are authorized to be accessed by any users regardless of the role.

This can be modified by specifying the role in the `hasRole()` method by restricting the users based on the assigned roles. The third chain is `.antMatchers("/**").permitAll()`, which indicates that any users can access all the URLs, and lastly, `sessionManagement().sessionCreationPolicy(SessionCreationPolicy.STATELESS)` indicates that no session should be created by Spring Security.

We have successfully created `SecurityConfig`, which contains all of our configurations for Spring Security; our code should look like the following:

```
@AllArgsConstructor
@Configuration
@EnableGlobalMethodSecurity(prePostEnabled = true)
public class SecurityConfig extends
WebSecurityConfigurerAdapter {
    // removed some code for brevety

    @Override
    protected void configure(HttpSecurity http) throws
      Exception {
        http
                // first chain
```

```
                        .csrf()
                        .disable()
                        // second chain
                        .antMatcher("/**")
                        .authorizeRequests()
                        // third chain
                        .antMatchers("/**")
                        .permitAll()
                        // fourth chain
                        .and()
                        .sessionManagement()
                        .sessionCreationPolicy(
                           SessionCreationPolicy.STATELESS);


        }
    }
```

Now, we will move on to the next step, where we will create our endpoints for our user entity.

Creating user endpoints

When implementing CRUD, we need to create our user endpoints. We need to develop these endpoints such that they will be used for the registration of a new user in our database. In this example, we will repeat the steps on how to develop endpoints discussed in *Chapter 6, Documenting APIs with OpenAPI Specification*, but we will also create a whole CRUD capability for the user entity.

Let's create a new user package and make the controller, data, entity, repository, and service packages under the user package.

Creating the user entity

Let's create the user entity first by creating a new class named UserEntity under the entity package, and we will place the following code:

```
@Entity
@Data
@AllArgsConstructor
@NoArgsConstructor
public class UserEntity {
```

```
@Id
@GeneratedValue(strategy = GenerationType.AUTO,
                generator = "UUID")
@Column(nullable = false, updatable = false)
private UUID id;

@Column(unique = true)
private String email;

private String mobileNumber;
private byte[] storedHash;
private byte[] storedSalt;

public UserEntity(String email, String mobileNumber) {
   this.email = email;
   this.mobileNumber = mobileNumber;
  }
}
```

In the preceding example, we have assigned several properties for UserEntity. We have annotated it with @Entity to indicate that this is a **Java Persistence API (JPA)** entity. We have configured it with an email address, mobile number, storedHash, and a storedSalt property. storedHash and storedSalt will be used for hashing and verifying the user's password.

Creating the user DTO

After creating the user entity, we will make the **Data Transfer Object (DTO)**. The DTO is an object that we commonly use for responses or to hide unnecessary properties. We will create a new class named UserDto under the data package, and we will place the following code:

```
@Data
@AllArgsConstructor
@NoArgsConstructor
public class UserDto {

   private UUID id;
```

```
    private String email;
    private String mobileNumber;
    private String password;
}
```

Creating the user repository

The next thing we need to do is create the repository for our user. Under the repository package, create a new class named UserRepository, and we will extend the class with JPARepository by adding the following code:

```
@Repository
public interface UserRepository extends
JpaRepository<UserEntity, UUID> {
    @Query(
        "" +
        "SELECT CASE WHEN COUNT(u) > 0 THEN " +
        "TRUE ELSE FALSE END " +
        "FROM UserEntity u " +
        "WHERE u.email = ?1"
    )
    Boolean selectExistsEmail(String email);

    UserEntity findByEmail(String email);
}
```

In the preceding example, we extended UserRepository with JPARepository, which grants all the CRUD capabilities to our repository. We have also created two methods with an @Query annotation, which checks whether the email address already exists.

Creating the user service

The next step is now to create our user service where we will implement the business logic of the application. Under the service package, we will create a new class named UserService, after the creation of the service.

We will place @AllArgsConstructor for the constructor injecting the dependencies and the @Service annotation to let Spring know that this is a service layer, and we will also inject ModelMapper and UserRepository into our service after the annotations and dependency injection.

We can create two methods that allow us to convert an entity into a DTO and vice versa by placing the following code:

```
private UserDto convertToDto(UserEntity entity) {
  return mapper.map(entity, UserDto.class);
}


private UserEntity convertToEntity(UserDto dto) {
  return mapper.map(dto, UserEntity.class);
}
```

Now, we will create the code for the basic CRUD functionalities:

- **Getting all users**: To get all of the users, we will place the following code:

  ```
  public List<UserDto> findAllUsers() {
    var userEntityList =
      new ArrayList<>(repo.findAll());

    return userEntityList
      .stream()
      .map(this::convertToDto)
      .collect(Collectors.toList());
  }
  ```

  The example code returns all the list of users converted into a DTO.

- **Getting users by ID**: To get a specific user by ID, we will place the following code:

  ```
  public UserDto findUserById(final UUID id) {
    var user = repo
      .findById(id)
      .orElseThrow(
        () -> new NotFoundException("User by id " + id +
                                    " was not found")
      );

    return convertToDto(user);
  }
  ```

  This example method retrieves a specific user using the `findByID()` method of the user repository.

- **Creating a new user**: The creation of a user is the most important method as this will be the registration method for the credentials. We will divide this into three methods – the first one is the createSalt() method, which will allow us to create a salt for the user's password.

Let's place the code for the createSalt() method:

```
private byte[] createSalt() {
    var random = new SecureRandom();
    var salt = new byte[128];
    random.nextBytes(salt);


    return salt;
}
```

The next method is createPasswordHash(), which will allow us to hash the user's password. We use the SHA-512 hashing algorithm and the provided salt to create the method. The following code is for the createPasswordHash() implementation:

```
private byte[] createPasswordHash(String password, byte[]
salt)
    throws NoSuchAlgorithmException {
    var md = MessageDigest.getInstance("SHA-512");
    md.update(salt);


    return md.digest(
        password.getBytes(StandardCharsets.UTF_8));
}
```

The last method is the createUser() method itself. We will first check whether a password is provided and then whether the email address already exists using the selectExistsEmail() method we have created. Next, after all the validations have passed, make a salt using the createSalt() method and hash the password using createPasswordHash(). Lastly, save the new user in the database. The following code is for the createUser() implementation:

```
public UserDto createUser(UserDto userDto, String
password)
    throws NoSuchAlgorithmException {
    var user = convertToEntity(userDto);


    if (password.isBlank()) throw new
        IllegalArgumentException(
        "Password is required."
```

```
    );

    var existsEmail =
      repo.selectExistsEmail(user.getEmail());
    if (existsEmail) throw new    BadRequestException(
      "Email " + user.getEmail() + " taken"
    );

    byte[] salt = createSalt();
    byte[] hashedPassword =
      createPasswordHash(password, salt);

    user.setStoredSalt(salt);
    user.setStoredHash(hashedPassword);

    repo.save(user);

    return convertToDto(user);
  }
```

- **Updating and deleting a user**: The last two methods we need to add are updateUser() and deleteUser(). This is a different method we can implement to give us the capability to edit the details of the user or delete the user in the database.

Let's see the following code implementation:

```
public void updateUser(UUID id, UserDto userDto, String
password)
  throws NoSuchAlgorithmException {
  var user = findOrThrow(id);
  var userParam = convertToEntity(userDto);

  user.setEmail(userParam.getEmail());
  user.setMobileNumber(userParam.getMobileNumber());

  if (!password.isBlank()) {
    byte[] salt = createSalt();
    byte[] hashedPassword =
```

```
            createPasswordHash(password, salt);

        user.setStoredSalt(salt);
        user.setStoredHash(hashedPassword);
    }

    repo.save(user);
}

public void removeUserById(UUID id) {
    findOrThrow(id);
    repo.deleteById(id);
}
private UserEntity findOrThrow(final UUID id) {
    return repo
        .findById(id)
        .orElseThrow(
            () -> new NotFoundException("User by id " + id +
                                    " was not found")
        );
}
```

We have already created the services needed for our user entity. Now, the last step is to make our controller.

Creating the user controller

The last requirement for the user is to create the controller. We will create a method for findAllUsers(), findUserById(), deleteUserById(), createUser(), and putUser() under the annotated services with specific HTTP requests.

Let's see the following code implementation:

```
@AllArgsConstructor
@RestController
public class UserController {

    private final UserService userService;

    @GetMapping("/api/v1/users")
```

```java
public Iterable<UserDto> getUsers() {
  return userService.findAllUsers();
}


@GetMapping("/api/v1/users/{id}")
public UserDto getUserById(@PathVariable("id") UUID id) {
  return userService.findUserById(id);
}


@DeleteMapping("/api/v1/users/{id}")
@ResponseStatus(HttpStatus.NO_CONTENT)
public void deleteUserById(@PathVariable("id") UUID id) {
  userService.removeUserById(id);
}


@PostMapping("/register")
@ResponseStatus(HttpStatus.CREATED)
public UserDto postUser(@Valid @RequestBody UserDto
                        userDto)
  throws NoSuchAlgorithmException {
  return userService.createUser(userDto,
                          userDto.getPassword());
}


@PutMapping("/api/v1/users/{id}")
public void putUser(
  @PathVariable("id") UUID id,
  @Valid @RequestBody UserDto userDto
) throws NoSuchAlgorithmException {
  userService.updateUser(id, userDto,
                      userDto.getPassword());
}
```

We have successfully created our endpoints for our user entity; we can now use the /register endpoint to create a new user for a valid authentication. Now, we will make the login endpoint using JWT.

JWT

JWT is a URL-safe method for communicating data. A JWT can be seen as an encrypted string containing a JSON object with a lot of information. It includes an additional structure consisting of a header payload that uses JSON format. JWTs can be encrypted or signed with a **Message Authentication Code** (**MAC**). A JWT is created by combining the header and payload JSON, and the whole token is Base64-URL-encoded.

When to use JWT

JWT is used chiefly on RESTful web services that cannot maintain a client state since JWT holds some information connected to the user. It can provide state information to the server for each request. JWT is utilized in applications that require client authentication and authorization.

JWT example

Let's have a look at the following JWT example:

```
eyJhbGciOiJIUzI1NiIsInR5cCI6IkpXVCJ9.eyJzdWIiOiIxMjM0NTY3ODkwIi
wibmFtZSI6IlNlaWppIFZpbGxhZnJhbmNhIiwiaWF0IjoxNTE2MjM5MDIyfQ.
uhmdFM4ROwnerVam-zdYojURqrgL7WQRBRj-P8kVv6s
```

The JWT in the given example is composed of three parts – we can notice that it is divided with a dot (.) character. The first string is the encoded header, the second string is the encoded payload, and the last string is the signature of the JWT.

The following block is an example of the decoded structure:

```
// Decoded header
{
   "alg": "HS256",
   "typ": "JWT"
}
// Decoded Payload
{
   "sub": "1234567890",
   "name": "Seiji Villafranca",
   "iat": 1516239022
}
// Signature
HMACSHA256(
   base64UrlEncode(header) + "." +
```

```
      base64UrlEncode(payload),
      secret-key
   )
```

We can see in the preceding example that the three parts are JSON objects, the headers, which contain the algorithm used for signing the JWT, the payload, which holds information that can be used to define the state, and the signature, which encodes both the headers and the payload appended by the secret key.

JWT implementation

We already know the concept and use of JWT; now, we will implement JWT generation in our Spring Boot project. We want to create an authentication endpoint that will return a valid JWT when a valid credential is submitted.

The first step is to add the JWT dependencies to our Spring Boot project.

Let's add the following XML code to pom.xml:

```xml
<dependency>
    <groupId>io.jsonwebtoken</groupId>
    <artifactId>jjwt-impl</artifactId>
    <version>0.11.2</version>
</dependency>
<dependency>
    <groupId>io.jsonwebtoken</groupId>
    <artifactId>jjwt-jackson</artifactId>
    <version>0.11.2</version>
</dependency>
```

Next, we need to create a package named jwt under our project package, and after its creation, create packages called controllers, filters, models, services, and util. We will start making the necessary models for our authentication endpoint.

Creating the authentication models

We need to create three models for our authentication. The first model is for the request, the next is for the response, and lastly, we have a model containing the user information and one to implement UserDetails from Spring Security.

For the request model, create a new class named `AuthenticationRequest` under the models' package. The implementation of the model is shown in the following code:

```
@Data
@NoArgsConstructor
@AllArgsConstructor
public class AuthenticationRequest implements Serializable {

    private String email;
    private String password;
}
```

The request only needs the email address and the password, since these are the credentials we need to validate.

Then, for the response model, create a new class named `AuthenticationResponse`; the implementation of the model is shown in the following code:

```
@Data
@NoArgsConstructor
@AllArgsConstructor
public class AuthenticationResponse implements Serializable {

    private String token;
}
```

The response model only contains the token; the JWT is returned once the credentials are validated.

Lastly, for the user principal model, create a new class named `UserPrincipal`; the implementation of the model is shown in the following code:

```
@AllArgsConstructor
public class UserPrincipal implements UserDetails {

    private final UserEntity userEntity;

    @Override
    public Collection<? extends GrantedAuthority>
      getAuthorities() {
      return null;
```

```
  }

  @Override
  public String getPassword() {
    return null;
  }

  @Override
  public String getUsername() {
    return this.userEntity.getEmail();
  }
  // Code removed for brevity. Please refer using the
  // GitHub repo.
  @Override
  public boolean isEnabled() {
    return false;
  }
 }
}
```

The use principal model implements `UserDetails` as this will be our custom user for Spring Security. We have overridden several methods, such as `getAuthorities()`, which retrieves the list of authorizations of the user, `isAccountNonLocked()`, which checks whether the user is locked, `isAccountNonExpired()`, which validates that the user is valid and not yet expired, and `isEnabled()`, which checks whether the user is active.

Creating the authentication utilities

We need to create the utilities for our authentication; the utilities will be responsible for the JWT creation, validation and expiration checks, and extraction of the information. These are the methods we will use to validate our token.

We will create a class named `JwtUtil` under the `util` package, and we will annotate this with an `@Service` annotation. Let's start with the methods needed for `util`.

Let's create the first two methods that we need to create a valid token:

```
 private String createToken(Map<String, Object> claims, String
 subject) {
   Keys.
   return Jwts
     .builder()
```

```
        .setClaims(claims)
        .setSubject(subject)
        .setIssuedAt(new Date(System.currentTimeMillis()))
        .setExpiration(new Date(System.currentTimeMillis() +
                          1000 * 60 * 60 * 10))
            .signWith(SignatureAlgorithm.HS256, SECRET_KEY)
        .compact();
}
public String generateToken(UserDetails userDetails) {
    Map<String, Object> claims = new HashMap<>();
    return createToken(claims, userDetails.getUsername());
}
```

The preceding implementation calls several methods from the JWT extension:

- The builder() method, which is responsible for the building of the JWT.
- The setClaims() method, which sets the claims of the JWT.
- The setSubject() method, which sets the subject; in this case, the value is the email address of the user.
- The setIssuedAt() method, which sets the date when the JWT is created.
- The setExpiration() method, which sets the expiration date of the JWT.
- The signWith() method, which signs the JWT with the provided key and algorithm.

The next method we need to implement is the claims extraction. We will use this method mainly to get useful information, such as the subject and the expiration of the token.

Let's have a look at the following code implementation:

```
public <T> T extractClaim(String token, Function<Claims, T>
claimsResolver) {
    final Claims claims = extractAllClaims(token);
    return claimsResolver.apply(claims);
}

private Claims extractAllClaims(String token) {
    return Jwts
        .parserBuilder()
        .setSigningKey(SECRET_KEY)
```

```
      .build()
    .parseClaimsJws(token)
    .getBody();
}
```

The `extractAllClaims()` method receives the token and uses the secret key provided by the application. We have called the `parseClaimsJWS()` method to extract the claims from the JWT.

Now, we will create the methods to extract and check whether the token is expired and extract the username using the `extractClaims()` method we have created.

Let's have a look at the following code implementation:

```
public Date extractExpiration(String token) {
    return extractClaim(token, Claims::getExpiration);
}
private Boolean isTokenExpired(String token) {
    return extractExpiration(token).before(new Date());
}
public String extractUsername(String token) {
    return extractClaim(token, Claims::getSubject);
}
```

We have used the `getExpiration` and `getSubject` built-in functions to get the expiration date and subject from the claims.

Lastly, we will create a method to validate that the token is not yet expired or a valid user is using the token.

Let's have a look at the following code implementation:

```
public Boolean validateToken(String token,
                             UserDetails userDetails) {
    final String username = extractUsername(token);
    return (
      username.equals(userDetails.getUsername()) &&
        !isTokenExpired(token)
    );
}
```

Creating the authentication service

Now, we will create the service for our authentication, as we know that services are responsible for the logic of our application. We will make the following methods, which will verify whether the password is correct using the hash, check whether the user has valid credentials, and provide a method that will override the default authentication.

The first step is to create a new class named `ApplicationUserDetailsService` under the service package, and we will implement the class using `UserDetailsService` from Spring Security. We will override the `loadUserByUsername()` method and execute the following code:

```
@Override
public UserDetails loadUserByUsername(String email)
  throws UsernameNotFoundException {
  return new UserPrincipal(
    userService.searchByEmail(email));
}
```

The preceding code calls the `searchByEmail()` method, which is our custom implementation for checking whether a user exists, and we will return the user as a `UserPrincipal` object.

The next step is to create the `verifyPasswordHash()` method, which will validate the user's password.

Let's have a look at the following code implementation:

```
private Boolean verifyPasswordHash(
  String password,
  byte[] storedHash,
  byte[] storedSalt
) throws NoSuchAlgorithmException {
  // Code removed for brevety. Please refer to the GitHub
  // repo

  for (int i = 0; i < computedHash.length; i++) {
    if (computedHash[i] != storedHash[i]) return false;
  }

  // The above for loop is the same as below

  return MessageDigest.isEqual(computedHash, storedHash);
}
```

The method we have created accepts the password, the stored salt, and the user's hash. We will first check whether storedHash has a length of 64 and storedSalt has a size of 128 to validate whether it is 64 bytes. We will get the computed hash by using the stored salt and message digest for the password, and lastly, we will check whether the passwords match by seeing whether the calculated hash and stored hash are equal.

The last method we need to implement is the authenticate() method. This is the primary method that our authenticate endpoint will call.

Let's have a look the following code implementation:

```
public UserEntity authenticate(String email, String password)
  throws NoSuchAlgorithmException {
  if (
    email.isEmpty() || password.isEmpty()
  ) throw new BadCredentialsException("Unauthorized");

  var userEntity = userService.searchByEmail(email);

  if (userEntity == null) throw new
      BadCredentialsException("Unauthorized");

  var verified = verifyPasswordHash(
    password,
    userEntity.getStoredHash(),
    userEntity.getStoredSalt()
  );

  if (!verified) throw new
      BadCredentialsException("Unauthorized");

  return userEntity;
}
```

The method first checks whether the user exists using the searchByEmail() method and checks whether the password is valid using the verifyPasswordHash() method that we have created.

Creating the authentication controller

Now, we will create the controllers of our authentication. This would create the primary endpoint for our login. The first step is to create a class named `AuthenticateController` under the controllers' package, and next, we will make `authenticate()` with the following implementation:

```
@RestController
@AllArgsConstructor
class AuthenticateController {

  private final AuthenticationManager
    authenticationManager;
  private final JwtUtil jwtTokenUtil;
  private final ApplicationUserDetailsService
    userDetailsService;

  @RequestMapping(value = "/authenticate")
  @ResponseStatus(HttpStatus.CREATED)
  public AuthenticationResponse authenticate(
    @RequestBody AuthenticationRequest req

  ) throws Exception {
    UserEntity user;

    try {

      user = userDetailsService.authenticate(
        req.getEmail(), req.getPassword());

    } catch (BadCredentialsException e) {
      throw new Exception("Incorrect username or password",
                          e);
    }
```

Then, we get the details of the user by calling `loadUserByUsername` from `userDetailsService` but don't forget to pass the email address of the user like so:

```
    var userDetails = userDetailsService.
  loadUserByUsername(user.getEmail());


    System.out.println(userDetails);
    var jwt = jwtTokenUtil.generateToken(userDetails);
```

```
        return new AuthenticationResponse(jwt);
    }
}
```

The `authenticate()` method accepts an `AuthenticationRequest` body, which requires an email address and password. We will use `service.authenticate()` we previously created to check whether the credentials are valid. Once this is confirmed, we can generate the token using `generateToken()` from our utilities and return an `AuthenticationResponse` object.

Creating the authentication filters

The last step we need to accomplish is to create the filter for our authentication. We will use filters to validate each HTTP request with a valid JWT in the request headers. We need to make sure that a filter is invoked only once for each request. We can achieve this by using `OncePerRequestFilter`. We will extend our filter class with the filter to ensure that the filter is only executed once for a specific request.

Now, let's create our authentication filter; first, let's create a class named `JwtRequestFilter` under the `filters` package, and we will extend this class with `OncePerRequestFilter`, then we will override the `doFilterInternal()` method, which has parameters of `HttpServletRequest`, `HttpServletResponse`, and `FilterChain`. We will also inject `ApplicationUserDetailsService` and `JwtUtil` for the credentials and token validation.

Our code will look like the following:

```
@AllArgsConstructor
@Component
public class JwtRequestFilter extends OncePerRequestFilter {

    private final ApplicationUserDetailsService
      userDetailsService;

    private final JwtUtil jwtUtil;

    @Override
    protected void doFilterInternal(
      HttpServletRequest request,
      HttpServletResponse response,
      FilterChain chain
    ) throws ServletException, IOException {
```

```
  }
}
```

Now, for the implementation of the method, the first thing we need to do is extract the JWT from the request header. Let's implement the following code:

```
//JWT Extraction
final String authorizationHeader =
  request.getHeader("Authorization");

    String username = null;
    String token = null;

    if (
      authorizationHeader != null &&
        authorizationHeader.startsWith("Bearer ")
    ) {
      token = authorizationHeader.substring(7);
      username = jwtUtil.extractUsername(token);
    }
```

The preceding code retrieves the JWT on the header with an *authorization* key, and when a token is retrieved, we will extract the username to check whether the user exists.

Then, the next step is to load the user's details using the retrieved username and check that the token is valid and not yet expired. If the token is good, we will create a UsernamePasswordAuthenticationToken from the user details and the list of the authorized users.

We will set the new authenticated principal in our security context; let's have a look the following code implementation:

```
//JWT Extraction section
// JWT Validation and Creating the new
// UsernamePasswordAuthenticationToken
if (
    username != null &&
    SecurityContextHolder.getContext()
      .getAuthentication() == null
  ) {
    UserDetails userDetails =
```

```
        this.userDetailsService
          .loadUserByUsername(username);

    if (jwtUtil.validateToken(token, userDetails)) {
      var usernamePasswordAuthenticationToken =
        new UsernamePasswordAuthenticationToken(
        userDetails,
        null,
        userDetails.getAuthorities()
      );
      usernamePasswordAuthenticationToken.setDetails(
        new WebAuthenticationDetailsSource()
           .buildDetails(request)
      );
      SecurityContextHolder
        .getContext()
        .setAuthentication(
          usernamePasswordAuthenticationToken);
    }
  }
  chain.doFilter(request, response);
}
```

We have successfully created a filter for our requests, and our authentication endpoints are all configured. The only thing we need to do is finalize our configuration. We would want to modify UserDetailsService with our custom authentication.

To achieve this, we will go back to our SecurityConfig file and place the following code implementation on our configure(AuthenticationManagerBuilder auth) method:

```
private final ApplicationUserDetailsService userDetailsService;


@Override
protected void configure(AuthenticationManagerBuilder auth)
throws Exception {
    auth.userDetailsService(userDetailsService);
}
```

The next step is we need to add the filter we have created; under the `configure(HttpSecurity http)` method, we will place the following code:

```
private final JwtRequestFilter jwtFilter;

@Override
protected void configure(HttpSecurity http) throws Exception {
    …. Http security configurations
    http.addFilterBefore(jwtFilter,
      UsernamePasswordAuthenticationFilter.class);
}
```

Now that our security configuration is complete, our final step is to add authentication to our anti-hero endpoints. A valid JWT is required upon making a request to the anti-hero endpoints.

To achieve this, we will annotate `AntiHeroController` with `@PreAuthorize("isAuthenticated()")` to configure the endpoints with the authentication process:

```
@PreAuthorize("isAuthenticated()")
public class AntiHeroController {
… methods

}
```

We have successfully implemented Spring Security and JWT on our application; let's simulate the endpoints created.

We will send an HTTP GET request for the anti-hero controller to get the list of all anti-heroes:

Figure 7.2 – 403 Forbidden on getting the anti-heroes list

When we send a sample request to one of the anti-heroes, this will now return a 403 error since it requires a valid token from our request headers. In this case, we need to create a new user using the `/register` endpoint:

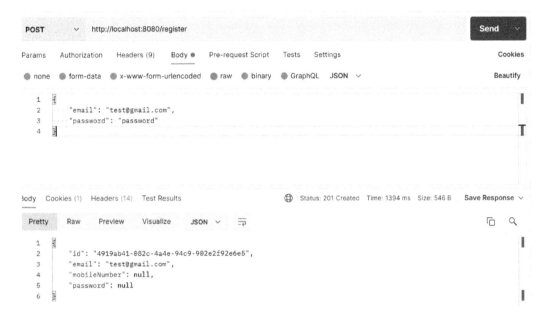

Figure 7.3 – User registration

After successfully creating our user, this is now a valid credential, and we can log in using the `/authenticate` endpoint:

Figure 7.4 – New credential login

We can see in the preceding example that our login is successful and the `/authenticate` endpoint returned a valid token. We can now use the token in the request header to send a request to anti-hero endpoints:

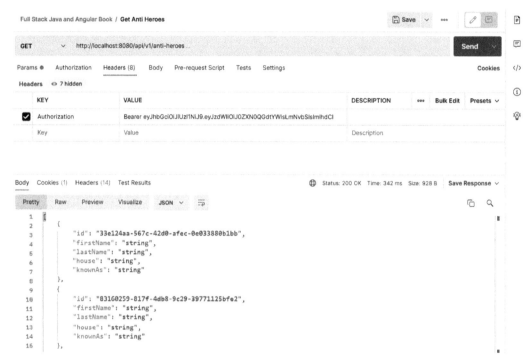

Figure 7.5 – Anti-hero endpoint returns the list successfully

We can see in the preceding example that we have used the generated token in our authorization header, and we have received a 200 response and returned the list of anti-heroes.

We have now successfully created the custom authentication and authorization for our Spring Boot application using Spring Security. In the next section, we will discuss an additional topic relating to security, called IDaaS.

IDaaS

In the previous section, we created our custom login authentication using Spring Security. We utilized some of the features of Spring Security and also used JWT to store user states and validate credentials. However, this example is not enough of a reliable and secure way of implementing authentication for our application.

Large and enterprise applications nowadays demand several security features to be able to prevent possible vulnerabilities that can occur. These features can include the architecture and the implementation of other services, such as SSO and **Multi-Factor Authentication** (**MFA**). These features can be cumbersome to work with and can require several sprints to modify, leading to a longer time to develop. This is where IDaaS comes to the rescue.

IDaaS is a delivery model that allows users to connect, authenticate, and use identity management services from the cloud. IDaaS helps speed up the development process as all authentication and authorization processes are provided under the hood.

It is commonly used by large and enterprise applications because of the advantages and features it offers. IDaaS systems utilize the power of cloud computing to handle **Identity Access Management** (**IAM**), which ensures that the right users access the resources. It is very helpful as companies do not need to worry about security and IAM responsibilities, which are very demanding due to the adaptation of cybersecurity threats.

Types of IDaaS

There are several types of IDaaS available on the market; some providers only provide clients with a directory, others offer several sets of features, which include SSO and MFA, but we will split IDaaS into two categories:

- Basic IDaaS
- Enterprise IDaaS

Basic IDaaS

Small- and medium-sized businesses commonly use basic IDaaS. It usually provides SSO and MFA and a cloud directory for storing credentials.

Basic IDaaS providers are also packaged with a more straightforward interface that gives users the capability to handle configuration and administrative tasks.

Enterprise IDaaS

Enterprise IDaaS, compared to basic IDaaS, is more complex and used by large and enterprise businesses. This is commonly used to extend the IAM infrastructure of the organization and provide access management to web, mobile, and API environments.

There are five requirements that an IDaaS should possess:

- **SSO**: Gives users the capability to access all platforms and applications using a single authentication
- **MFA**: Increases the layers of security, requiring the user to present two valid pieces of evidence to prove their identity
- **Cloud directory**: Provides a cloud directory where data and credentials can be stored
- **Access security**: Policy-based management for applications for increasing security

- **Provisioning**: Provides capabilities to automate the exchange of user identities between applications and service providers using **System for Cross-Domain Identity Management (SCIM)**

Those are the five characteristics required of an IDaaS.

If you are wondering about any examples of an IDaaS that you can use, here are some service providers:

- **Google Cloud Identity**: Google Cloud Identity provides a wide range of security features for users to enable authentication, access management, and authorization. It is an enterprise IDaaS with several security features, such as SSO, MFA, automated user provisioning, and context-aware access.

  To learn more about Google Cloud Identity, you can visit `https://cloud.google.com/identity`.

- **Okta Workforce Identity**: Okta is one of the top IDaaS providers on the market. It is also an enterprise IDaaS provider that has several basic and advanced features, such as SSO, MFA, Universal Directory, B2B integration, and API Access Management.

  Okta and Auth0 joined forces around 2021, providing identity platforms and solutions such as universal login, password-less authentication, and machine-to-machine communication.

  To learn more about Auth0 and Okta, you can visit the following links: `https://auth0.com/` and `https://www.okta.com/workforce-identity/`.

- **Azure Active Directory**: Azure Active Directory is also an enterprise-grade IDaaS solution, the same as the other providers. It offers a wide range of security solutions, has several features, such as identity governance, unified identity management, and password-less authentication, for users, and best of all has a basic tier that is free to use.

  To learn more about Azure Active Directory, you can visit `https://azure.microsoft.com/en-us/services/active-directory/`.

Summary

With this, we have reached the end of this chapter. Let's have a recap of the valuable things you have learned. You have learned about the concept and importance of CORS and how it can provide security for accessing resources. We have discussed the different ways that we can implement CORS in our Spring Boot applications, which are at the method level, at the controller level, and a combination of both approaches.

We have also learned about the concept and features of Spring Security and discussed the implementation of custom authentication and authorization in our application. Lastly, we have also learned about IDaaS, a delivery model that allows users to connect, authenticate, and use identity management services from the cloud.

In the next chapter, we will be learning about the integration of event loggers into our Spring Boot application.

Logging Events in Spring Boot

In the previous chapter, we discussed the ideas, features, and implementation of **Cross-Origin Resource Sharing** (**CORS**) in securing our application. We also learned about **JSON Web Tokens** (**JWTs**) and how to generate one by creating authentication endpoints.

This chapter will focus on logging events in our Spring Boot application. We will discuss the popular packages for logging in to and configuring Spring Boot, where to save them, and what to do with logs as we develop our application.

In this chapter, we will cover the following topics:

- Getting started with SLF4J and Log4j2

- Setting up SLF4J and Log4j2

- Using logs

Technical requirements

The finished version of this chapter's code may be seen at the following link: `https://github.com/PacktPublishing/Spring-Boot-and-Angular/tree/main/Chapter-08/superheroes`.

Getting started with SLF4J and Log4j2

Logging is considered one of the most important aspects of developing an application. Its importance tends to be underrated and, worse, we forget to apply it to our applications.

Event logging is used in most tech industries, especially those providing enterprise applications. It is applied with a given standard to prevent complex debugging and allow for an easier understanding of the code we are reading. A well-written and structured log can benefit developers, especially when maintaining or debugging code from another developer. Instead of searching exhaustively for an error, records will expedite the debugging process, providing information on where and why the error occurred, and what has happened in our application.

Logging has also evolved with improvements in languages and frameworks; in backend development, several logging frameworks have been developed to provide more flexible logging capabilities. Some of the example frameworks that we will discuss are SLF4J and Log4j2 for Java Spring Boot. Before proceeding, let's discuss the features of a logging framework.

Features of a logging framework

A logging framework contains the following three features for us to display and capture events in our application:

- **Logger**: Gets the messages and the metadata
- **Formatter**: Formats messages retrieved from the logger
- **Handler**: Responsible for printing the messages in the debug console or inserting them in the database for the developer

A logging framework also displays messages with different severity levels, allowing the developer to quickly identify which event has occurred. The severity levels in a logging framework are as follows:

- **FATAL**: Level 1; considered a critical issue that can cause an application to pause or terminate
- **ERROR**: Runtime errors in the application
- **WARNING**: Logs that usually display deprecated APIs
- **INFO**: Logs that display events on the runtime of the application
- **DEBUG**: Logs that display information on the flow of the application
- **TRACE**: Logs that display more detailed information on the flow of the application

Logging using SLF4J

One of the popular logging frameworks being used with Java is **Simple Logging Façade for Java**, or **SLF4J**. It is one of the most widely used frameworks since it allows users to use any logging frameworks, such as Log4j, Logback, the `java.util.logging` package, or Java's own logging engine, JUL, using only a single dependency. This means that we can switch from one logging framework to another depending on what is needed.

There are several advantages to using SLF4J:

- SLF4J enables us to switch from one framework to another at runtime or deployment.
- SLF4J has a migrator tool that allows us to migrate existing projects using the Java Class Library from Log4j to SLF4J.
- SLF4J supports parameterized logging messages to bind dynamic values for our logs.

- SLF4J decouples the application from the logging framework. We do not need to worry about which logging framework is being used when developing our application.

Methods and classes of SLF4J

SLF4J provides several classes and methods for displaying messages with severity levels, profiling the time of execution, or simply returning the instance of the logger. Let's discuss the provided methods and classes.

Logger interface

The logger interface is mainly used to display the messages or logs provided with the severity level. This is also the entry point of the SLF4J API.

- `void debug(String message)`: Logs the message at the **DEBUG** level
- `void error(String message)`: Logs the message at the **ERROR** level
- `void info(String message)`: Logs the message at the **INFO** level
- `void trace(String message)`: Logs the message at the **TRACE** level
- `void warn(String message)`: Logs the message at the **WARN** level

The LoggerFactory class

The `LoggerFactory` class is the SLF4J utility class, commonly used to create loggers using frameworks such as JUL and Log4j.

`Logger getLogger(String name)` generates the logger object with a specified name. The following example uses the `getLogger()` method:

```
private static final org.SLF4J.Logger log = org.SLF4J.
LoggerFactory.getLogger(LogClass.class);
```

The Profiler class

The `Profiler` class is mainly used to identify the execution time of a specific task in our application, also known as the **poor man's profiler**.

Various methods may be used:

- `void start(string name)` creates a new child stopwatch with a specific name and stops the previously created stopwatches.
- `TimeInstrument stop()` stops the recent child and global stopwatches and will return the current time execution.

- void log() logs the details of the current time instruments with the logger.
- void print() prints the details of the current time instrument.

Features of SLF4J

SLF4J has several features that make logs more helpful in debugging. It provides support for parameterized logging, which allows us to display dynamic values in our messages. Another feature is profiling, which is commonly used to measure different attributes such as the memory and execution time of specific tasks in an application.

Let's discuss the concept and implementation of each feature.

Parameterized logging

To use parameterized logging in SLF4J, we will include placeholders { } in the message where we want to pass the value.

Let's have a look at the following example:

```
public class LoggerExample {
    public static void main(String[] args) {

        //Creating the Logger object
        Logger logger =
          LoggerFactory.getLogger(LoggerExample.class);
        String name = "seiji";

        //Logger using info level
        logger.info("Hello {}, here is your log", name);
    }
```

In the preceding example, we have created a parameter in our message to display the value of the name variable. Once we execute the application, the output will be as follows:

```
INFO: Hello seiji, here is your log
```

Parameterized logging also supports multiple parameters in messages, as in the following example:

```
public class LoggerExample {
    public static void main(String[] args) {

        //Creating the Logger object
```

```
Logger logger =
LoggerFactory.getLogger(LoggerExample.class);
Integer x = 3;
Integer y = 5;

//Logging the information
logger.info("The two numbers are {} and {}", x, y);
logger.info("The sum of the two number is" + (x +
            y));

}
```

In the preceding example, we can display the x and y variables in a single log. We can also execute operations directly in our messages. The output would be as follows:

```
INFO: The two numbers are 3 and 5
INFO: The sum of the two numbers is 8
```

Profiling

SLF4J also provides profiling, which is used to measure the memory, usage, and execution time of specific tasks in an application. The profiling feature can be used by a class named `Profiler`.

To implement a profiler in our code, we have to execute the following steps:

1. **Create a new Profiler class**: We need to create a new instance of `Profiler` with a specific name. Once we have done so, remember that we have started a global stopwatch. The following example shows how to create a new `Profiler`:

   ```
   Profiler profiler = new Profiler("ExampleProfiler");
   ```

2. **Start a child stopwatch**: We use the child stopwatch if we want to measure specific methods in our app. To create one, we will call the `start()` method. Remember that starting a child stopwatch terminates other running stopwatches. This example shows how to start a stopwatch:

   ```
   profiler.start("Example1");
   class.methodExample();
   ```

3. **Stop the stopwatches**: We call the `stop()` method to stop the running stopwatch and global stopwatch. This will also return the Time instrument:

   ```
   TimeInstrument tm = profiler.stop();
   ```

4. **Print the contents of the instrument**: We execute the `print()` method to display the contents and information of the Time instrument.

Now we have learned the concepts, features, and advantages of SLF4J, we will discuss a framework called Log4j2.

Logging using Log4j2

Log4j2 is one of the most common logging frameworks used with Java. Since SLF4J is an abstraction of logging frameworks, Log4j2 can be used with SLF4J. Log4j2 is very flexible and offers different ways to store log information for debugging; it also supports asynchronous logging and displays logs with a severity level to quickly identify the importance of messages.

Let's discuss the following features of Log4j2:

- The Log4j2 Logger
- Log4j2 Appenders
- Log4j2 Layouts
- Log4j2 Markers
- Log4j2 Filters

The Log4j2 Logger

The **Logger** is the main feature used by our application to create `LogRecord` instances. This means the logger is responsible for dispatching the messages. To create a Log4j2 Logger, we only need the following code:

```
Logger log = LogManager.getLogger(ExampleClass.class);
```

After creating a new Logger, we can now use it to call several methods, such as `info()`, to dispatch messages.

Log4j2 Appenders

Appenders are responsible for placing the logs dispatched by the Logger. In Log4j2, there are a wide range of Appenders that help us decide where to store our logs.

Here are some of the Appenders that are available from Log4j2:

- `ConsoleAppender`: Writes logs to the console (`System.out` or `System.err`). This is the default Appender.
- `FileAppender`: Writes logs to a file using `FileManager`.

- JDBCAppender: Writes logs to a database using a JDBC driver.

- HTTPAppender: Writes logs to a specific HTTP endpoint.

- KafkaAppender: Writes logs to Apache Kafka.

- AsyncAppender: Encapsulates another Appender and uses another thread to write logs, making it asynchronous logging.

- SyslogAppender: Writes logs to a syslog destination.

You can visit the Log4j2 documentation for other available Appenders at the following link: `https://logging.apache.org/log4j/2.x/manual/appenders.html`.

Log4j2 Layouts

Appenders use **Layouts** to format the output of a LogEvent. Log4j2 has different Layouts we can choose from to format our logs:

- **Pattern**: The default Layout used by Log4j2 uses a string pattern to display the logs. For example, the `%d{HH:mm: ss} %msg%n;` pattern would give the following result:

    ```
    14:25:30 Example log message
    ```

- **CSV**: The Layout for generating logs using CSV format.

- **HTML**: The Layout for generating logs in HTML format.

- **JSON**: The Layout for generating logs in JSON format.

- **XML**: The Layout for generating logs in XML format.

- **YAML**: The Layout for generating logs in YML format.

- **Syslog**: The Layout for generating logs into a syslog-compatible format.

- **Serialized**: Serializes the logs into a byte array using Java serialization.

Log4j2 Markers

Markers are objects commonly used to mark a single log statement to identify whether we need to execute certain actions to specific logs. For example, we can mark a single log statement using the IMPORTANT Marker, which can indicate to the Appender that it needs to store the log in a different destination.

Let's have a look at an example of how to create and use Markers:

```
public class Log4j2Marker {
    private static Logger LOGGER =
```

```
      LoggerFactory.getLogger(Log4j2Marker.class);
    private static final Marker IMPORTANT =
      MarkerFactory.getMarker("IMPORTANT");
    public static void main(String[] args) {
        LOGGER.info("Message without a marker");
        LOGGER.info(IMPORTANT,"Message with marker"
    }
  }
```

In the preceding example, we can create a new Marker using the `MarkerFactory.getLogger()` method. To use the new Marker, we can apply it to a specific logger that indicates a particular action needed for significant events.

Log4j2 Filters

Log4j2 Filters are another valuable feature for use in displaying loggers. This gives us the capability to control log events that we want to say or publish based on the given criteria. In executing a Filter, we can set it with the `ACCEPT`, `DENY`, or `NEUTRAL` values. Here are some of the Filters we can use to display loggers:

- **Threshold**: Applies filtering to log events using the severity level
- **Time**: Applies filtering to log events with a given time range
- **Regex**: Filters the log events based on a given regex pattern
- **Marker**: Filters the log events based on the given Marker
- **Composite**: Provides a mechanism to combine multiple filters
- **Dynamic Threshold**: Applies filtering to log events using the severity level and includes additional attributes

In the following section, we will configure the logging frameworks in our project.

Setting up SLF4J and Log4j2

We will now implement several logging frameworks, including **Logback** and **Log4j2**, in our Spring Boot application. Remember that SLF4J is already included.

Configuring Logback

Logback is the default logger used by Spring Applications, so no dependencies need to be installed to use it. The `spring-boot-starter-logging` dependency is already included once we create our Spring Boot application. The first step we need to take is to make our Logback configuration file.

In our project, under the `resources` folder, we will add the `logback-spring.xml` file. This is where we will place our Logback configuration. The following is an example configuration:

```xml
<?xml version="1.0" encoding="UTF-8"?>
<configuration>

    <property name="LOGS" value="./logs" />
    <!—Please refer to the logback-spring.xml of
        the GitHub repo. Thank you. -->
    <!-- LOG everything at INFO level -->
    <root level="info">
        <appender-ref ref="RollingFile" />
        <appender-ref ref="Console" />
    </root>

    <logger name="com.example" level="trace"
      additivity="false">
        <appender-ref ref="RollingFile" />
        <appender-ref ref="Console" />
    </logger>

</configuration>
```

In the preceding XML, several configurations were defined to format our log events. We have created two Appenders – `Console` and `RollingFile`. Configuring the two appender tags will create logs in System.out and File Output.

We have also used a pattern that modifies the look and format of the log display. In this example, we have used the `%black(%d{ISO8601}) %highlight(%-5level) [%blue(%t)] %yellow(%C{1.}): %msg%n%throwable` pattern to display the logs in `System.Out`. It shows the date in black, the severity level in highlight, the thread name in blue, the class name in yellow, and the message assigned to the logs.

After successfully configuring Logback, we can run the application and see the logs in our console:

```
2022-03-29 12:04:04,687 INFO  [background-preinit] org.hibernate.validator.internal.util.Version: HV000001: Hibernate Validator 6.2.0.Final
2022-03-29 12:04:04,728 INFO  [restartedMain] org.springframework.boot.StartupInfoLogger: Starting SuperheroesApplication using Java 17 on LAPTOP-NEIIT559 with PID 9512 (C:\Users\Sei
2022-03-29 12:04:04,728 DEBUG [restartedMain] org.springframework.boot.StartupInfoLogger: Running with Spring Boot v2.6.2, Spring v5.3.14
2022-03-29 12:04:04,729 INFO  [restartedMain] org.springframework.boot.SpringApplication: No active profile set, falling back to default profiles: default
2022-03-29 12:04:04,805 INFO  [restartedMain] org.springframework.boot.logging.DeferredLog: Devtools property defaults active! Set 'spring.devtools.add-properties' to 'false' to disa
2022-03-29 12:04:04,805 INFO  [restartedMain] org.springframework.boot.logging.DeferredLog: For additional web related logging consider setting the 'logging.level.web' property to 'D
2022-03-29 12:04:06,376 INFO  [restartedMain] org.springframework.data.repository.config.RepositoryConfigurationDelegate: Multiple Spring Data modules found, entering strict reposito
2022-03-29 12:04:06,379 INFO  [restartedMain] org.springframework.data.repository.config.RepositoryConfigurationDelegate: Bootstrapping Spring Data JPA repositories in DEFAULT mode.
```

Figure 8.1 – Log events using Logback

We will now use the Log4j2 framework for our logs.

Configuring Log4j2

We can also use a different framework for logging events in our application. In this example, we will use Log4j2 to handle our logs:

1. The first step is to add the Log4j2 dependency to our pom.xml file. To do this, we will add the following code:

    ```
    <dependency>
        <groupId>org.springframework.boot</groupId>
        <artifactId>spring-boot-starter-Log4j2</artifactId>
    </dependency>
    ```

2. After successfully adding the dependency, we must exclude the spring-boot-starter-logging dependency in our Spring Boot application, allowing us to override Logback and use the Log4j2 framework in logging events.

    To do so, we must add the following XML code to the dependencies under the org.springframework.boot group:

    ```
    <exclusions>
        <exclusion>
            <groupId>org.springframework.boot</groupId>
            <artifactId>
                spring-boot-starter-logging</artifactId>
        </exclusion>
    </exclusions>
    ```

3. After including the Log4j2 dependency, we will add a file named log4j2-spring.xml to the resources folder and add the following XML configuration:

    ```
    <?xml version="1.0" encoding="UTF-8"?>
    <Configuration>
    ```

```
<!--Please refer to the log4j2-spring.xml  of the
    GitHub repo. -->

<Loggers>
    <Root level="info">
        <AppenderRef ref="Console" />
        <AppenderRef ref="RollingFile" />
    </Root>

    <Logger name="com.example"
      level="trace"></Logger>
</Loggers>

</Configuration>
```

The preceding configuration is almost the same as the one we have implemented using Logback. We have also created two Appenders – `Console` and `RollingFile`; the only significant difference is the pattern for the log events. We have now successfully configured Log4j2. When we run our application, we will see the following log output:

```
2022-03-29T12:49:34,334 INFO  [restartedMain] o.a.j.l.DirectJDKLog: Initializing Spring embedded WebApplicationContext
2022-03-29T12:49:34,334 INFO  [restartedMain] o.s.b.w.s.c.ServletWebServerApplicationContext: Root WebApplicationContext: initialization
2022-03-29T12:49:34,409 INFO  [restartedMain] c.z.h.HikariDataSource: HikariPool-1 - Starting...
2022-03-29T12:49:34,765 INFO  [restartedMain] c.z.h.HikariDataSource: HikariPool-1 - Start completed.
2022-03-29T12:49:34,780 INFO  [restartedMain] o.s.b.a.h.H2ConsoleAutoConfiguration: H2 console available at '/h2-console'. Database
2022-03-29T12:49:35,008 INFO  [restartedMain] o.h.j.i.u.LogHelper: HHH000204: Processing PersistenceUnitInfo [name: default]
2022-03-29T12:49:35,156 INFO  [restartedMain] o.h.Version: HHH000412: Hibernate ORM core version 5.6.3.Final
2022-03-29T12:49:35,536 INFO  [restartedMain] o.h.a.c.r.j.JavaReflectionManager: HCANN000001: Hibernate Commons Annotations {5.1.2.Final
2022-03-29T12:49:35,827 INFO  [restartedMain] o.h.d.Dialect: HHH000400: Using dialect: org.hibernate.dialect.PostgreSQLDialect
2022-03-29T12:49:36,775 INFO  [restartedMain] o.h.e.t.j.p.i.JtaPlatformInitiator: HHH000490: Using JtaPlatform implementation: [org.hibe
2022-03-29T12:49:36,782 INFO  [restartedMain] o.s.o.j.AbstractEntityManagerFactoryBean: Initialized JPA EntityManagerFactory for persist
2022-03-29T12:49:37,464 DEBUG [restartedMain] o.s.w.f.GenericFilterBean: Filter 'jwtRequestFilter' configured for use
```

Figure 8.2 – Log events using Log4j2

Having configured and modified the configuration of our logs using the Log4j2 framework, we will now use it to add logs to our code.

Using logs

We can now use the log frameworks we have configured in our Spring Boot application to define logs on the different parts of our code. To do so, we must first create a new logger instance.

An example would be creating a log when a user attempts to get a list of all anti-heroes. In `AntiHeroeController`, we will add the following code to create a new logger instance:

```
private static final Logger LOGGER = LoggerFactory.
getLogger(AntiHeroController.class);
```

We must also be aware that `LoggerFactory` and `Logger` should be under the SLF4J dependency. It is always recommended to use **SLF4J** as this is an abstraction of logging frameworks and makes it easier to switch between them.

In this case, our import should be as follows:

```
import org.slf4j.Logger;
import org.slf4j.LoggerFactory;
```

Once we have created a new logger instance, we can now use it in our methods, for example, if we want to display a log when the user attempts to get a list of anti-heroes.

To accomplish this, under the `getAntiHeroes()` method, we will add the following code:

```
public List<AntiHeroDto> getAntiHeroes(Pageable pageable) {
    int toSkip = pageable.getPageSize() *
                pageable.getPageNumber();
    //SLF4J
    LOGGER.info("Using SLF4J: Getting anti hero
                list - getAntiHeroes()");


    // Mapstruct is another dto mapper, but it's not
    // straightforward
    var antiHeroList = StreamSupport
                .stream(
                service.findAllAntiHeroes().spliterator(),
                false)
            .skip(toSkip).limit(pageable.getPageSize())
            .collect(Collectors.toList());


    return antiHeroList
            .stream()
            .map(this::convertToDto)
```

```
            .collect(Collectors.toList());
}
```

In the preceding example, we have invoked `info(String message)`. Every time the user calls the get anti-heroes endpoint, the log will be displayed. We can also invoke the following methods:

- `trace()`: Displays the log events on the **TRACE** level
- `debug()`: Displays the log events on the **DEBUG** level
- `warn()`: Displays the log events on the **WARN** level
- `error()`: Displays the log events on the **ERROR** level
- `getName()`: Retrieves the name of the logger
- `isInfoEnabled()`: Checks whether the logger is enabled on the **INFO** level
- `isDebugEnabled()`: Checks whether the logger is enabled on the **DEBUG** level
- `isWarnEnabled()`: Checks whether the logger is enabled on the **WARN** level
- `isErrorEnabled()`: Checks whether the logger is enabled on the **ERROR** level

Annotations in Lombok

Now let's see how Lombok, a library in our Spring Boot application, can help us. Lombok can simplify our code by using annotations, but it also offers annotations for SLF4J and Log4j2 as follows:

- `@log4j2`: This annotation will generate a new Log4j2 instance in our class. The following example code will be generated:

```
public class LogExample {
        private static final org.SLF4J.Logger log =
          org.SLF4J.LoggerFactory.getLogger(
            LogExample.class);
    }
```

- `@slf4j`: This annotation will generate a new SLF4J instance in our class. The following example code will be generated:

```
public class LogExample {
    private static final org.SLF4J.Logger log =
       org.SLF4J.LoggerFactory.getLogger(
          LogExample.class);
    }
```

- The `slf4j` annotation is recommended as it allows the switching of logging frameworks.

  Once we have used the annotations in our class, we don't need to create a new instance and we can use the log directly in our methods:

  ```
  //LOMBOK SLF4J
  log.info("Using SLF4J Lombok: Getting anti-hero list -
  getAntiHeroes()");
  ```

Summary

This chapter has explained the concept and importance of loggers and how they can help developers in debugging and maintaining applications. It has introduced Log4j2, a third-party framework for Spring Boot that offers several features, such as **Appenders**, **Filters**, and **Markers**, which can assist in categorizing and formatting log events for developers. It has also introduced the concept of SLF4J, which is an abstraction of logging frameworks that allows us to switch between different frameworks at runtime or deployment.

In the following chapter, we will learn about the concepts and integration of unit testing in our Spring Boot application.

9

Writing Tests in Spring Boot

In the previous chapter, you have learned about the importance of loggers, their concepts, and how they can help developers debug and maintain applications. You have learned about Log4j2, which is a third-party framework for Spring Boot that offers several features such as **Appenders**, **Filters**, and **Markers** that can assist in making log events categorized and formatted for developers. We have also discussed SLF4J, which is an abstraction of logging frameworks that allows us to switch between different frameworks during runtime or at deployment, and lastly, we have implemented and configured the logging frameworks with XML configuration and Lombok.

This chapter will now focus on writing unit tests for our Spring Boot application; we will discuss the most commonly used testing frameworks with Java, JUnit, and **AssertJ** and implement them in our application. We will also be integrating Mockito with our unit test for mocking objects and services.

In this chapter, we will cover the following topics:

- Understanding JUnit and AssertJ
- Writing a test
- Writing tests in a service using Mockito

Technical requirements

The link to the finished version of this chapter is here: `https://github.com/PacktPublishing/Spring-Boot-and-Angular/tree/main/Chapter-09`.

Understanding JUnit and AssertJ

After every development of an application, testing will always be the next step, and this is one of the most important tasks before delivering or deploying our application into production for the world. The testing phase is critical for companies, as this ensures the quality and effectiveness of their products.

As this is one of the essential processes, there should be little room for errors in testing, and manual testing is not enough, as this is prone to human errors and has a more significant chance of missing the existing issues in an application. This is where unit testing comes to the rescue – unit testing is automated testing that allows the developer to write tests for a single class or entity.

It is a form of **regression testing** that runs all of the tests to validate whether the code still passes the test cases after several changes or updates have been applied to the application code. Unit tests help maintain the quality of our applications, as they bring the following benefits:

- **Speed**: Unit testing will be less time-consuming compared to manual testing, as this is programmable and will deliver the results in a short period.

- **Cost reduction**: Unit testing is automated, which means fewer testers will be required for testing the application.

- **Fewer errors**: Unit testing will significantly reduce the number of errors made, as testing is not done manually by humans.

- **Programmable**: Unit tests can produce sophisticated tests that detect hidden information in the application.

Unit tests are widely used now in both frontend and backend development, especially in Java, because of their advantages and testing. There are already several testing frameworks available in Java, but we will discuss the first and most commonly used framework, **JUnit**.

JUnit framework

JUnit is a regression testing framework mainly used for writing tests and assertions for single classes in a Java application; it promotes the idea of *first testing and then coding*, which states that we need to create test data for a piece of code to be tested before implementation. JUnit is also an open source framework, which makes it more reliable.

There is a large community supporting the framework, it uses assertions to test expected results and annotations to identify the methods for testing, and it can be efficiently utilized and integrated with Maven and Gradle projects.

Let's discuss the features of JUnit that we will use for writing tests:

- **Fixtures**: These are objects that we can consider constants or the baseline for running tests. The primary use of fixtures is to ensure that variables that have the same value throughout testing will be used. There are two types of fixtures, and these are as follows:

  - `setUp()`: This method is executed *before* every test is invoked.

- `tearDown()`: This method is executed *after* every test is invoked:

```java
public class JavaTest extends TestCase {
    protected int value1, value2;
    // will run before testSubtract and testMultiply
    protected void setUp() {
        value1 = 23;
        value2 = 10;
    }
    public void testSubtract() {
        double result = value1 - value2;
        assertTrue(result == 13);
    }
    public void testMultiply() {
        double result = value1 * value2;
        assertTrue(result == 230);
    }}
```

In the preceding code example, we can see that there are two test methods defined, which are `testSubtract()` and `testMultiply()`, before each method is called. The `setUp()` fixture will be called first to assign the values of the `value1` and `value2` variables.

- **Test suites**: Group several unit test cases and execute them together, using the `@RunWith` and `@Suite` annotations to run the tests. Let's have a look at the following example:

```java
//JUnit Suite Test
@RunWith(Suite.class)
@Suite.SuiteClasses({
    TestOne.class, TestTwo.class
});
public class JunitTestSuite {
}
public class TestOne {
    int x = 1;
    int y = 2;
    @Test
    public void TestOne() {
        assertEquals(x + y, 3);
    }
```

```
}
public class TestTwo {
    int x = 1;
    int y = 2;
    @Test
    public void TestTwo() {
        assertEquals(y - x, 1);
    }
}
```

In the preceding code example, we can see that we have two defined classes with a method with the `@Test` annotation; the test methods will be executed together, as we have bundled them using the `@Suite.SuiteClasses` method.

- **Test runners**: Mainly used for running the test cases, we use the `runClasses()` method to run the test cases inside a specific class. Let's have a look at a basic example here:

```
public class JUnitTestRunner {
    public static void main(String[] args) {
        Result result =
            JUnitCore.runClasses(TestJunit.class);

        for (Failure failure : result.getFailures()) {
            System.out.println(failure.toString());
        }

        System.out.println(result.wasSuccessful());
    }
}
```

- **Classes**: JUnit classes are mainly used for writing the tests for our application; these include the following:

  - **Assert**: Includes the set of assert methods

  - **Test case**: Includes the test cases that contain the fixtures for running multiple tests

  - **Test result**: Includes the methods to gather all of the results from an executed test case

Assertions in JUnit

Assertions are the way to validate whether our tests are valid by checking the outcome of the written code. In JUnit, all assertions are under the `Assert` class, and some of the essential methods from Assert are as follows:

- `void assertTrue(boolean condition)`: Validates whether the condition is `true`

- `void assertFalse(boolean condition)`: Validates whether the condition is `false`

- `void assertNotNull(Object obj)`: Checks whether the object is not null

- `void assertNull(Object obj)`: Checks whether the object is null

- `void assertEquals(Object obj1, Object obj2)`: Checks whether two objects or primitives are equal

- `void assertArrayEquals(Array array1, Array array2)`: Validates whether two arrays are equal to each other

Annotations

Annotations are meta tags that we add to methods and classes; this provides additional information to JUnit about which methods should run before and after the test methods and which will be ignored during the test execution.

Here are the annotations that we can use in JUnit:

- `@Test`: This annotation is used for a `public void` method to signify that the method is a test case that can be executed.

- `@Ignore`: This annotation is used to ignore a test case not being executed.

- `@Before`: This annotation is used for a `public void` method to run the method before each test case method. This is commonly used if we want to declare similar objects used by all test cases.

- `@After`: The annotation is used for a `public void` method to run the method after each test case method; this is commonly used if we want to release or clean several resources before running a new test case.

- `@BeforeClass`: The annotation allows a `public static void` method to run once before all of the test cases are executed.

- `@AfterClass`: The annotation allows a `public static void` method to run once all test cases are executed.

Let's have an example test with annotations and their sequence of execution:

```java
public class JunitAnnotationSequence {

    //execute once before all test
    @BeforeClass
    public static void beforeClass() {
        System.out.println("beforeClass()");
    }
    //execute once after all test
    @AfterClass
    public static void  afterClass() {
        System.out.println("afterClass()");
    }


    //execute before each test
    @Before
    public void before() {
        System.out.println("before()");
    }
    //execute after each test
    @After
    public void after() {
        System.out.println("after()");
    }
    @Test
    public void testMethod1() {
        System.out.println("testMethod1()");
    }
    @Test
    public void testMethod2() {
        System.out.println("testMethod2();");
    }
}
```

In the preceding code example, we have a `JunitAnnotationSequence` class that has several annotated methods. When we execute the test, we will have the following output:

```
beforeClass()
before()
testMethod1()
after()
before()
testMethod2()
after()
afterClass()
```

We can see in the preceding example that the methods annotated with `@BeforeClass` and `@AfterClass` are only called once and they are called at the start and end of the test execution. On the other hand, the methods annotated with `@Before` and `@After` are called at the beginning and the end of each test method.

We have learned about the basics of JUnit in unit testing; now, let's discuss the concepts of AssertJ.

Using AssertJ

We have just explored the concepts and features of JUnit in the last part, and we have learned that in JUnit alone, we can apply assertions using the `Assert` class, but we can make our assertions more fluent and flexible by using AssertJ. **AssertJ** is a library mainly used for writing assertions; its primary goal is to improve the readability of test code and make the maintenance of tests simpler.

Let's compare how to write assertions in JUnit and AssertJ:

- JUnit checking whether the condition returns `true`:

    ```
    Assert.assertTrue(condition)
    ```

- AssetJ checking whether the condition returns `true`:

    ```
    Assertions.assertThat(condition).isTrue()
    ```

We can see in the preceding example that in AssertJ, we will always pass the object to be compared in the `assertThat()` method, and we will call the next method, which is the actual assertion. Let's have a look at the different kinds of assertions we can use in AssertJ.

Boolean assertions

Boolean assertions are used to check whether conditions return `true` or `false`. The assertion methods are as follows:

- `isTrue()`: Checks whether the condition is `true`:

  ```
  Assertions.assertThat(4 > 3).isTrue()
  ```

- `isFalse()`: Checks whether the condition is `false`:

  ```
  Assertions.assertThat(11 > 100).isFalse()
  ```

Character assertions

Character assertions are used to compare the object to a character or check whether the character is in the Unicode table; the assertion methods are as follows:

- `isLowerCase()`: Reviews whether the given character is lowercase:

  ```
  Assertions.assertThat('a').isLowerCase();
  ```

- `isUpperCase()`: Checks whether the character is uppercase:

  ```
  Assertions.assertThat('a').isUpperCase();
  ```

- `isEqualTo()`: Checks whether the two given characters are equal:

  ```
  Assertions.assertThat('a').isEqualTo('a');
  ```

- `isNotEqualTo()`: Checks whether the two given characters are not equal:

  ```
  Assertions.assertThat('a').isEqualTo('b');
  ```

- `inUnicode()`: Checks whether the character is included in the Unicode table:

  ```
  Assertions.assertThat('a').inUniCode();
  ```

These are just some of the assertions available under `AbstractCharacterAssert`. For the complete documentation, you can go to `https://joel-costigliola.github.io/assertj/core-8/api/org/assertj/core/api/AbstractCharacterAssert.html`.

Class assertions

Class assertions are used to check the fields, types, access modifiers, and annotations in a specific class. The following are some of the class assertion methods:

- `isNotInterface()`: Verifies that the class is not an interface:

  ```
  Interface Hero {}
  class Thor implements Hero {}
  Assertions.assertThat(Thor.class).isNotInterface()
  ```

- `isInterface()`: Verifies that the class is an interface:

  ```
  Interface Hero {}
  class Thor implements Hero {}
  Assertions.assertThat(Hero.class).isInterface()
  ```

- `isPublic()`: Verifies that the class is public:

  ```
  public class Hero {}
  protected class AntiHero {}
  Assertions.assertThat(Hero.class).isPublic()
  ```

- `isNotPublic()`: Verifies that the class is not public:

  ```
  public class Hero {}
  protected class AntiHero {}
  Assertions.assertThat(Hero.class).isNotPublic()
  ```

These are just some of the assertions available under `AbstractClassAssert`. For the complete documentation, you can go to `https://joel-costigliola.github.io/assertj/core-8/api/org/assertj/core/api/AbstractClassAssert.html`.

Iterable assertions

Iterable assertions are used to verify an iterable or array object based on its length and contents. The following are some of the iterable assertion methods:

- `contains()`: Demonstrates that the iterable has the given values:

  ```
  List test = List.asList("Thor", "Hulk",
                           "Dr. Strange");
  assertThat(test).contains("Thor");
  ```

- `isEmpty()`: Verifies whether the given iterable has a length greater than 0:

```
List test = new List();
assertThat(test).isEmpty();
```

- `isNotEmpty()`: Verifies whether the given iterable has a length of 0:

```
List test = List.asList("Thor", "Hulk",
                         "Dr. Strange");
assertThat(test).isNotEmpty ();
```

- `hasSize()`: Verifies whether the length of the iterable is equal to the given value:

```
List test = List.asList("Thor", "Hulk",
                         "Dr. Strange");
assertThat(test).hasSize(3);
```

These are just some of the assertions available under `AbstractIterableAssert`. For the complete documentation, you can go to the link provided here: `https://joel-costigliola.github. io/assertj/core-8/api/org/assertj/core/api/AbstractIterableAssert. html`.

File assertions

File assertions are used to verify whether a file exists, can be written, or is readable, and also verify its contents. The following are some of the file assertion methods:

- `exists()`: Proves that the file or directory exists:

```
File file = File.createTempFile("test", "txt");
assertThat(tmpFile).exists();
```

- `isFile()`: Verifies whether the given object is a file (providing a directory will result in a failed test):

```
File file = File.createTempFile("test", "txt");
assertThat(tmpFile).isFile();
```

- `canRead()`: Verifies whether the given file is readable by the application:

```
File file = File.createTempFile("test", "txt");
assertThat(tmpFile).canRead();
```

- `canWrite()`: Verifies whether the given file is modifiable by the application:

```
File file = File.createTempFile("test", "txt");
assertThat(tmpFile).canWrite();
```

These are just some of the assertions available under `AbstractFileAssert`. For the complete documentation, you can go to the link provided here: `https://joel-costigliola.github.io/assertj/core-8/api/org/assertj/core/api/AbstractFileAssert.html`.

Map assertions

Map assertions are used to check a map based on its entries, keys, and size. The following are some of the map assertion methods:

- `contains()`: Verifies whether the map contains the given entries:

```
Map<name, Hero> heroes = new HashMap<>();
Heroes.put(stark, iron_man);
Heroes.put(rogers, captain_america);
Heroes.put(parker, spider_man);
assertThat(heroes).contains(entry(stark, iron_man),
   entry(rogers, captain_america));
```

- `containsAnyOf()`: Verifies whether the map contains at least one of the entries:

```
Map<name, Hero> heroes = new HashMap<>();
Heroes.put(stark, iron_man);
Heroes.put(rogers, captain_america);
Heroes.put(parker, spider_man);
assertThat(heroes).contains(entry(stark, iron_man),
entry(odinson, thor));
```

- `hasSize()`: Verifies that the size of the map is equal to the given value:

```
Map<name, Hero> heroes = new HashMap<>();
Heroes.put(stark, iron_man);
Heroes.put(rogers, captain_america);
Heroes.put(parker, spider_man);
assertThat(heroes).hasSize(3);
```

- `isEmpty()`: Verifies that the given map is empty:

```
Map<name, Hero> heroes = new HashMap<>();
assertThat(heroes).isEmpty();
```

- `isNotEmpty()`: Verifies that the given map is not empty:

```
Map<name, Hero> heroes = new HashMap<>();
Heroes.put(stark, iron_man);
Heroes.put(rogers, captain_america);
Heroes.put(parker, spider_man);
assertThat(heroes).isNotEmpty();
```

These are just some of the assertions available under `AbstractMapAssert`. For the complete documentation, you can go to the link provided here: `https://joel-costigliola.github.io/assertj/core-8/api/org/assertj/core/api/AbstractMapAssert.html`.

We have learned about the different assertion methods using AssertJ; now, we will implement and write our unit test in our Spring Boot application.

Writing a test

In this section, we will now start writing our unit tests in our Spring Boot application. As we go back to our application, the **services** and **repository** are the essential parts of our application where we need to implement unit tests, as the services contain the business logic and can be modified often, especially when new features are added. The repository includes methods for CRUD and other operations.

We will be implementing two approaches in writing our unit tests. The first method is using an in-memory database such as H2 to store our created data when running unit tests. The second method is mocking our objects and repository using the Mockito framework.

Testing with the H2 database

The first approach that we will implement in writing our tests is using JUnit and AssertJ with the H2 database. The H2 database is an in-memory database that allows us to store data in the system memory. Once the application is closed, it will delete all the stored data. H2 is usually used for **Proof-of-Concept** or unit testing.

We have already added an H2 database in *Chapter 4*, *Setting Up the Database and Spring Data JPA*, but if you have missed this part, in order for us to add the H2 dependency, we will add the following into our `pom.xml` file:

```
<dependency>
<groupId>com.h2database</groupId> <artifactId>h2</artifactId>
```

```
<scope>runtime</scope>
</dependency>
```

After successfully adding the dependency, we will add our h2 configuration under our test/java folder. We will add a new resource bundle and create a new application to accomplish this. A properties file will be used for the unit tests and we will place the following configuration:

```
spring.datasource.url=jdbc:h2://mem:testdb;DB_CLOSE_DELAY=-1
spring.datasource.username={username}
spring.datasource.password={password}
spring.datasource.driver-class-name=org.h2.Driver
spring.jpa.hibernate.ddl-auto=create-drop
spring.jpa.show-sql=true
spring.jpa.properties.hibernate.dialect=org.hibernate.dialect.
PostgreSQLDialect
spring.jpa.properties.hibernate.format_sql=true
```

In the preceding example configuration, first, we have specified that we want to store our data in a test.mv.db file using the spring.datasource.url property. We can also override the username and password for our *H2* console using the spring.datasource.username and spring.datasource.password properties, and we have also specified that the tables will be created once the application starts and will be dropped when the application stops.

Testing a service

Now, we will create a package under our test/java folder. This is where we will write our tests. We will create a similar package from our main folder. In this case, we will make com.example. springbootsuperheroes.superheroes.antiHero.h2.service. Under the newly created package, we will create a new class named AntiHeroH2ServiceTest, where we will start writing our tests for AntiHeroService.

The first step we need to take is to annotate our class using the @DataJpaTest annotation. The annotation allows the service to focus only on the JPA components by disabling the full auto-configuration and just applying the configuration related to the tests. The next step is to add the dependency of our AntiHeroService, which is AntiHeroRepository. We will declare a new AntiHeroRepository and use the @Autowired annotation to inject the dependency, and we will also declare AntiHeroService, as this is the service that we need to test. We will have the following code:

```
@DataJpaTest
public class AntiHeroH2ServiceTest {
    @Autowired
```

```
    private AntiHeroRepository repo;
    private AntiHeroService service;


}
```

After injecting our dependency and annotating our class, the next thing we would want to consider is what the possible properties we want to have before running each of the tests are; in this case, we would like to have an instance of `AntiHeroService` created before running a test case. To accomplish this, we will make a method annotated with the `@BeforeEach` annotation, and create a new instance of `AntiHeroService` with `AutoWired` `AntiHeroRepository` as the parameter:

```
@BeforeEach
public void setup() {
    service = new AntiHeroService(repo);


}
```

Now, we can write a test case for our service; our goal is to write a test for each method that `AntiHeroService` possesses.

Let's have the list of the methods for `AntiHeroService`:

- `Iterable<AntiHeroEntity> findAllAntiHeroes`: Should return the list of anti-heroes.
- `AntiHeroEntity addAntiHero(AntiHeroEntity antiHero)`: Should add a new anti-hero entity.
- `void updateAntiHero(UUID id, AntiHeroEntity antiHero)`: Should update the anti-hero based on the given ID.
- `AntiHeroEntity findAntiHeroById(UUID id)`: Should return the anti-hero with the given ID; if it is not found, it will return `NotFoundException`.
- `void removeAntiHeroById(UUID id)`: Should remove the anti-hero in the database based on the given ID.

Let's first write a test for the `findAllAntiHeroes()` method. The possible test case for the method is to check whether the method retrieves all the anti-heroes successfully in the database. To test this scenario, we would want to add a single entity or a list of test anti-hero entities to our H2 database first. We can call the `findAllAntiHeroes()` method to retrieve the newly added entities in the database. Let's see the example unit test here:

```
@Test
public void shouldFindAllAntiHero() {
```

```
AntiHeroEntity antiHero = new AntiHeroEntity();
antiHero.setFirstName("Eddie");
antiHero.setLastName("Brock");
antiHero.setHouse("MCU");

service.addAntiHero(antiHero);

Iterable<AntiHeroEntity> antiHeroList =
  service.findAllAntiHeroes();
AntiHeroEntity savedAntiHero =
  antiHeroList.iterator().next();

assertThat(savedAntiHero).isNotNull();
}
```

In the preceding code example, we can see that we have created a new anti-hero instance to be an exemplary piece of data in the database memory first. We have added the data to our database using the addAntiHero() method. After successfully inserting the data, we can check or assert whether we can retrieve the newly created anti-hero using the findAllAntiHeroes() method. In the scenario here, we have retrieved the first data in our anti-hero list. We used assertThat(savedAntiHero). isNotNull() to validate that the first element of the list is not null.

Now, let's write a test for the addAntiHero() method. The test that we will create for the following method is mostly similar to the test that we have created for the findAllAntiHeroes() method. The possible test case for the following method is to check whether the entity is being added to our database successfully.

Let's have a look at the following example unit test:

```
@Test
public void shouldAddAntiHero() {
    AntiHeroEntity antiHero = new AntiHeroEntity();
    antiHero.setFirstName("Eddie");
    antiHero.setLastName("Brock");
    antiHero.setHouse("MCU");
    service.addAntiHero(antiHero);

    Iterable<AntiHeroEntity> antiHeroList =
      service.findAllAntiHeroes();
```

```
AntiHeroEntity savedAntiHero =
   antiHeroList.iterator().next();

assertThat(antiHero).isEqualTo(savedAntiHero);


}
```

We created a new anti-hero entity in the preceding code example and inserted it into our database using the addAntiHero() method. After adding the latest data, we can retrieve the list and validate whether our new data is in the database. In the given scenario, we retrieved the first piece of data in our anti-hero list, and we used assertThat(antiHero).isEqualTo(savedAntiHero); to check whether the data we retrieved was equal to the data we instantiated.

Next, let's now write the test for updateAntiHeroMethod();. The possible test case for the following method is to check whether the method successfully modifies a piece of information for a specific entity in our database.

Let's have a look at the example unit test that satisfies the test case here:

```
@Test
public void shouldUpdateAntiHero() {
    AntiHeroEntity antiHero = new AntiHeroEntity();
    antiHero.setFirstName("Eddie");
    antiHero.setLastName("Brock");
    antiHero.setHouse("MCU");

    AntiHeroEntity savedAntiHero  =
       service.addAntiHero(antiHero);

    savedAntiHero.setHouse("San Francisco");
    service.updateAntiHero(savedAntiHero.getId(),
                           savedAntiHero);
    AntiHeroEntity foundAntiHero =
       service.findAntiHeroById(savedAntiHero.getId());

    assertThat(foundAntiHero.getHouse()).isEqualTo(
       "San Francisco");

}
```

We created a new anti-hero entity in the preceding code example and inserted it into our database using the addAntiHero() method. After adding the entity, we updated the added anti-hero's house information to "San Francisco" and saved it in our database using updateAntiHeroMethod(). Lastly, we have retrieved the modified anti-hero using its ID and validated that the house information was modified by adding the assertThat(foundAntiHero.getHouse()).isEqualTo("San Francisco"); assertion.

Next, we would now create a unit test for the removeAntiHeroById() method. The possible test case for the method is to validate whether an entity with a corresponding ID has successfully been deleted from the database.

Let's have a look at the example unit test that satisfies the test case:

```
@Test
public void shouldDeleteAntiHero() {
    assertThrows(NotFoundException.class, new Executable() {
        @Override
        public void execute() throws Throwable {
            AntiHeroEntity savedAntiHero =
                service.addAntiHero(antiHero);

            service.removeAntiHeroById(
                savedAntiHero.getId());
            AntiHeroEntity foundAntiHero =
                service.findAntiHeroById(
                    savedAntiHero.getId());

            assertThat(foundAntiHero).isNull();
        }
    });
}
```

In the preceding example, we can see that we have added some additional elements in writing our unit test; we have created a new instance of Executable(), where we have placed our main code. We have asserted our Executable() with NotFoundException.class. The main reason for this is that we expect that findAntiHeroByID() will return the NotFoundException error, as we have deleted the entity in our database.

Remember that when asserting errors, we should use assertThrows().

We have successfully written a test for our services and now, we will implement unit tests at the repository level.

Testing a repository

Writing a test for the repository of our application is mostly the same as how we write our tests at the service level; we also treat them as services and we test them if there are additional methods added to the repository.

The example that we will take is writing a unit test for our `UserRepository`. Let's have a recap of the methods that `UserRepository` possesses:

- `Boolean selectExistsEmail(String email)`: Returns `true` when the user exists with the given email
- `UserEntity findByEmail(String email)`: Returns the user when the given email exists in the database

To start writing our test, first, we will create a new package named `user.repository` under the `com.example.springbootsuperheroes.superheroes` package, and we will make a new class called `UserRepositoryTest`. After successfully creating the repository, we will annotate the class with `@DataJPATest` so that it focuses only on the JPA components and inject `AntiHeroRepostiory` using the `@Autowired` annotation.

Our class will now look as follows:

```
@DataJpaTest
class UserRepositoryTest {

    @Autowired
    private UserRepository underTest;

}
```

Now, we can write our tests after successfully injecting the repository. First, we want to write a test for the `selectExistsEmail()` method. The possible test case for the method is that it should return `true` if the email exists in our database.

Let's have a look at the following example code:

```
@Test
void itShouldCheckWhenUserEmailExists() {
    // give
    String email = "seiji@gmail.com";
    UserEntity user = new UserEntity(email, "21398732478");
```

```
    underTest.save(user);

    // when
    boolean expected = underTest.selectExistsEmail(email);

    // then
    assertThat(expected).isTrue();
}
```

We have added an example user entity into our database in the example unit test. The selectExistsEmail() method is expected to return true. This should retrieve the added user with the given email.

The next test is for the findByEmail() method; this is almost similar to the test we have created for the selectExistsEmail() method. The only thing we need to modify is the assertion, as we are expecting a return value of the User type.

Let's have a look at the following example code:

```
@Test
void itShouldFindUserWhenEmailExists() {
    // give
    String email = "dennis@gmail.com";
    UserEntity user = new UserEntity(email, "21398732478");

    underTest.save(user);

    // when
    UserEntity expected = underTest.findByEmail(email);

    // then
    assertThat(expected).isEqualTo(user);
}
```

We have successfully written a test for our services and repository with JUnit, AssertJ, and the H2 database. In the next section, we will use the second implementation on writing unit tests using JUnit and AssertJ with Mockito.

Writing tests in a service using Mockito

In the previous section, we created our unit tests using the H2 database; in this approach, we will completely omit the use of the database and utilize the concept of mocking in creating sample data in our unit tests. We will achieve this by using **Mockito**. Mockito is a mocking framework in Java that allows us to test classes in isolation; it does not require any databases.

It will enable us to return dummy data from a mocked object or service. Mockito is very useful, as this makes unit testing less complex, especially for larger applications, as we don't want to test the services and dependencies simultaneously. The following are the other benefits of using Mockito:

- **Supports return values**: Supports mocking return values.

- **Supports exceptions**: Can handle exceptions in unit tests.

- **Supports annotation**: Can create mocks using annotation.

- **Safe from refactoring**: Renaming method names or changing the order of parameters will not affect the tests, as mocks are created at runtime.

Let's explore the different features of Mockito for writing unit tests.

Adding behavior

Mockito contains the when() method where we can mock the object return value. This is one of the most valuable features of Mockito, as we can define a dummy return value of a service or a repository.

Let's have a look at the following code example:

```
public class HeroTester {
    // injects the created Mock
    @InjectMocks
    HeroApp heroApp = new HeroApp();
    // Creates the mock
    @Mock
    HeroService heroService;
    @Test
    public void getHeroHouseTest(){
        when(heroService.getHouse())).thenReturn(
            "San Francisco ");
    assertThat(heroApp.getHouse()).isEqualTo(
        "San Francisco");
  }
}
```

In the preceding code example, we can see that we have mocked `HeroService` in our test. We have done this to isolate the class and not test the functionality of `Heroservice` itself; what we want to test is just the functionality of `HeroApp`. We have added behavior for the `heroService.getHouse()` method by specifying a mock return `thenReturn()` method. In this case, we expect that the `getHouse()` method will return a value of `"San Francisco"`.

Verifying behavior

The next feature that we can use from Mockito is behavior verification in unit tests. This allows us to verify whether the mocked method is called and executed with parameters. This can be achieved using the `verify()` method.

Let's take the same class example:

```
public class HeroTester {
    // injects the created Mock
    @InjectMocks
    HeroApp heroApp = new HeroApp();
    // Creates the mock
    @Mock
    HeroService heroService;
    @Test
    public void getHeroHouseTest(){
        when(heroService.getHouse())).thenReturn(
            "San Francisco ");
    assertThat(heroApp.getHouse()).isEqualTo(
        "San Francisco");
    verify(heroService).getHouse();
  }
}
```

In the preceding code example, we can see that we have added `verify(heroService).getHouse()` to our code. This validates whether we have called the `getHouse()` method. We can also validate whether the method is called with some given parameters.

Expecting calls

Expecting calls is an extended feature for behavior verification; we can also check the number of times that the mocked method has been called. We can do so by using the `times(n)` method. At the same time, we can also validate whether it has been called using the `never()` method.

Let's have a look at the following example code:

```
public class HeroTester {
    // injects the created Mock
    @InjectMocks
    HeroApp heroApp = new HeroApp();
    // Creates the mock
    @Mock
    HeroService heroService;
    @Test
    public void getHeroHouseTest(){
      // gets the values of the house
      when(heroService.getHouse())).thenReturn(
        "San Francisco ");
      // gets the value of the name
      when(heroService.getName())).thenReturn("Stark");
      // called one time
      assertThat(heroApp.getHouse()).isEqualTo(
        "San Francisco");
      // called two times
      assertThat(heroApp.getName()).isEqualTo("Stark");
      assertThat(heroApp.getName()).isEqualTo("Stark");

      verify(heroService, never()).getPowers();
      verify(heroService, times(2)).getName();
    }
}
```

In the preceding code example, we can see that we have used the `times(2)` method to validate whether the `getName()` method from `heroService` has been called two times. We have also used the `never()` method, which checks that the `getPowers()` method has not been called.

Mockito, other than `times()` and `never()`, also provides additional methods to validate the expected call counts, and these methods are the following:

- `atLeast (int min)`: Validates whether the method is called at least *n* times
- `atLeastOnce ()`: Validates whether the method is called at least once
- `atMost (int max)`: Validates whether the method is called at most *n* times

Exception handling

Mockito also provides exception handling in unit tests; it allows us to throw exceptions on mocks to test errors in our application.

Let's have a look at the following example code:

```
public class HeroTester {
    // injects the created Mock
    @InjectMocks
    HeroApp heroApp = new HeroApp();
    // Creates the mock
    @Mock
    HeroService heroService;
    @Test
    public void getHeroHouseTest(){
    doThrow(new RuntimeException("Add operation not
            implemented")).when(heroService.getHouse()))
    .thenReturn("San Francisco ")
  assertThat(heroApp.getHouse()).isEqualTo(
    "San Francisco");
  }
}
```

In the preceding example, we have configured `heroService.getHouse()`, once it is called, to throw `RunTimeException`. This will allows us to test and cover the error blocks in our application.

We have learned about the different features available in Mockito. Now, let's proceed with writing our tests in our Spring Boot application.

Mockito in Spring Boot

In this section, we will now implement Mockito for writing unit tests in our Spring Boot application. We will be writing tests for our service again, and we will create another package under our `test/java` folder, which will be used for our unit tests using Mockito; we will make `com.example.springbootsuperheroes.superheroes.antiHero.service`. Under the newly created package, we will create a new class named `AntiHeroServiceTest`, where we will start writing our tests for `AntiHeroService`.

After successfully creating our class, we will need to annotate the class with `@ExtendWith(MockitoExtension.class)` to be able to use the Mockito methods and features. The next step is to mock our `AntiHeroRepository` and inject it into our `AntiHeroRepositoryService`. To accomplish this, we would use the `@Mock` annotation with the declared repository and the `@InjectMocks` annotation with the declared service, and our class would now look as follows:

```
@ExtendWith(MockitoExtension.class)
class AntiHeroServiceTest {

    @Mock
    private AntiHeroRepository antiHeroRepository;

    @InjectMocks
    private AntiHeroService underTest;
}
```

In the preceding example, we successfully mocked our repository and injected it into our service. We can now start mocking our repository's return values and behavior in our tests.

Let's have some example tests in our `AntiHeroService`; in an example scenario, we will write a test for the `addAntiHero()` method. The possible test case for this one is to verify whether the `save()` method from the repository is called and the anti-hero is successfully added.

Let's have a look at the example code here:

```
@Test
void canAddAntiHero() {
    // given
    AntiHeroEntity antiHero = new AntiHeroEntity(
            UUID.randomUUID(),
            "Venom",
            "Lakandula",
            "Tondo",
            "Datu of Tondo",
            new SimpleDateFormat(
               "dd-MM-yyyy HH:mm:ss z").format(new Date())
        );
```

```
// when
underTest.addAntiHero(antiHero);

// then
ArgumentCaptor<AntiHeroEntity>
antiHeroDtoArgumentCaptor =
  ArgumentCaptor.forClass(
        AntiHeroEntity.class
);
verify(antiHeroRepository).save(
  antiHeroDtoArgumentCaptor.capture());
AntiHeroEntity capturedAntiHero =
  antiHeroDtoArgumentCaptor.getValue();

assertThat(capturedAntiHero).isEqualTo(antiHero);
}
```

In the preceding example, the first step is always to create a sample entity that we can use as a parameter for adding a new anti-hero; after invoking the addAntiHero() method that we are testing, we have verified whether the save() method of AntiHeroRepository has been invoked using the verify() method.

We have also used ArgumentCaptor to capture the argument values we have used in the previous way, which will be used for further assertions. In this case, we have asserted that the captured anti-hero is equal to the anti-hero instance we have created.

Summary

With this, we have reached the end of this chapter. Let's have a recap of the valuable things you have learned; you have learned about the concepts of JUnit, which is a testing framework that offers features such as fixtures, test suites, and classes to test the methods in our application. You have also learned about the application of AssertJ with JUnit, which provides a more flexible way of asserting objects in our unit tests; and lastly, you have also learned about the importance of Mockito, which provides us with the ability to mock objects and services.

In the next chapter, we will now develop our frontend application using Angular. We will discuss how to organize our features and modules, structure our components inside our Angular file structure, and add Angular Material to the user interface.

Part 3:
Frontend Development

This part contains a real-world scenario of developing an Angular 13 application. The following chapters are covered in this part:

Setting Up Our Angular Project and Architecture

In the previous chapter, you learned about the concepts of **JUnit**, which is a testing framework that offers features such as fixtures, test suites, and classes to test the methods in our application. You also learned the application of **AssertJ** with JUnit, which gives a more flexible way of asserting objects in our unit tests, and lastly, you also understood the importance of Mockito, which provides us with the ability to mock objects and services, omitting the use of the database in unit tests.

In this chapter, we will start building our frontend application using Angular; we will be tackling the main fundamentals of Angular, such as components, modules, directives, and routes. We will also point out some of the best practices for organizing our Angular project.

In this chapter, we will cover the following topics:

- Organizing features and modules
- Structuring components
- Adding Angular material

Technical requirements

The link to the finished version of this chapter is here: `https://github.com/PacktPublishing/Spring-Boot-and-Angular/tree/main/Chapter-10/superheroes`.

Organizing features and modules

In this section, we will be discussing how we can organize and structure our Angular project to make it optimized and maintainable. Since Angular is considered a **Model View Whatever** (**MVW**) framework, Angular developers have the freedom to implement their choice of pattern in developing the project. This could be confusing, as you will experience different structures and standards switching from one project to another. To solve this dilemma, we will present a commonly used structure in the industry or some kind of baseline structure that you will typically find in Angular projects.

However, before we proceed to our main topic, let us first discuss how to create our Angular project and what the basic concepts that we need to know before coding Angular are. You can skip this part if you are already knowledgeable about Angular and proceed to the *Organizing the folder structure* section.

Generating an Angular project

We can create or set up the dependencies of our Angular project using a tool known as the **Angular CLI**. We can scaffold the project by using a single command responsible for downloading the dependencies and generating the required files for our Angular project to run. The **Angular CLI** is a handy tool in that it also provides several commands that will help us generate boilerplate codes in Angular.

To install the Angular CLI, we should make sure that we have Node.js installed on our machine, and we will execute the `npm install -g @angular/cli` command. After executing the command, we can verify whether our Angular CLI has been successfully installed – we will have a new global `ng` command that we can use to check the version of the installed CLI.

To check the version, we will execute the `ng --version` command, and we will get the following output:

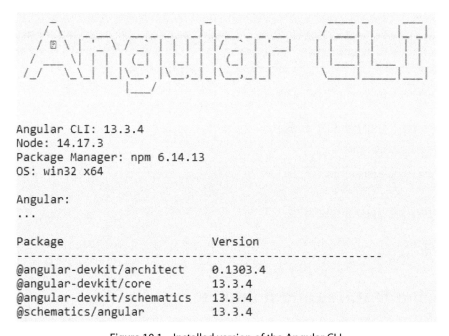

```
Angular CLI: 13.3.4
Node: 14.17.3
Package Manager: npm 6.14.13
OS: win32 x64

Angular:
...

Package                      Version
--------------------------------------------------------
@angular-devkit/architect    0.1303.4
@angular-devkit/core         13.3.4
@angular-devkit/schematics   13.3.4
@schematics/angular          13.3.4
```

Figure 10.1 – Installed version of the Angular CLI

In the preceding output, we can see that the version of the Angular CLI and Node.js installed on your machine is displayed after executing the `ng -- version` command. Currently, we have Angular CLI Version 13 installed, which means that once we scaffold an Angular project, it will be on **Version 13**.

After successfully installing the Angular CLI, we can now execute several commands for our project. Here are some of the commands that we can use in the Angular CLI:

- `ng new <project name> [options]`: Creates or scaffolds a new Angular project

- `ng serve <project> [options]`: Builds and serves your Angular application

- `ng generate <schematic> [options]`: Generates and modifies files with a specific schematic

  Some schematics we can generate are as follows:

  - Component

  - Module

  - Directive

  - Guard

- `ng build<project> [options]`: Compiles the Angular application into an output directory named `dist`, which will be used for production

- `ng test <project> [options]`: Runs the unit test in the Angular project

These are just some of the most commonly used commands of the Angular CLI. For the complete commands, you can visit the documentation for Angular at `https://angular.io/cli`.

We know the commands we can use in the Angular CLI. Now, let's generate our Angular project by executing the `ng new superheroes` command on our desired path. This will ask several questions, such as "*would you like to add Angular routing?*" and "*which stylesheet format would you like to use?*" We can select *Yes* and **Syntactically Awesome Style Sheet (SASS)** for these questions, as we need routes and SASS to build our application later.

After this step, this will now scaffold a new Angular project named superheroes and will be responsible for configuring the web pack, creating the required settings, and downloading the project's dependencies. After the scaffold is accomplished, open the superheroes project in Visual Studio Code or any IDE you prefer. We will see that the Angular application is configured and ready to run on our local server.

```
> .angular
> .vscode
> node_modules
∨ src
  ∨ app
    TS app-routing.module.ts
    <> app.component.html
    𝒫 app.component.scss
    TS app.component.spec.ts
    TS app.component.ts
    TS app.module.ts
  > assets
  > environments
  ★ favicon.ico
  <> index.html
  TS main.ts
  TS polyfills.ts
  𝒫 styles.scss
  TS test.ts
  ≡ .browserslistrc
  ⚙ .editorconfig
  ◆ .gitignore
  {} angular.json          M
  K karma.conf.js
  {} package-lock.json
  {} package.json
  ⓘ README.md
  {} tsconfig.app.json
  ⬛ tsconfig.json
  {} tsconfig.spec.json
```

```
You, 6 minutes ago | 1 author (You)
 1  {
 2    "name": "superheroes",
 3    "version": "0.0.0",
       ▷ Debug
 4    "scripts": {
 5      "ng": "ng",
 6      "start": "ng serve",
 7      "build": "ng build",
 8      "watch": "ng build --watch --configuration development",
 9      "test": "ng test"
10    },
11    "private": true,
12    "dependencies": {
13      "@angular/animations": "~13.3.0",
14      "@angular/common": "~13.3.0",
15      "@angular/compiler": "~13.3.0",
16      "@angular/core": "~13.3.0",
17      "@angular/forms": "~13.3.0",
18      "@angular/platform-browser": "~13.3.0",
19      "@angular/platform-browser-dynamic": "~13.3.0",
20      "@angular/router": "~13.3.0",
21      "rxjs": "~7.5.0",
22      "tslib": "^2.3.0",
23      "zone.js": "~0.11.4"
24    },
25    "devDependencies": {
26      "@angular-devkit/build-angular": "~13.3.4",
27      "@angular/cli": "~13.3.4",
28      "@angular/compiler-cli": "~13.3.0",
29      "@types/jasmine": "~3.10.0",
30      "@types/node": "^12.11.1",
31      "jasmine-core": "~4.0.0",          You, 6 minutes ago • initial commit …
32      "karma": "~6.3.0",
33      "karma-chrome-launcher": "~3.1.0",
34      "karma-coverage": "~2.1.0",
35      "karma-jasmine": "~4.0.0",
36      "karma-jasmine-html-reporter": "~1.7.0",
37      "typescript": "~4.6.2"
38    }
39  }
40
```

Figure 10.2 – Folder structure and dependencies installed after scaffolding

To run our project, we can open the VS Code terminal with the *Ctrl +* ` shortcut and execute the ng serve command. We can also use the defined scripts in our package.json file. In this case, we can perform npm run start to run our application. We will see in the terminal whether Angular is running successfully on our local server in the following screenshot:

```
> ng serve

√ Browser application bundle generation complete.

Initial Chunk Files    | Names      | Raw Size
vendor.js              | vendor     |   1.97 MB |
polyfills.js           | polyfills  | 294.85 kB |
styles.css, styles.js  | styles     | 173.69 kB |
main.js                | main       |  50.13 kB |
runtime.js             | runtime    |   6.52 kB |

                       | Initial Total |  2.49 MB

Build at: 2022-05-01T06:57:57.874Z - Hash: 5cb655001d470ea8 - Time: 3719ms

** Angular Live Development Server is listening on localhost:4200, open your browser on http://localhost:4200/ **

√ Compiled successfully.
```

Figure 10.3 – Folder structure and dependencies installed after scaffolding

After successfully running our Angular application, we can now open the app using the default URL (`http://localhost:4200`) in our browser, and we will see the default page of our Angular project:

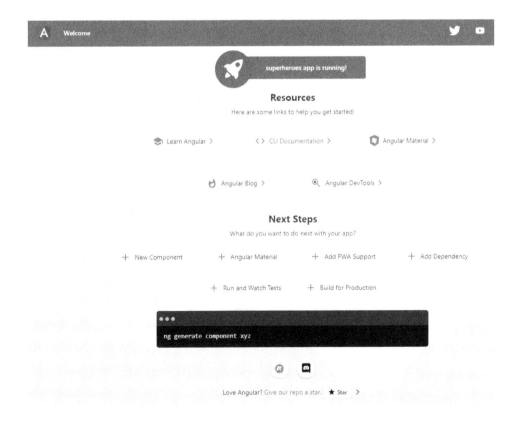

Figure 10.4 – Angular default page

We have successfully configured and started our Angular application locally. Now, let's discuss the concepts we will use to build our application.

Angular features

The Angular framework is a component-based framework that allows us to develop reusable components to promote the reusability and maintainability of code. It offers many features that will make our frontend development more powerful. In this section, we will discuss the basic features and fundamentals of Angular that serve as its building blocks; take note that we will not discuss all of the features here, as we will focus more on the organization of the project.

To learn more about the features, you can visit the official documentation for Angular: `https://angular.io/start`.

Components

Components are the main building blocks in Angular. They are responsible for defining what the behavior and the look of the view will be. Components are annotated with the @Component decorator, which assigns several types of metadata that describe the component's HTML, CSS, and selector.

The following are the commands to generate a component:

```
ng generate component <component-name>
ng g c <component-name>
```

The following is a code example for a component:

```
import { Component } from '@angular/core';

@Component({
    selector: 'app-root',
    templateUrl: './app.component.html',
    styleUrls: ['./app.component.scss']
})
export class AppComponent {
    title = 'superheroes';
}
```

Components have a feature called **data binding**, which allows us to pass data into the view. Data binding can be used to display values to the user, respond to user events, and modify the styles. Angular binding is classified into two groups:

- One-way binding
- Two-way binding

One-way binding

As can be inferred from the name, data only flows in one direction here. It can be from a component to the view or vice versa.

There are several ways to achieve one-way binding in Angular, and the two most common ways are using interpolation and property binding.

Interpolation

Interpolation is a one-way binding technique that allows us to display expressions to a string literal in HTML. Interpolation uses { { } } (double curly braces) for expressions inside HTML code.

Let's have a look at the following example code:

```
// app.component.ts
export class AppComponent {
  title = 'superheroes';
}
<!—app.component.html ->
<!-- INTERPOLATE TITLE -->
<span> Title:  {{title}} </span>
```

In the preceding example, we have used interpolation to display the value of the `title` variable in the view. Using interpolation, we can also use operators in the template expression.

Property binding

Property binding allows us to bind HTML element properties in the component. Since we bind the HTML element properties, when the bound value changes, the view also changes. We can bind to HTML element properties such as `class`, `href`, `disabled`, and `src`.

Let's have a look at the following example code on how to use property binding:

```
// app.component.ts
export class AppComponent {
  isDisabled = true;
}
<!—app.component.html ->
<button [disabled]="isDisabled">Can't be clicked</button>
```

In the preceding example, we have bound the `isDisabled` variable to the disabled property of the button. The button will be disabled, as we have set the value of the `isDisabled` to `true`.

Two-way binding

Two-way binding is a two-way data flow. Any changes applied to the model will be reflected in the view simultaneously and any modifications involved in the view are updated in the component. Two-way data binding helps handle forms, as we want our model to be updated once the values of the form are also updated and vice versa.

To achieve two-way binding, the ngModel directive is used.

ngModel

ngModel is a directive used to achieve two-way binding in Angular. This is under the Forms module in @angular/forms. ngModel, once it is bound to an input field or other form element, gives that element a property binding and an event binding. Let's have a look at the following example code:

```
// app.component.ts
export class AppComponent {
   model = 'seiji';
}
<!--app.component.html -->
<input [(ngModel)]="model"/>
```

In the preceding example code, we have bound the model value to an input element using the ngModel directive. This syntax is also known as the *banana in a box*, which encloses ngModel with a square bracket and parenthesis. The directive will bind the model's value with the input field using property binding and listen to the input value changes by utilizing ngModelChange.

Directives

Directives are an Angular feature that helps us manipulate the **Document Object Model** (**DOM**). We can modify a DOM element's layout, behavior, and view. Directives are classified into three parts: **components** are one of the classifications, and the other two are **attribute** and **structural** directives.

Structural directives

Structural directives are directives that can modify the layout of the DOM by adding, updating, or removing elements, listed below are some of the structural directives in Angular:

- *ngIf: A directive that is used to add or remove elements in the DOM based on a condition:

  ```
  <div *ngIf="condition">Will show if the condition is
  true</div>
  ```

- *ngFor: A directive that is used to repeat HTML elements from the items iterated in a specific list:

```
// this will display all the users for each row
<tr *ngFor="let user of users;">
    <td>{{user.firstName }}</td>
    <td>{{user.lastName}}</td>
</tr>
```

- *ngSwitch: A directive that allows us to add or remove HTML elements using a switch case mechanism. The HTML elements will be displayed if the provided expression is matched:

```
//evaluates the hero variable and displays the name of
the hero base on its value
<div [ngSwitch]="hero">
   <div *ngSwitchCase="'Dr. Strange'">
      Stephen Strange</div>
   <div *ngSwitchCase="'Hawkeye'">Clint Barton</div>
   <div *ngSwitchCase="'Hulk'">Bruce Banner</div>
</div>
```

Attribute directives

Attribute directives are directives used for changing or modifying the appearance or behavior of the element. Compared to structural directives, attribute directives cannot add or remove elements in the DOM.

Listed here are some of the attribute directives in Angular:

- **ngClass**: A directive used to add CSS classes to or remove them from an HTML element; this allows us to change the appearance of elements dynamically:

```
//adds an error class on the input element if the
//control value is invalid
<input type="text" [ngClass]="control.isInvalid ?
'error': ''" />
```

- **ngStyle**: A directive that allows us to change the styles of HTML elements:

```
// the color of the element will base on the value of
// the color variable
<div [ngStyle]="{'color': color}"> Angular Framework </
div>
```

Modules

Modules are one of the essential features of the Angular framework. As our application gets more complex, it will consist of large blocks of components, directives, and services. This will affect the maintainability of the application's code base. The Angular framework provides a way of organizing and grouping blocks, known as modules.

Modules in the Angular framework help us develop our application promoting the separation of concerns. They allow us to classify and organize blocks based on their functionality. Angular is also built using modules; the @angular/core framework is the primary Angular module, which provides Angular's core functionalities and services.

Creating a module

We will use the @NgModule decorator to create a module. It consists of several types of metadata that allow us to define the component, services, pipes, and other modules included in the created module.

The following example code shows the properties available for a module:

```
@NgModule({
    declarations:[],
    imports:[],
    providers:[],
    exports: [],
    bootstrap:[],
    entrycomponents:[]
})
```

Let's now discuss the functionality of each property:

- **Declarations**: This is where we place the components, directives, and pipes of our applications. Remember that components, directives, and pipes must be declared in only one module.

- **Providers**: This is where we place services to allow them to be available for dependency injection.

- **Imports**: This is where we place one or more other modules in our application. Once we import a specific module, all components, pipes, and directives in the imported module can be used.

- **Exports**: This is where we place the components, directives, and pipes to be available to other modules once imported.

- **Bootstrap**: This is where we place the main component of the module. The Bootstrap property is used mainly for the root module of the Angular application (AppModule), as the root module's responsibility is to load the first view as our application starts.

- **Entry components**: This is where we place components that should be dynamically loaded in our application.

  The following diagram shows how NgModule works in an Angular application:

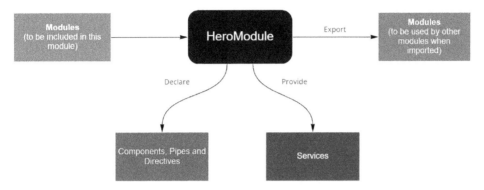

Figure 10.5 – Diagram for the flow of an Angular module

Services and dependency injection

Services are also one of the valuable features of Angular. It is code that can be reused in different components of your application.

The primary responsibility of services is the following:

- Reusing logic on different components

- Implementing API communication and data access

- Promoting single responsibility, as it separates the independent features of components

To create a service in the application, we will create a class and annotate it with the @Injectable decorator. To register the service at the root level of your application, we will add the following to our @Injectable decorator:

```
@Injectable({
  providedIn: 'root',
})
```

Once we have set the value of the providedIn metadata in the root, this will create a single, shared instance of the service throughout the application. On the other hand, if we want to provide the service in a specific module, we will place the service in the provider metadata of @NgModule:

```
@NgModule({
    providers: [Service1]
})
```

Now that we have discussed some of the essential features of Angular, we will focus on how to structure your Angular application.

Creating the Angular folder structure

The Angular framework is considered an MVW framework, which means that there are many possible ways of structuring our application. In this case, we would discuss one of the best practices or most commonly used structures that can help your Angular application be scalable and maintainable.

In the previous part, we learned that Angular blocks could be grouped and organized into modules; modules are a good starting point for structuring our Angular application. The first step we can implement is to group and classify modules based on their functionality. Listed here is the classification of our modules.

Root module

The **root** module is the application's main module. This is the first module loaded as the Angular application starts. The root module is automatically generated when we scaffold an Angular application called `AppModule` and is found under the `src/app` folder.

Feature module

The **feature** module is where we place modules that apply a specific feature of our application. This means that most of what our code uses is inside this module. We will create the components, pipes, and directives under the module where they should be included and we can also separate components by placing the components that have a route in a page folder.

Let's have a look at an example folder structure of a feature module called `AntiHeroModule`:

```
├── src
│   ├── app
│   │   ├── anti-hero
│   │   │   ├── components
│   │   │   │   ├── shared.component.ts
│   │   │   ├── directives
│   │   │   │   ├── first.directive.ts
│   │   │   │   ├── another.directive.ts
│   │   │   ├── pages
│   │   │   │   ├── form
│   │   │   │   │   ├── form.component.ts
│   │   │   │   ├── list
│   │   │   │   │   ├── list.component.ts
```

```
|    |    |    |    |       ├── anti-hero.component.ts
|    |    |    |    |       ├── anti-hero.component.html
|    |    |    |    |       ├── anti-hero.component.css
|    |    |    |    |       ├── index.ts
|    |    |    |    ├── pipes
|    |    |    |    |    ├── first.pipe.ts
|    |    |    |    ├── anti-hero.module.ts
|    |    |    |    ├── anti-hero.routing.module.ts
|    |    |    |    ├── index.ts
```

In the folder structure here, we have divided our anti-hero module into several parts. The first folder is the `components` folder, which contains all of the components shared throughout this module. These can also be called **dumb** components, which we will discuss in the next section.

The next two are the `directives` and `pipes` folders, which contain the directives and pipes used in `AntiHeroModule`. Lastly, the `pages` folder includes the components in `AntiHeroModule` that have a direct route. These can also be called **smart** components. We have also included the `index. ts` file, known as a barrel file, which will provide a centralized place for exporting components, directives, and pipes.

Shared module

The **shared** module is a module that is used and shared throughout the application; this is composed of the components, pipes, and directives that we are required to use in different parts of the application. Remember that a shared module should not have a dependency on other modules in the application.

Shared modules are created under the `src/app/shared` folder.

Let's have a look at the example folder structure of a shared module in our application:

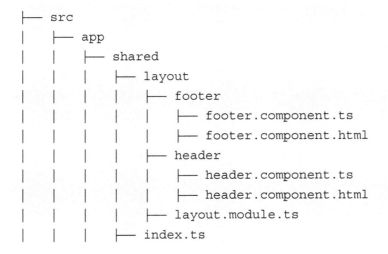

```
├── src
|    ├── app
|    |    ├── shared
|    |    |    ├── layout
|    |    |    |    ├── footer
|    |    |    |    |    ├── footer.component.ts
|    |    |    |    |    ├── footer.component.html
|    |    |    |    ├── header
|    |    |    |    |    ├── header.component.ts
|    |    |    |    |    ├── header.component.html
|    |    |    |    ├── layout.module.ts
|    |    |    ├── index.ts
```

In the preceding folder structure, we can see that we have created two components named `footer` and `navbar`; these are some of the most commonly shared components in applications.

Core module

The **core** module is a module for services shared throughout the applications. These are singleton services, having only one instance in the application. The services that are included in the core module are usually authentication services.

Since it should only have one instance, the core module must only be imported into the application's root module.

We can add the following code to our core module to prevent it from being imported into other modules:

```
@NgModule({})
export class CoreModule {
  constructor(@Optional() @SkipSelf() core:CoreModule ){
    if (core) {
        throw new Error("Core module should only be
                        imported to the Root Module")
    }
  }
}
```

In the preceding code example, we have added a `CoreModule` parameter to our constructor with `@Optional` and `@SkipSelf` decorators – this will throw an error if the core returns a value indicating that `CoreModule` has already been imported into the root module.

Let's now proceed to learn how to implement the structure on an Angular application.

Implementing the structure

Now that we have learned the different module categories for our Angular application, let's apply the folder structure to our superheroes project.

Our goal here is to create a frontend application with a simple **Create, Read, Update, and Delete (CRUD)** functionality for heroes and anti-heroes.

First, we will create the shared features and the `core` folder under the `app` directory, and after completing the three main categories, we will make the blocks needed for each module.

Blocks under the features module

We want to create the blocks under our features module; the first thing we need to scaffold is `AntiHeroModule`. Execute the `ng g m anti-hero` command to generate the module under the `src/app` folder.

Now, under the anti-hero folder, we will create the following folders:

- `components`: This will contain components that will be shared in this module.

- `pipes`: This will contain all the pipes used by the anti-hero module.

- `directives`: This will contain all the directives that the anti-hero module will use.

- `pages`: This will contain components that have a direct route.

After creating the folders, we will now make the page components for our anti-hero module. We will add two pages where the first one will be the page for displaying the list of anti-heroes and the second one will be a form that allows us to view, create, or modify the selected hero in the list. We can execute the `ng g c anti-hero/pages/pages/form` and `ng g c anti-hero/pages/list` commands to make the two pages. This will create two new components, `form` and `list`, under the `pages` folder.

After successfully creating the page components, we will also add a routing module for our anti-hero module. We will execute the `ng g m anti-hero/anti-hero-routing --flat` command and we will place the following code in our routing module:

```
import {NgModule} from "@angular/core";
import {RouterModule, Routes} from "@angular/router";
import {ListComponent} from "./pages/list/list.component";
import {FormComponent} from "./pages/form/form.component";

const routes: Routes = [
  {
    path: "",
    component: ListComponent,
  },
  {
    path: "form",
    component: FormComponent,
  },
];
@NgModule({
```

```
   declarations: [ListComponent, FormComponent],
   imports: [RouterModule.forChild(routes)],
   exports:[RouterModule]
})
export class AntiHeroRoutingModule {}
```

In the preceding example code, we have defined routes for our `form` and `list` pages. This means that the page components will have direct routes in our application, and we have also defined `ListComponent` as the base route for this module.

After successfully creating the page components and defining routes, we want our root module (`AppModule`) to have a route for `AntiHeroModule`.

To implement this, we will place the following code in `app-routing.module.ts`:

```
import { NgModule } from '@angular/core';
import { RouterModule, Routes } from '@angular/router';
const routes: Routes = [
   {
     path: "",
     redirectTo: "anti-heroes",
     pathMatch: "full",
   },
   {
     path: "anti-heroes",
     loadChildren: () =>
       import("./anti-hero/anti-hero.module").then((m) =>
            m.AntiHeroModule),
   }
];
@NgModule({
   imports: [RouterModule.forRoot(routes)],

})
export class AppRoutingModule { }
```

In the preceding example code, we have used lazy loading to create a route for `AntiHeroModule`. Once we visit the `{baseUrl}/anti-heroes` URL, this will load `AntiHeroModule` and redirect to the base route, which is `ListComponent`. We have also used `RouterModule.forRoot()` to import the routes, as this is the root module.

After successfully defining the routes for our `AppModule`, we can now see the current structure of our application:

Figure 10.6 – Folder structure after creating the anti-hero feature

Now that we have completed our feature module in Angular, we have only the `pages` folder. We will add other blocks such as the components and directives later as we develop the application. The next step is to make the shared module.

Blocks under the shared module

Now, our next goal is to create the blocks under the shared module. We defined the shared module as components, directives, and pipes that are shared throughout the application and must not have a dependency on other modules. To create our shared module, we will execute the `ng g m shared` command. This will create a new shared folder and a module file inside the new shared folder.

Now after completing the shared module, we can generate the blocks that will be categorized in this module. In our application, we can include `navbar` and `footer` as shared components, as they will be used in every part of our application.

We will execute the `ng g c shared/layout/navbar` and `ng g c shared/layout/footer` commands to scaffold `navbar` and `footer`. We can see that `FooterComponent` and `NavbarComponent` are automatically added to the `shared.module.ts` file as Angular detects the module closest to the components:

```
@NgModule({
  declarations: [
    NavbarComponent,
    FooterComponent
  ],
  imports: [CommonModule]
})
export class SharedModule { }
```

Remember to add the `navbar` and `footer` components in the `exports` metadata of `NgModule` and we will import the shared module in different modules:

```
@NgModule({
  declarations: [
    NavbarComponent,
    FooterComponent
  ],
  exports: [NavbarComponent, FooterComponent]
  imports: [CommonModule]
})
```

We can also add shared directives and pipes under the shared folder by executing the `ng g c shared/directive/directive-name` and `ng g c shared/pipes/pipe-name` commands depending on the needs of our application. After successfully creating the blocks, we will have the following folder structure:

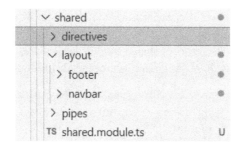

Figure 10.7 – Folder structure after creating the shared module

We must also remember that a shared module does not need a routing module since it does not have components that require routes in our application.

Blocks under the core module

The last module that we need to create is the core module. Core modules are services that we share throughout the application and they have only one instance. One service that always goes into the core module is the authentication service.

To create our shared module, we will execute the `ng g m core;` command after completing the core module. We will scaffold the authenticate service by running the `ng g s core/services/authenticate` command.

After successfully creating the authenticate service, we will provide it under the `core.module.ts` file to include the service in the module. We can also add shared models under the core module by adding a `models` folder depending on the need of our application. Now, we have the following folder structure:

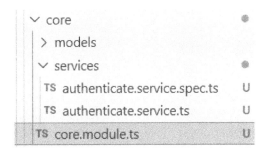

Figure 10.8 – Folder structure after creating the shared module

We will make the contents of the authenticate service as we go through the development of the application but now that we have created the base structure of our Angular application, we will use this structure to build other parts of the project. Now, we will discuss how we can structure our components in Angular.

Structuring components

We have already structured our Angular application by categorizing our modules based on their use and functionality, which will benefit code reusability and maintainability. However, there is still the possibility that a large number of components could be created under a specific module, which would further improve the maintainability of an application. In this section, we will discuss another strategy for building your Angular architecture at the component level.

Smart and dumb or presentation components

The most common and recommended **component-level architecture** for building Angular applications is the smart and dumb component architecture. In the previous section, we split the modules into different categories based on how we were using them in the application.

This architecture also offers the same concept. We will divide the components into two different types – namely, **smart components** and **dumb** or **presentation components**.

Let's discuss the characteristics of each component type.

Smart components

Smart components are also known as application-level components or container components. The primary responsibility of these components is to communicate with services and consume data from a request. Since they are smart, they contain all the dependencies and subscriptions required to get the data for the application.

Smart components can be considered page components that have direct routes in our application and they are the parent components holding the dumb components. Let's have a look at the following example code for creating smart components:

```
@Component({
    selector: 'app-home',
    template: `
      <h2>User List</h2>
      <div>
          <table class="table">
              <tbody>
              <tr (click)="selectUser(user)" *ngFor="let user
                of users">
                  <td> {{user.firstName}} </td>
                  <td>
                      <span>{{user.lastName}}</span>
                  </td>
              </tr>
              </tbody>
          </table>
      </div>
      `,
    styleUrls: ['./home.component.css']
```

```
})
export class HomeComponent implements OnInit {
  users: User[] = [];
  constructor(private userService: UserService) {
  }
  ngOnInit() {
      this. userService.getUsers()
          .subscribe(users => this.users = users);
  }
  selectUser(user: User) {
     // action
  }
}
```

In the preceding example code, we have created a component named HomeComponent that will display a list of users in the table. We have also injected UserService to get the users from an HTTP request. We know that this component will successfully display the users, but we can see that our template is extensive and might get too complicated as we add more features to this component.

What we would want to do is omit elements that are only for presentation purposes. In this scenario, we would like to remove the table in our HomeComponent, and we would have the following code:

```
@Component({
  selector: 'app-home',
  template: `
    <h2>User List</h2>
    <div>
       <!--we will place that dumb component here later-->
    </div>
  `,
  styleUrls: ['./home.component.css']
})
export class HomeComponent implements OnInit {
  users: User[] = [];
  constructor(private userService: UserService) {
  }
  ngOnInit() {
      this. userService.getUsers()
```

```
          .subscribe(users => this.users = users);
   }
   selectUser(user: User) {
      // action
   }
}
```

In the preceding refactored code, we have removed the table displaying the list of users. We only want smart components to handle dependency injections, subscriptions, and actions. We have now successfully created our smart components and the next step is to make the presentation components.

Dumb or presentation components

Dumb components, also known as presentation components, are responsible for displaying data in the application. They should not have dependencies and subscriptions, as their only purpose is to present the data in the view.

Let's create the table we omitted a while ago as a dumb component:

```
@Component({
   selector: 'users-list',
   template: `
        <table class="table">
            <tbody>
            <tr (click)="selectUser(user)" *ngFor="let user
             of users">
                <td> {{user.firstName}} </td>
                <td>
                    <span>{{user.lastName}}</span>
                </td>
            </tr>
            </tbody>
        </table>
    `,
   styleUrls: ['./users-list.component.css']
})
export class UsersListComponent {
   @Input()
   users: User[];
```

```
@Output('user')
userEmitter = new EventEmitter<User>();
  selectUser(user:User) {
      this.userEmitter.emit(user);
  }
}
```

In the preceding example code, we have created a separate component for the table that displays the list of users. Since dumb components have no dependencies injected, the component will need to receive the data from the smart components. To achieve this, we have added an @Input binding property to accept the list of users from HomeComponent; on the other hand, we have also added an @Output binding property to bubble actions to the parent or smart component.

Remember that dumb components must not have any logic or actions; in this case, we will pass the event in the parent component with the use of EventEmitter and the parent component will be responsible for the steps needed to be accomplished. In the example code, once a row is clicked, we are passing the user to the userEmitter that HomeComponent will retrieve.

After successfully creating UserListComponent, we can now use this in our HomeComponent, and we will have the following code:

```
@Component({
  selector: 'app-home',
  template: `
    <h2>User List</h2>
    <div>
       <users-list users="users"
       (user)="selectUser($event)"/>
    </div>
  `,
  styleUrls: ['./home.component.css']
})
export class HomeComponent implements OnInit {
  users: User[] = [];
  constructor(private userService: UserService) {
  }
  ngOnInit() {
      this. userService.getUsers()
```

```
                    .subscribe(users => this.users = users);
    }
    selectUser(user: User) {
        // action
    }
}
```

In the preceding example code, we can see that we have used `UsersListComponent` as a child component of `HomeComponent`. It accepts the list of the users retrieved by `HomeComponent` and emits an event once a specific row is clicked. With that, we have now finished discussing the concepts of smart and dumb components.

Let's apply the architecture to our application now.

Implementing smart and dumb components in the project

Let's now implement the smart and dumb component architecture in our Angular project. We will create our components under `AntiHeroModule`. We have already made our **smart components** and these are the `form` and `list` components in the `pages` folder.

We will always place our smart components in the `pages` folder, as these will be our container components throughout the application. The next step is to create our dumb components. We will create two dumb components, namely the `anti-hero-form` and `anti-hero-list` components. To make the components, execute the `ng g c anti-hero/components/anti-hero-form anti-hero/components anti-hero-list` command. After successfully generating the two dumb components, let's place the following code.

For `AntiHeroListComponent`, we will place the following code into the `anti-hero-list.component.html` file:

```html
<table>
    <thead>
        <th *ngFor="let item of headers">{{item.headerName}}</
th>
    </thead>
    <tbody>
        <tr (click)="selectAntiHero(item)"
  *ngFor ="let item of antiHeroes">
            <ng-container *ngFor="let header of headers">
                <td>{{item[header.fieldName]}}</td>
            </ng-container>
```

```
        </tr>
      </tbody>
  </table>
```

In the preceding HTML code, we have created a table where the headers and the items are bound to the `antiHeroes` variable. We have also bound the headers and the key values of the anti-hero to display the values dynamically.

Now, let's add the properties for receiving and emitting data into our `AntiHeroList` component:

---

anti-hero-list.component.ts

```
export class AntiHeroListComponent implements OnInit {
  @Input() headers: Array<{headerName: string, fieldName:
    keyof AntiHero}> = [];
  @Input() antiHeroes: Array<AntiHero> = [];
  @Output() antiHero = new EventEmitter();

  constructor() { }
  ngOnInit(): void {
  }
  selectAntiHero(antiHero: AntiHero) {
    this.antiHero.emit(antiHero);
  }
}
```

Now, in the `TypeScript` file of the anti-hero component, we have defined three properties that we need for the dumb component to accept data from and emit events to the smart component.

The first property is the `headers` property, which has the `@Input` annotation. This will get an array of the `{headerName: string, fieldName: keyof AntiHero}` type, which will be iterated to display the column headers and display the values of each field of an anti-hero item. The second property is `antiHeroes`, which also has an `@Input` annotation. This will accept the list of anti-heroes to be displayed in each row, and lastly, the `antiHero` property, which is annotated with `@Output`. This emits the selected anti-hero to the parent component once a user clicks a single row.

We have also added an interface named `AntiHero` in `anti-hero/models/anti-hero.interface.ts` that will be used to cast object types.

We will have the following code for `interface`:

```
export interface AntiHero {
    firstName: string;
    lastName: string;
    house: string;
    kownAs: string;
}
```

In the preceding code example, we have created an `AntiHero` interface that will be used as the blueprint of our object. The properties of the anti-hero object are the same as the properties we defined in our Spring application.

After creating the interface for our object, we will now declare and import our components and modules into `AntiHeroModule`.

Let's have a look at the following code:

---

anti-hero.module.ts

```
@NgModule({
    declarations: [
        AntiHeroListComponent,
        AntiHeroFormComponent,
        ListComponent,
        FormComponent
    ],
    imports: [
        CommonModule,
        AntiHeroRoutingModule,
    ]
})
export class AntiHeroModule { }
```

In our `anti-hero.module.ts` file, we want to make sure that our smart components and dumb components are declared; otherwise, we will have errors at compilation. We also want to check whether our `AntiHeroRoutingModule` is imported for use of the routes.

Let's now add additional styling to improve the user interface of our application. Let's have a look at the following code:

anti-hero-list.component.scss

```scss
table, th, td {
    border: 1px solid;
    border-collapse: collapse;
    border: 1px solid;
}
```

We have also added a simple CSS code to style our table in the component. Now, we have successfully created our `AntiHeroListComponent`. The next step is to use this presentation component on the `ListComponent` page. Let's have a look at the following code example:

```typescript
export class ListComponent implements OnInit {
  // sample data of anti-hero
  antiHeroes: AntiHero[] = [
    {
      firstName: "Eddie",
      lastName: "Brock",
      house: "New York",
      kownAs: "Venom"
    }
  ]
  headers: {headerName: string, fieldName: keyof
            AntiHero}[] = [
    {headerName: "First Name", fieldName: "firstName"},
    {headerName: "Last Name", fieldName: "lastName"},
    {headerName: "House", fieldName: "house"},
    {headerName: "Known As", fieldName: "kownAs"},
  ]
  constructor() { }
  ngOnInit(): void {
  }
  selectAntiHero(antiHero: AntiHero) {}
}
```

In the `TypeScript` file of `ListComponent`, we have created the definition of the headers and an example list of `antiHeroes` for the anti-hero list to display. This will only be temporary, as we just want to test whether our presentation component displays the list of anti-heroes successfully. We have also created the `selectAntiHero()` function for future implementation once a specific anti-hero is selected.

Let's now define the input and output properties for `AntiHeroList`. Let's have a look at the following code:

list.component.html

```
<!-- Dumb component anti hero list -->
<app-anti-hero-list [antiHeroes]="antiHeroes"
[headers]="headers" (antiHero)="selectAntiHero($event)"></app-
anti-hero-list>
```

Now, in the HTML file of `ListComponent`, we have bound `headers` and `antiHeroes` to the properties of `app-anti-hero-list`. We have also used the `selectAntiHero()` function to catch the event once `antiHero` has emitted an action.

After successfully implementing our presentation component, we can run the application and open the application in the browser. We should see the following results:

First Name	Last Name	House	Known As
Eddie	Brock	New York	Venom

Figure 10.9 – AntiHeroList presentation component

We can see in the results that our presentation component has successfully displayed the data coming from the parent component. For the form component, we will implement its functionalities in the next chapter, as creating forms will be another different topic.

Now, we have learned about the concepts, structure, and implementation of smart and dumb components. In the next section, we will now use a UI framework that will help us improve the interface of our Angular application.

Adding Angular Material

We have already organized our Angular application using the **core**, **feature**, and **shared** architecture at the module level and the smart and dumb architecture at the component level. Now, we are ready to customize and improve the look and UI by styling our components. We all know that writing CSS code from scratch and developing a base style is another challenge for us developers. It creates additional effort for us beyond just worrying about the logical side of the code. This is where Angular Material saves the day!

Angular Material is a library created by Google that provides a wide range of UI components for use in Angular applications, such as tables, cards, inputs, and date pickers. This means that we don't have to style components from scratch, as a list of components from the material library is ready to use.

Angular Material has a wide range of growing components under the hood. It provides modules containing the components that can be used in Angular applications which can be imported into a specific application module; components are reusable and easy to customize in terms of their look and feel, as they have built-in properties that we can use.

Let's configure Angular Material in our Angular project.

Configuring Angular Material

Angular Material is easy to configure in Angular projects, as it provides a schematic to install all the dependencies of Angular Material in just one command. To install Angular Material, we will execute the following command:

```
ng add @angular/material
```

After executing the command, it will ask some questions before installing the resources:

- **Choose a prebuilt theme name or "custom" for a custom theme**: Angular Material provides prebuilt themes or you can configure your custom theme.

- **Set up global Angular Material typography styles**: Choosing **yes** will apply the global typography of Angular Material.

- **Set up browser animations for Angular Material**: Choosing **yes** will install `BrowserAnimationsModule` in our root module. This is important when we want to use animations from Angular Material.

After completing all the questions, it will now install Angular Material. This will execute the following actions for our project:

1. Adding dependencies to `package.json` (`@angular/material` and `@angular/cdk`).

2. Adding the `Roboto` font to the `index.html` file:

   ```
   <link href="https://fonts.googleapis.com/
   css2?family=Roboto:wght@300;400;500&display=swap"
   rel="stylesheet">
   ```

3. Adding the Material Design icon font to the `index.html` file:

   ```
   <link href="https://fonts.googleapis.com/
   icon?family=Material+Icons" rel="stylesheet">
   ```

4. Adding the following CSS styles:

    - Setting `height` to `100%` for `html` and `body`

    - Setting `Roboto` as the default font

    - Removing margins from the body:

    ```
    html, body { height: 100%; }
    body { margin: 0; font-family: Roboto, "Helvetica Neue",
    sans-serif; }
    ```

After successfully installing Angular Material in our application, we are now ready to use the components in our application.

Implementing Angular Material

We will now implement Angular Material components in our Angular project. As we mentioned a while ago, Angular Material offers a wide range of components that we can use for building our application. In this example project, we will only define the components that we will use in our application. Let's list the components that we will implement.

Button component

The native `<button>` or `<a>` elements that are enhanced with Material Design styling.

We can import the button component using the following code:

```
import {MatButtonModule} from '@angular/material/button';
```

Here's an example of the button component:

```
<div class="example-button-row">
    <button mat-raised-button>Basic</button>
    <button mat-raised-button
      color="primary">Primary</button>
    <button mat-raised-button
      color="accent">Accent</button>
    <button mat-raised-button color="warn">Warn</button>
    <button mat-raised-button disabled>Disabled</button>
    <a mat-raised-button href="
      https://material.angular.io/target=" _blank>Link</a>
</div>
```

In the preceding code example for the **Material** button, we can see that we are using built-in directives from Material Design to change the style and look of the button. The example code will have the following output:

Figure 10.10 – Example output for the Material button

Icon component

This component allows us to add vector-based icons to the application and supports both icon fonts and SVG icons.

We can import the icon component using the following code:

```
import {MatIconModule} from '@angular/material/icon';
```

Here's an example of the icon component:

```
<mat-icon color="primary">delete</mat-icon>
<mat-icon color="accent">fiber_new</mat-icon>
<mat-icon color="warn">pageview</mat-icon>
```

In the preceding code example, we can create icons by using the mat-icon component. This has several input properties such as color that allow us to customize the color of the icon. The example code will have the following output:

Figure 10.11 – Example output for the Material icon

Table component

This component allows us to add a data table with Material Design styling. The Material table is based on the foundation of the **CDK data table**. For more information on how to implement a CDK data table, see the documentation at https://material.angular.io/cdk/table/overview.

We can import the table component using the following code:

```
import {MatTableModule} from '@angular/material/table';
```

Here's an example of the table component:

```
<table mat-table [dataSource]="data" class="mat-elevation-z8">
  <!-- Position Column -->
  <ng-container matColumnDef="id">
    <th mat-header-cell *matHeaderCellDef> ID </th>
    <td mat-cell *matCellDef="let element">
    {{element.position}} </td>
  </ng-container>

  <!-- Name Column -->
  <ng-container matColumnDef="name">
    <th mat-header-cell *matHeaderCellDef> Name </th>
    <td mat-cell *matCellDef="let element">
      {{element.name}} </td>
  </ng-container>

  <tr mat-header-row *matHeaderRowDef="columns"></tr>
  <tr mat-row *matRowDef="let row; columns: columns;"></tr>
</table>c
```

In the preceding example, we can see the table uses several properties. The first property is the `dataSource` property, which will be the one accepting the list of data to be displayed. The next property is `matColumnDef`, which defines the field name of each column that should be included in the columns variable that is bound to the `matHeaderRowDef` property. Lastly, the `matHeaderCellDef` and `mattCelDef` properties display the actual column name and the associated values, as shown in the following screenshot:

Figure 10.12 – Example output for the Material table

Toolbar component

This component allows us to add a toolbar with Material Design styling. This is commonly used as a container for headers, titles, and navigation buttons.

We can import the toolbar component using the following code:

```
import {MatToolbarModule} from '@angular/material/toolbar';
```

Here's an example of the toolbar component:

```
<p>
  <mat-toolbar color="primary">
    <button mat-icon-button class="example-icon"
      aria-label="Example icon-button with menu icon">
      <mat-icon>menu</mat-icon>
    </button>
    <span>Angular CRUD</span>
  </mat-toolbar>
</p>
```

In the preceding code example, we have created a toolbar element using the mat-toolbar component. The mat-toolbar component uses content projection that allows us to customize its contents. The example code will have the following output:

Figure 10.13 – Example output for the Material toolbar

Form field component

This component allows us to wrap Material components to apply text field styles such as underlining, hint messages, and floating labels. The following components can be used inside <mat-form-field>:

- input matNativeControl> and <textarea matNativeControl>: Can be used by adding import {MatInputModule} from '@angular/material/input';
- <mat-select>: Can be used by adding import {MatSelectModule} from '@angular/material/select';
- <mat-chip-list>: Can be used by adding import {MatChipsModule} from '@angular/material/chips';

Here's an example of the form field component:

```
<p>
  <mat-form-field appearance="legacy">
```

```
        <mat-label>Legacy form field</mat-label>
        <input matInput placeholder="Placeholder">
      </mat-form-field>
  </p>
  <p>
    <mat-form-field appearance="standard">
      <mat-label>Standard form field</mat-label>
      <input matInput placeholder="Placeholder">
    </mat-form-field>
  </p>
  <p>
    <mat-form-field appearance="fill">
      <mat-label>Fill form field</mat-label>
      <input matInput placeholder="Placeholder">
    </mat-form-field>
  </p>
  <p>
    <mat-form-field appearance="outline">
      <mat-label>Outline form field</mat-label>
      <input matInput placeholder="Placeholder">
    </mat-form-field>
  </p>
```

In the preceding code example, we have created a toolbar element using the `mat-form-field` component. The `mat-form-field` component should have the `mat-label` component and an input element with the `matInput` directive as its contents. The example code will have the following output:

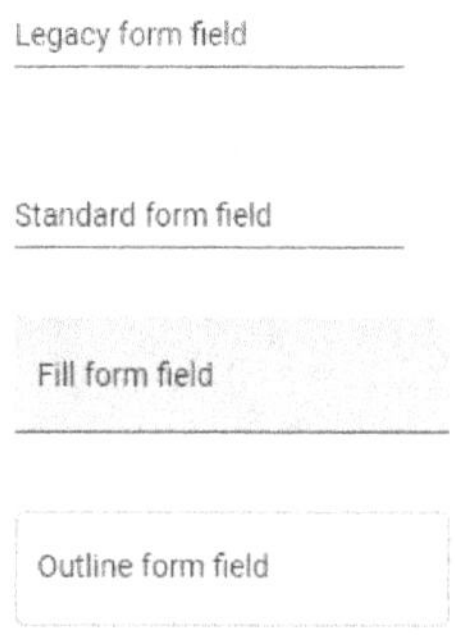

Legacy form field

Standard form field

Fill form field

Outline form field

Figure 10.14 – Example output for the Material form field

For more information on the list of components from Angular Material, see the documentation at `https://material.angular.io/components`.

Now that we have listed the Material components we will use in our application, let's apply Material Design to our components.

The first step we need to do is to create our Material module. The Material modules will be included in the shared module so that we can use Material design components throughout the application. To generate our Material module in our Angular application, we will execute the following command: `ng g m material`. After successfully generating the Material module, we will add the necessary modules from Angular Material:

```
@NgModule({
  imports: [
    CommonModule,
    MatToolbarModule,
    MatIconModule,
    MatButtonModule,
    MatTableModule,
    MatFormFieldModule,
    MatSelectModule,
    MatInputModule,
  ],
  exports: [
    MatToolbarModule,
    MatIconModule,
    MatButtonModule,
    MatTableModule,
    MatFormFieldModule,
    MatSelectModule,
    MatInputModule,
  ]
})
export class MaterialModule { }
```

We can see in the preceding example that we have also exported the Material modules, as we will use them on different modules in the application.

Now that we have imported the needed modules for our application, let's convert the components.

Navbar component

The **navbar component** is found under the shared module. We will use the toolbar material to create our navbar component. To implement this, we will place the following code:

```
<p>
    <mat-toolbar color="primary">
        </button>
        <span>Angular CRUD</span>
    </mat-toolbar>
</p>
```

In the preceding example, we have used the `mat-toolbar` element to use the toolbar material. We can also add a color property to style the toolbar and add additional elements inside.

We also need to import `MaterialModule` under `SharedModule` for this to recognize `MatToolbarModule` and it will output the following:

Figure 10.15 – The look of the navbar component after implementing Material

Anti-hero list component

This component is found under the anti-hero module. We will use the table material to create our list component. To implement this, we will place the following code for `anti-hero-list.component.html`:

```
<table mat-table [dataSource]="antiHeroes" class="mat-
elevation-z8">
    <!-- Data for columns -->
    <ng-container *ngFor="let item of headers"
      [matColumnDef]="item.fieldName">
        <th mat-header-cell *matHeaderCellDef>
            {{item.headerName}} </th>
        <td mat-cell *matCellDef="let element">
            {{element[item.fieldName]}} </td>
    </ng-container>
    <!-- Actions for specific item -->
```

```html
<ng-container matColumnDef="actions">
    <th mat-header-cell *matHeaderCellDef>
      Actions </th>
    <td mat-cell *matCellDef="let element">
        <button (click)="selectAntiHero(element, 0)"
          mat-raised-button color="primary">
            <mat-icon>pageview</mat-icon> View
        </button>
         
        <button (click)="selectAntiHero(element, 1)"
          mat-raised-button color="warn">
            <mat-icon>delete</mat-icon> Delete
        </button>
    </td>
</ng-container>
<tr mat-header-row *matHeaderRowDef="headerFields">
</tr>
<tr mat-row *matRowDef="let row; columns:
  headerFields"></tr>
</table>
```

We will place this for `anti-hero-list.component.ts`:

```typescript
export class AntiHeroListComponent implements OnInit {
  @Input() headers: Array<{headerName: string, fieldName:
    keyof AntiHero}> = [];
  @Input() antiHeroes: Array<AntiHero> = [];
  @Output() antiHero = new EventEmitter<{antiHero:
    AntiHero, action :TableActions}>();
  headerFields: string[] = [];

  ngOnInit(): void {
    this.getHeaderFields();
  }
  getHeaderFields() {
    this.headerFields = this.headers.map((data) =>
      data.fieldName);
```

```
        this.headerFields.push("actions");
    }
    selectAntiHero(antiHero: AntiHero, action: TableActions) {
        this.antiHero.emit({antiHero, action});
    }
}
```

In the preceding example code, we have still used the same variables in our application; the antiHeroes variable that holds the list of anti-heroes is now bound to the dataSource property and we have also iterated the headers property to display the column name and its associated values. Lastly, we have created a new variable named headerFields that contains the fieldName to display the values of an anti-hero item.

We also need to import MaterialModule under AntiHeroModule for this to recognize MatTableModule and it will have the following output:

Figure 10.16 – The look of the table component after implementing Material

Command bar component

We will create a new dumb component under the anti-hero module. We will execute the ng g c anti-hero/components/anti-hero-command-bar command and we will place the following code for anti-hero-command-bar.html:

```
<p>
    <mat-toolbar>
        <button mat-raised-button color="primary"
            (click)="emitAction(0)">
                <mat-icon>fiber_new</mat-icon> Create
        </button>
         
        <button  mat-raised-button color="warn"
            (click)="emitAction(0)">
                <mat-icon>delete</mat-icon> Delete All
        </button>
    </mat-toolbar>
</p>
```

We will place this for `anti-hero-command-bar.ts`:

```
export class AntiHeroCommandBarComponent implements OnInit {
  @Output() action = new EventEmitter<CommandBarActions>()
  constructor() { }
  ngOnInit(): void {
  }
  emitAction(action: CommandBarActions) {
    this.action.emit(action);
  }
}
```

In the preceding example code, we have also used the toolbar module to create our command bar component. Since this is a dumb component, we should only emit the actions to its parent component and not hold any dependencies. After successfully creating the command bar, we will get the following output:

Figure 10.17 – The look of the command bar component after implementing Material

Now, we will finalize the application layout by placing the components on the following page:

- `app.component.html`:

```
<app-navbar></app-navbar>
<div class="container">
    <router-outlet></router-outlet>
</div>
```

- `list.component.html`:

```
<!—Dumb component command bar →
<app-anti-hero-command-bar>
</app-anti-hero-command-bar>—- Dumb component anti hero
list -->
<app-anti-hero-list [antiHeroe"]="antiHer"es"
[header"]="head"rs"></app-anti-hero-list>
```

After successfully implementing the preceding code, we will now have the following layout:

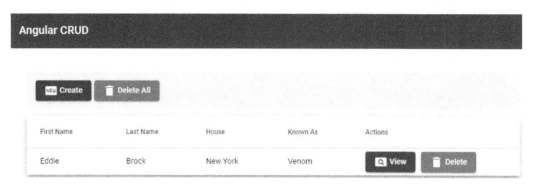

Figure 10.18 – Layout for the list component page

We have now created our anti-heroes page component with Material Design. As we go through the following chapters, we will implement the features for the action buttons and the form component.

Summary

With this, we have reached the end of this chapter. Let's have a recap of the valuable things you have learned; you have learned about the concepts and fundamentals of Angular and, at the same time, how to scaffold an Angular project and create components, directives, and modules using the Angular CLI. You have also learned some of the best practices for organizing our Angular components, modules, and other parts of our Angular project. This will be very useful for the maintainability of the project, especially for enterprise applications.

In the next chapter, we will learn how to build Reactive forms, essential form control, and grouping form controls in Angular. We will also implement `FormBuilder` and validate form input.

11

Building Reactive Forms

In the previous chapter, we have already learned how to structure our Angular application at the module and component level, which promotes the maintainability of code, especially in enterprise applications. We have organized modules into three categories: core modules, shared modules, and feature modules. We have also grouped components into two classifications: Smart and Dumb components, which separate components that retrieve data and have dependencies from components that are for presentation purposes only.

We have also discussed how to configure and implement Angular Material, which is a UI library that provides ready-to-use components and base styling for our Angular application.

In this chapter, we will now start learning how to build forms using reactive forms in Angular. We will understand form groups, form controls, and form arrays and create validations in our form.

In this chapter, we will cover the following topics:

- Understanding reactive forms
- Basic form controls
- Grouping form controls
- Using the `FormBuilder` service to generate controls
- Validating form input

Technical requirements

Here is a link to the finished version of this chapter:

https://github.com/PacktPublishing/Spring-Boot-and-Angular/tree/main/Chapter-11

Understanding reactive forms

One of the advantages of the **Angular** framework is that it already provides its form extensions. We can find these extensions under the @angular/forms package once we have created our Angular application. There are two available ways to build forms. These are **template-driven forms** and **reactive forms**; them having their own form extension is advantageous to the developers as this does not require installing under packages to create forms.

At the same time, we can make sure that every Angular application uses a single library for building forms. In this section, we will be focusing more on how to implement reactive forms in our application as this is the commonly used method in developing forms in Angular applications, but first, let's discuss a basic introduction to the template-driven approach before proceeding to reactive forms.

The template-driven approach

Template-driven forms, as the name suggests, are forms declared and validated on the template (HTML). It uses the ngForm directives, which transforms the HTML form into a template-driven form and creates a top-level FormGroup, and the ngModel directive makes a FormControl for the form elements.

To use template-driven forms, we must import FormsModule into the module where we want to use the template-driven forms. In the following code example, we have imported FormsModule into the app.module.ts file:

```
...
import { FormsModule } from '@angular/forms';
@NgModule({
  declarations: [
    AppComponent
  ],
  imports: [
    BrowserModule,
    AppRoutingModule,
    FormsModule
  ],
  providers: [],
  bootstrap: [AppComponent]
})
export class AppModule { }
```

We must not forget to import FormsModule as our application will not recognize the ngForm and ngModel directives.

Creating a template-driven form

The first step in creating template-driven forms is to create an HTML form template. Let's have a look at the following code example for an illustration of how to do this:

```
<form>
  <p>
    <label for="email">Email </label>
    <input type="text" id="email" name="email">
  </p>
  <p>
    <label for="firstname">First Name</label>
    <input type="text" id="firstname" name="firstname">
  </p>
  <p>
    <label for="lastname">Last Name</label>
    <input type="text" id="lastname" name="lastname">
  </p>
  <button type="submit">Submit</button>
</form>
```

In the preceding code example, we have created our HTML form template and have added three form elements: the email, first name, and last name input, which will be our form controls. We have also enclosed the elements with a `<form>` tag.

After successfully creating an HTML form template, this form will be automatically converted into a template-driven form. It is not required for us to add the ngForm directive to the form tag as Angular finds all form tags in our application to convert it into a template-driven form, although we can still use the ngForm directive to be assigned in a local template variable for us to access the properties and method of the ngForm directive. We can also use the variable template for submitting our forms. Let's have a look at the following code example:

```
<form #userForm="ngForm">
```

Now, we can convert our elements into form controls by adding the ngModel directive to each input; this allows us to track the values, validation status, and user interaction of each form element. Let's have a look at the following code example with the added form controls:

```
<form #userForm="ngForm">
  <p>
    <label for="firstname">First Name</label>
```

```
    <input type="text" name="firstname" ngModel>
  </p>
  <p>
    <label for="lastname">Last Name</label>
    <input type="text" name="lastname" ngModel>
  </p>
  <p>
    <label for="email">Email </label>
    <input type="text" id="email" name="email" ngModel>
  </p>
</form>
```

Lastly, we will add an ngSubmit event to submit the data of the form component. We will add the ngSubmit event to the form tag and add a method to the component class to receive the data. Let's have a look at the following code example:

```
<!—HTML template -- >
<form #userForm="ngForm"  (ngSubmit)="onSubmit(userForm)">

<!—typescript file (Component class) -- >
onSubmit(contactForm) {
    console.log(userForm.value);
 }
```

In the preceding code example, once the user has clicked the **Submit** button of the form, this will call the onSubmit() method, and it will display the form control values as a JSON object in our console; this will now allow us to use the form values in sending data implementing business logic.

After successfully implementing all the steps, we will now have a final template for the template-driven form:

```
<form #userForm="ngForm" (ngSubmit)="onSubmit(userForm)">>
  <p>
    <label for="firstname">First Name</label>
    <input type="text" name="firstname" ngModel>
  </p>
  <p>
    <label for="lastname">Last Name</label>
    <input type="text" name="lastname" ngModel>
  </p>
```

```
  <p>
    <label for="email">Email </label>
    <input type="text" id="email" name="email" ngModel>
  </p>
  <button type="submit">Submit</button>
</form>
```

When to use template-driven forms

Template-driven forms are very flexible and easy to implement in Angular applications. However, this approach has some limitations and can cause an impact in terms of maintainability; some of the best scenarios for using a template-driven approach in building forms are set out here:

- It's easier to use template-driven forms when migrating from AngularJS to Angular2, such that both use the ngModel directive.

- Template-driven forms are more suitable in simple and small forms that do not require complex validations since validation is applied at the template level. This could be a disadvantage as it will be hard to maintain validations on larger applications at the same time. It has limitations on applying validations to the form controls.

In the second of the aforementioned scenarios, reactive forms are chosen over template-driven forms as complex forms can be handled better with reactive forms, especially in implementing validations. Let's now understand the concept of reactive forms.

The reactive approach

A reactive form is the second approach in building forms in Angular applications; this is the most commonly used approach as it is more effective in handling complex forms than template-driven forms. Reactive forms are also known as **model-driven forms**, in which we define the structure of our forms in the component class instead of defining it in the template.

We also define the validations in the class before we bind it in to our HTML form, which means that the logic and validation patterns will now be separated from the HTML template and will be maintained by the TypeScript side of our component.

Using reactive forms

The first step for us to use reactive forms is to import ReactiveFormsModule; this is usually imported into the root module or the shared module of the application. ReactiveFormsModule contains all directives—such as formGroup and formControlName—that will allow us to implement reactive forms; this is also found under the @angular/forms package.

After successfully importing `ReactiveFormsModule`, the next step is to create our HTML form template and create a model using `FormGroup`, `FormControl`, and `FormArray`. These are the three building blocks of reactive forms that we will use to bind our form templates and are outlined in more detail here:

- `FormControl`: This represents a single form element inside a form; it stores the value of a form element that allows us to retrieve data from each input.

- `FormArray`: This is a collection of form controls that allows us to dynamically add and remove controls to accept more values from the form.

- `FormGroup`: This is a collection of form controls; it can also contain another form group or form arrays.

Assuming we have a `HeroesComponent`, we will create a `FormGroup` by writing the following code in the class component:

```
userForm = new FormGroup({})
```

In the preceding code example, we have instantiated a new `FormGroup` and assigned it to the `userForm` variable; this is only a form group, and we have not yet added form controls to the model. To add a form control, we will place the following code:

```
userForm = new FormGroup({
   email: new FormControl(),
   firstName: new FormControl(),
   lastName: new FormControl(),
});
```

We can see in the preceding example that we have added three form controls to our `FormGroup`; this can now be bound to the HTML form template in our application to capture the values and state of form elements.

Let's now create an HTML form template with `formGroup` and `formControlName` directives:

```
<form [formGroup]="userForm" (ngSubmit)="onSubmit()">
   <p>
     <label for="email">Email </label>
     <input type="text" id="email" name="email"
       formControlName="email">
   </p>
   <p>
     <label for="firstname">First Name </label>
```

```
      <input type="text" id="firstname" name="firstName"
        formControlName="firstname">
    </p>
    <p>
      <label for="lastname">Last Name </label>
      <input type="text" id="lastname" name="lastname"
        formControlName="lastName">
    </p>
    <p>
      <button type="submit">Submit</button>
    </p>
  </form>
```

In the example code, we can see that the template is almost the same as the template-driven forms. The only difference is that we use `formGroup` and `formControlName` directives to bind our form. The `formGroup` directive is used to bind the `userFrom` form group in our component class; on the other hand, the `formControlName` directive is used to bind the values and the state of the form controls defined in the `userForm` form group. Lastly, we are still using the `ngSubmit` event to call a method when the **Submit** button in the form is clicked.

We have now successfully created a reactive form in our application, but this only covers the basic features and concepts of reactive forms. In the following sections of this chapter, we will be discussing the functionalities and capabilities of form controls and form groups.

Basic form controls

This section will now discuss more of the concepts of form controls in reactive forms. We have already created an example of form controls in the previous section, but now, we will discover more about the functions and capabilities of form controls in Angular.

Form controls represent a single form element inside a form; they store the value of a form element that allows us to retrieve data of each input. This can be `input`, `textarea`, or any element that accepts values. When used in Angular, form controls can be instantiated by adding `new FormControl('')` code; we can see that it takes a single argument that defines the values of the control. These values can be `null` as form controls can be reset.

Form controls are like the properties of a JSON object, but compared to JSON, each control has its methods that will help us control, modify, and validate the values.

Next, let's have a look at the different methods and features of form controls.

Form control methods

Let's have a look at the different form control methods and their parameters that we can use for modifying controls:

- `setValue()`: A method that sets the new value for the control.

    Parameters:

    - `value`: The new value assigned to the form control.

    - `options`: An object that defines the configuration of the controls on how it will propagate changes and emit events when the value changes. Here are the options that we can set in the form control:

        - `onlySelf`: When set to `true`, the changes from the control will not affect the other controls.

        - `emitEvent`: When set to `true` or not supplied, `statusChanges` and `valueChanges` observables are emitted when the status and the value of the form control are updated.

        - `emitModelToViewChange`: When set to `true` or not supplied, a change from the form control will call the `onChange` event to update the view.

        - `emitViewToModelChange`: When set to `true` or not supplied, a change from the form control will call the `onModelChange` event to update the view.

    Here's the code for using the `setValue()` method:

    ```
    setValue(value: TValue, options?: { onlySelf?: boolean;
    emitEvent?: boolean; emitModelToViewChange?: boolean;
    emitViewToModelChange?: boolean; }): void
    ```

- `patchValue()`: Patches the value of a control. The parameters of the `patchValue` method are the same as the `setValue()` method.

    Here's the code for using the `patchValue()` method:

    ```
    patchValue(value: TValue, options?: { onlySelf?: boolean;
    emitEvent?: boolean; emitModelToViewChange?: boolean;
    emitViewToModelChange?: boolean; }): void
    ```

- `getRawValue()`: Retrieves the value of a form control. This is commonly used on disabled form controls.

    Here's the code for using the `getRawValue()` method:

    ```
    getRawValue(): TValue
    ```

- reset(): Resets the form control from its default value. It will also mark the control as pristine and untouched.

  Parameters:

  - formState: Defines the initial value and the disabled state of the control.
  - options: An object that defines the configuration of the controls on how it will propagate changes and emit events when the value changes. We can set the following option in the form control:

    - onlySelf: When set to true, changes from the control will not affect the other controls.

  Here's the code for using the reset() method:

  ```
  reset(formState?: TValue | FormControlState<TValue>,
  options?: { onlySelf?: boolean; emitEvent?: boolean; }):
  void
  ```

- registerOnChange(): Registers a listener to emit events once the form control value is changed.

  Parameters:

  - function: The method that is called when the value changes, as illustrated here:

    ```
    registerOnChange(fn: Function): void
    ```

- registerOnDisabledChange(): Registers a listener to emit events once the isDisabled status of the control changes.

  Parameters:

  - function: The method that is called when the disabled status changes, as illustrated here:

    ```
    registerOnDisabledChange(fn: (isDisabled: boolean) =>
    void): void
    ```

We have now learned about the different methods we can use in form controls. Now, let's have a look at some examples of different usage of form controls.

Initializing form controls

There are several ways to initialize our form controls. We can set the value, the disabled state, and the validators of a specific form control. Let's have a look at the following examples:

- **Initializing a form control with an initial value**:

  ```
  const control = new FormControl('Hero!'); console.
  log(control.value); // Hero
  ```

In the preceding code example, we instantiated a form control with a default value of Hero. We can access the value by accessing the value property inherited from AbstractControl.

- **Initializing a form control with an initial value and the disabled state**:

```
const control = new FormControl({ value: 'Hero',
disabled: true });
// get the status
console.log(control.value, control.status); //Hero,
                                            //DISABLED
```

In the preceding code example, we instantiated a form control with an object value. This initializes the value and the disabled state of the form control. We can access the value by accessing the status property inherited from AbstractControl.

- **Initializing a form control with an initial value and an array of built-in validators**:

```
const control = new FormControl('', [Validators.email,
Validators.required);
// get the status
console.log(control.status); // INVALID
```

We instantiated a form control with an empty string value in the preceding code example. With the second parameter of an array of validators, this will return an invalid status since there should not be an empty value and should be a valid email format.

Resetting form controls

We can use the reset() method to reset the value and the disabled state of a form control. Let's have a look at the following code examples of different usage:

- **Resetting controls to a specific value**:

```
const control = new FormControl('Tony Stark')
console.log(control.value); // Tony Stark
control.reset('Iron Man');
console.log(control.value); // Iron Man
```

In the preceding code example, we have used the reset() method with a parameter. The parameter allows us to reset the form control to a specific value.

- **Resetting controls to an initial value**:

```
const control = new FormControl('Tony Stark')
console.log(control.value); // Tony Stark
```

```
control.reset();
console.log(control.value); // Tony Stark
```

In the preceding code example, we used the `reset()` method without a parameter. This would reset the form control's value with its initial value.

- **Resetting controls with a value and a disabled state**:

```
const control = new FormControl('Tony Stark'); console.
log(control.value); // Tony Stark console.log(control.
status); // VALID
control.reset({ value: 'Iron Man', disabled: true });
console.log(control.value); // Iron Man console.
log(control.status); // DISABLED
```

In the preceding code example, we have used an object parameter in calling the `reset()` method, and we have indicated the value and disabled state of the form control. In this case, it will disable the control and change the status to `DISABLED`.

Listening to events

In using form controls, we can listen to several events such as changing values and status. Let's have a look at the following code examples on how to listen to events of form controls:

- **Listening to value changes**:

```
control = new FormControl('');
this.control.valueChanges.subscribe((data) => {
        console.log(data); // Iron Man
    });
this.control.setValue('Iron Man')
```

In the preceding code example, we have called the `valueChanges` property that has an `Observable` type, which we can subscribe to listen to changes to the form control value. In this case, once we set the value of the form control, the `valueChanges` property will emit the new value.

- **Listening to status changes**:

```
control = new FormControl('');
this.control.statusChanges.subscribe((data) => {
        console.log(data); // DISABLED
    });
This.control.disable ()
```

In the preceding code example, we have called the `statusChanges` property that has an `Observable` type, which we can subscribe to listen to changes to the form control status. In this case, once we disable the form control, this will emit the new status, which is `DISABLED`.

We have already learned about the features and functionalities of form controls; now, we will discuss how to group form controls using form groups and form arrays.

Grouping form controls

This section will now discuss how to group form controls in our application. Forms contain several related controls, which is why it is necessary to group them for a better structure. Reactive forms provide two ways to group form controls, as follows:

- **Form group**: Creates a form with a fixed set of form controls. Form groups can also contain another set of form groups to handle complex forms.

- **Form array**: Creates a form with dynamic form controls. It can add and remove form controls and at the same time can contain other form arrays to handle complex forms.

Creating form groups

Form groups allow us to control the values and status of form controls by groups. We can also access a single form control inside a form group using its name. To create a form group, let's follow the next steps:

1. Let's say we have a `HeroComponent`; for example, the first step is to import the `FormGroup` and `FormControl` classes from the `@angular/forms` package, like so:

   ```
   import { FormGroup, FormControl } from '@angular/forms';
   ```

2. The next step is to create a `FormGroup` instance. In this example, we want to create a new form group with `firstName`, `lastName`, and `knownAs` form controls:

   ```
   export class HeroComponent {
     heroForm = new FormGroup({
         firstName: new FormControl(''),
         lastName: new FormControl(''),
         knownAs: new FormControl('')
   });
   }
   ```

In the preceding code example, we have created a new form group named `heroForm`. Simultaneously, we have added three form controls as object parameters included in the `heroForm` form.

3. The next step is to bind our form group instance with the form element in our view:

```
<form [formGroup]=" heroForm ">
  <label for="first-name">First Name: </label>
  <input id="first-name" type="text"
    formControlName="firstName">
  <label for="last-name">Last Name: </label>
  <input id="last-name" type="text"
    formControlName="lastName">
  <label for="known-as">Known As: </label>
  <input id="known-as" type="text"
    formControlName="knownAs"> </form>
```

In the preceding code example, we have used the formGroup directive to bind our heroForm form in our form element. We must also bind each form control with the input elements by using the formControlName directive.

4. The last step is to get the value of the whole form group. We will use the ngSubmit event to call a method and will retrieve the form value by accessing the value property, like so:

```
//hero.component.html
<form [formGroup]="heroForm" (ngSubmit)="onSubmit()">
//hero.component.ts
onSubmit() {
// Will display value of form group in a form of JSON
  console.warn(this.heroForm.value);
}
```

We have created and bound an example form group, but this is only a simple form group and introduces a linear structure of controls. Now, let's create a form group that contains form groups.

Creating nested form groups

Form groups can also have another form group instead of having a list of controls. Imagine a JSON object that has properties with the value of another JSON object. This cannot be handled by a simple linear of form controls, and we must create another set of form groups to take this kind of object.

Let's follow the next steps to develop nested form groups:

1. We will be using the previous form example; in this case, we would want to add a new `address` property in our form, but instead of having it as a new instance of the form control, we will declare it as a new instance of the form group:

```
export class HeroComponent {
  heroForm = new FormGroup({
        firstName: new FormControl(''),
  lastName: new FormControl(''),
  knownAs: new FormControl('')
  address: new FormGroup({
      street: new FormControl('')
      city: new FormControl('')
      country: new FormControl('')
  })
  });
}
```

In the preceding code example, we have added an `address` property as a new form group instance. We have also added new form controls inside the form group—namely, `street`, `city`, and `country`. This is now considered a nested form group.

2. The next step is to bind the nested form group with our form element in the view:

```
<div formGroupName="address">
        <label for="street">Street: </label>
        <input id="street" type="text"
          formControlName="street">
        <label for="city">City: </label>
        <input id="city" type="text"
          formControlName="city">

        <label for="country">Country: </label>
        <input id="country" type="text"
          formControlName="country">
    </div>
```

In the preceding code example, we have used the `formGroupName` directive to bind our address form group. Remember that this element should be inside the `heroForm` form group; we have also used the `formControlName` directive to bind the controls under the nested form group. Now, we can also use the `ngSubmit` event again and call the `value` property as we did in the previous example to get the value of the whole form.

We have created simple and complex forms using form groups. Let's now discuss another way of grouping controls using form arrays.

Creating form arrays

Form arrays are helpful, especially if we want to add or remove controls in our form at runtime. This allows us to have flexible forms in our application and at the same time handle a more complex set of objects to process. To create a form array, let's have a look at the following steps:

1. We will be using the previous form example; in this case, we would want to add a new `powers` property to our form and declare it as a new `FormArray` instance:

```
export class HeroComponent implements OnInit {
  powerFormArray: FormArray;
  constructor() {
     this.powerFormArray=
        this.heroForm.get("powers") as FormArray;
  }
  ngOnInit() {
     heroForm = new FormGroup({
        ... controls from previous example
        powers: new FormArray([])
     })
  }
}
```

In the preceding code example, we have created a new `FormArray` instance inside our `heroForm` form group. This accepts an empty array having no form controls on initialization. We have also assigned the instance of the form array into a variable for us to access the array in our view.

2. The next step is to create methods that can add and remove an instance of a form control in the form array:

```
addPower() {
   (this.form.get("powers") as FormArray).push(new
```

```
        FormControl());
    }
    deletePower(i: number) {
        (this.form.get("powers") as
        FormArray).removeAt(i);
    }
```

In the preceding code example, we have created two methods that we will use for the form array. The addPower() method allows us to add a new form control instance in the power form array; this gets the instance of the form array by name and pushes a new form control instance.

On the other hand, the deletePower() method gets the instance of the form array by name and removes a specific form control using the removeAt() method and the index of the control to be deleted.

3. The last step is to bind the form array instance with the form element in the view:

```
<ng-container formArrayName="powers">
    <label for="tags">Tags</label>
    <div class="input-group mb-3" *ngFor="let _ of
      powerFormArray.controls; index as i">
        <input type="text" class="form-control"
          [formControlName]="i" placeholder="Power
          Name">
        <button (click)="deletePower(i)"
          class="btn btn-danger"
          type="button">Delete</button>
</div>
        <button class="btn btn-info me-md-2"
          type="button" (click)="addPower()">
          Add</button>
</ng-container>
```

In the preceding code example, we have bound the powers to form an array with the view using the formArrayName directive. We have also used the ngFor directive to iterate all the controls inside form array; we would also need to get the index of each control to pass it on to our deletePower() method.

After successfully creating the form arrays, we will now have a view of the form:

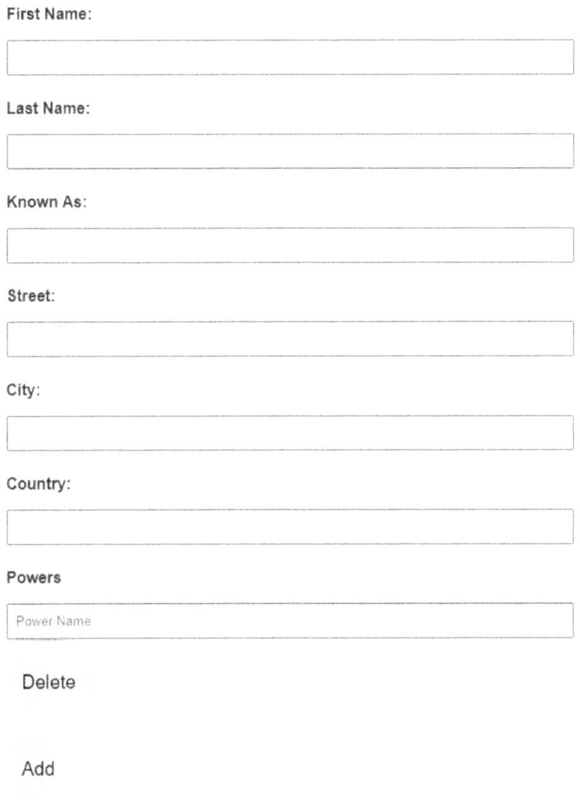

First Name:

Last Name:

Known As:

Street:

City:

Country:

Powers

Power Name

Delete

Add

Figure 11.1 – Hero form with a form group and form arrays

We have successfully created reactive forms using form groups and form arrays. Now, we will use the FormBuilder service to simplify the syntax in creating forms in our application.

Using the FormBuilder service to generate controls

In the previous section, we successfully created reactive forms using form groups, form arrays, and form controls. However, as we can see from the syntax, creating forms becomes repetitive. We are always instantiating new instances of form controls, form arrays, and form groups, and this is not ideal in larger forms. FormBuilder provides the solution for this issue.

This is a service that can be injected into our components to generate groups, controls, and arrays without instantiating new ones. To create a reactive form using `FormBuilder`, we will be following the next steps:

1. We will be transforming the form in the previous section using `FormBuilder`. The first step is to import the `FormBuilder` service into our component from @angular/forms:

    ```
    import { FormBuilder } from '@angular/forms';
    ```

2. The next step is to inject the `FormBuilder` service into our component:

    ```
    export class HeroComponent implements OnInit {
     powerFormArray: FormArray;
     constructor(private fb: FormBuilder) {}
     ... code implementation
     }
    ```

3. The last step is now to create and generate controls using the methods of the `FormBuilder` service:

    ```
    export class HeroComponent implements OnInit {
     heroForm = this.fb.group({
        firstName: [''],
       lastName: [''],
       knownAs: [''],
       address:  this.fb.group({
          street: [''],
          city: [''],
          country: [''],
       }),
         powers: this.fb.array([])
    });

    constructor(private fb: FormBuilder) {}
    ... code implementation
    }
    ```

We can see in the preceding example that our form has the same structure as the form we created in the previous section. The major difference is that we are using the methods of `FormBuilder` to create forms. We have used the `group()` method to generate form groups, the `array()` method to generate a form array, and an array with an empty string value to generate a control and set its default value.

The output for this code will be the same. `FormBuilder` methods are mainly for making our reactive forms clean and readable. Now, we will discuss how to add validations to our controls.

Validating form input

We have now created and simplified our reactive form in the previous section, but we want to make our forms accurate in accepting data and at the same time create a user-friendly experience for the user to let them know easily what the valid values for each control are. Now, we will learn how to add validations to our reactive forms.

In reactive forms, we are adding validators as parameters directly to the form controls in the component class instead of adding them as an attribute in the template.

Built-in validators

Angular provides several built-in validator functions that we can use directly in our forms. Let's have a look at some of these:

- `static min(min: number)` —Requires the value of the control to be equal to or greater than the given number:

```
form = this.fb.group({
  name: [10, [Validators.min(4)]]
});
console.log(this.form.status) // returns VALID
static max(max: number) - requires the value of the
control to be equal to or less than the given number.
form = this.fb.group({
  name: [3, [Validators.max (4)]]
});
console.log(this.form.status) // returns VALID
```

- `static required(control: AbstractControl<any, any>)` —Controls must not have a non-empty value:

```
form = this.fb.group({
  name: ['test value', [Validators.required]]
});
console.log(this.form.status) // returns VALID
```

- `static requiredTrue(control: AbstractControl<any, any>)` —Controls must have a value of `true`:

```
form = this.fb.group({
  name: [true, [Validators.requiredTrue]]
});
console.log(this.form.status) // returns VALID
```

- `static minLength(minLength: number)` —Used for arrays and strings, this requires that the length of the value should be equal to or greater than the given number:

```
form = this.fb.group({
  name: ['test', [Validators.minLength (4)]]
});
console.log(this.form.status) // returns VALID
```

- `static maxLength(maxLength: number)` —Used for arrays and strings, this requires that the length of the value should be equal to or less than the given number:

```
form = this.fb.group({
  name: ['test', [Validators.maxLength (4)]]
});
console.log(this.form.status) // returns VALID
```

Custom validators

Other than the built-in validators, we can also create custom validators, which is helpful if our forms require more complex verification and checking.

Let's have a look at the following example custom validator:

```
import { AbstractControl, ValidationErrors, ValidatorFn } from
"@angular/forms";
export function checkHasNumberValidator(): ValidatorFn {
    return (control: AbstractControl): ValidationErrors |
      null => {
      const error = /\d/.test(control.value);
      return error ? {hasNumbers: {value: control.value}} :
        null;
    };
}
```

In the preceding code example, we have created a new validator named checkHasNumberValidator(). The main use of this validator is to invalidate control values that have a number. We have retrieved the form control where the validator is assigned, then we have tested the value of the control and will return a custom error named hasNumbers if the regex is true.

After successfully creating the custom validator, we can now use it in our controls, like so:

```
heroForm = this.fb.group({
    firstName: ['', [checkHasNumberValidator]],
    lastName: ['', [checkHasNumberValidator]],
    knownAs: [''],
    address:  this.fb.group({
        street: [''],
        city: [''],
        country: [''],
    }),
      powers: this.fb.array([])
});
```

In the preceding example code, we want our first name and last name field to be restricted to letters only. In this case, we have used checkHasNumberValidator as a second parameter for the firstName and lastName controls.

Let's now proceed to the implementation of reactive forms.

Implementing reactive forms in our project

We have now successfully learned how to develop reactive forms using FormBuilder, and at the same time, added validations to our controls. Now, we will implement these reactive forms in our project.

The first step is to create our form group instance. Under the anti-hero/components/anti-hero-form file, we will create our form group using the FormBuilder service in the class component, and at the same time, we will create our form elements in our HTML template. Follow the next steps:

1. Create a form group instance by executing the following code:

    ```
    export class AntiHeroFormComponent implements OnInit {
      @Input() selectedId = "";
      @Input() actionButtonLabel: string = 'Create';
      form: FormGroup;
    ```

```
constructor(private fb: FormBuilder) {
  this.form = this.fb.group({
    id: [''],
    firstName: [''],
    lastName: [''],
    house: [''],
    knownAs: ['']
  })
}
<! - Please refer to the anti-hero-form.component.ts file
in the GitHub repo, Thank you ->
}
```

2. Then, create an HTML template, like so:

```
<! - Please refer to the anti-hero-form.component.html
file in the GitHub repo, Thank you ->
```

In the implemented code in our `component` class, the first thing we did was create a form group object. We have added several controls that resemble the properties of the anti-hero object. Our goal here is to use the same form for creating and updating an anti-hero detail. In this case, we have also added several `Input()` bindings and methods to our class to help the form identify which actions are currently being done:

- `selectedId`: This will accept the ID of the anti-hero if the actions are updated.
- `actionButtonLabel`: This will change depending on the action being done (`Create` or `Update`).
- `checkAction()`: If `selectedId` has a value, this will change the value of `actionButtonLabel` to `"Update"`.
- `patchDataValues()`: This will be used for patching the values of the selected anti-hero in the form controls.
- `emitAction()`: Emits the value of the form and the action into the parent component.
- `clear()`: Calls the `reset()` method to clean the form.

3. The next step is to use the anti-hero form in our form page component. Under the `anti-hero/pages/form` file, we will place the anti-hero form in the HTML template, and at the same time, check the current route if it has the ID of the selected anti-hero in the parameters. Here are the steps:

   i. Add the anti-hero form to the HTML template:

   ```
   <app-anti-hero-form [selectedId]="id"></app-anti-hero-
   form>
   ```

ii. Add the activated router to capture the ID:

```
export class FormComponent implements OnInit {
  id = "";
  constructor(private router: ActivatedRoute) { }
  ngOnInit(): void {
    this.id = this.router.snapshot.params['id'];
  }
}
```

4. The next step is now to create a route for our page form component. In the `anti-hero-routing.module.ts` file, we will add the following entry to our routes:

```
{
  path: "form",
  children: [
    {
      path: "",
      component: FormComponent
    },
    {
      path: ":id",
      component: FormComponent
    }
  ]
},
```

In the preceding code example, we have created two routes that redirect to `FormComponent`. The first route is for the `create` action, which has a `baseURL/anti-heroes/form` route, and the second route is for the `update` action, which has a `baseURL/anti-heroes/form/:id` route. This means that we are using the same components for our two actions, and the `id` parameters act as our indicator of which action is currently being done.

5. The last step is to add navigations to the `list` component. We will add several methods that will call navigate methods to redirect us to the form component depending on the selected action, as follows:

- `list.component.html`:

```
<!-- Dumb component command bar -->
<app-anti-hero-command-bar
```

```
    (action)="executeCommandBarAction($event)"></app-anti-
    hero-command-bar>
    <!-- Dumb component anti hero list -->
    <app-anti-hero-list [antiHeroes]="antiHeroes"
    (antiHero)="selectAntiHero($event)"
    [headers]="headers"></app-anti-hero-list>
```

- `list.component.ts`:

```
    selectAntiHero(data: {antiHero: AntiHero, action:
    TableActions}) {
    <! - Please refer to the list.component.ts file in the
    GitHub repo, Thank you->
      this.router.navigate(['anti-heroes', 'form',
                            data.antiHero.id]);
    }
    executeCommandBarAction(action: CommandBarActions) {
      switch(action) {
        case CommandBarActions.Create: {
          this.router.navigate(["anti-heroes", "form"]);
          return;
        }
        case CommandBarActions.DeleteAll: {
          return;
        }
        default: ""
      }
    }
```

After accomplishing all the steps, we will now have the following form output:

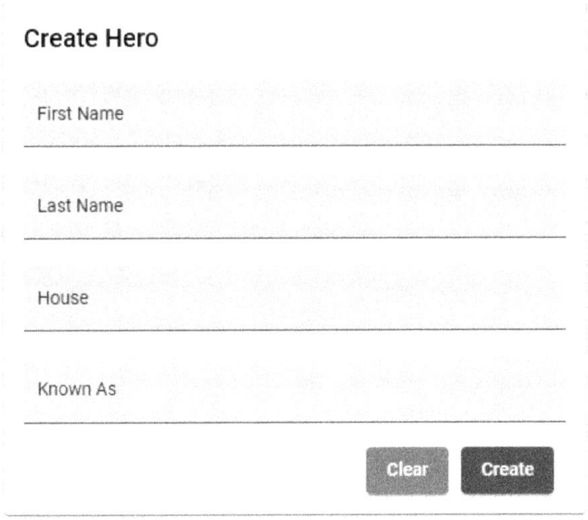

Figure 11.2 – Form UI for creating an anti-hero

Summary

With this, we have reached the end of this chapter; let's have a recap of the valuable things you have learned. You have learned about the concepts and implementation of Angular reactive forms, and we have implemented FormGroup, FormBuilder, and formControlName directives to bind input values to capture data in our form. We have also discussed how to group form controls for binding nested properties and create form arrays in our reactive forms. This is primarily useful if some objects we want to display have array values.

At the same time, we want to accept a list of entries from users. Lastly, we have also learned how to implement validations for form controls to handle and verify user input, which will be beneficial for the user experience and help avoid unexpected errors.

In the next chapter, we will learn about the concepts and implementation of state management in Angular applications; we will discuss the idea of the Redux pattern and the **NgRx** library in terms of how they can improve the application architecture.

12

Managing States with NgRx

In the previous chapter, we learned about the concepts and features of Reactive forms. We implemented `FormGroup`, `FormBuilder`, and `formControlName` to bind input values in the form elements in the application. We also discussed how to group form control to bind nested properties and create form arrays in our Reactive forms.

After that, we learned how to implement validations for form controls to handle and verify user input. This will be beneficial for the user experience and help us avoid unexpected errors.

In this chapter, we will add a new recipe to our application and learn how to implement state management, specifically **NgRx**, for handling data in our Angular application.

In this chapter, we will cover the following topics:

- Understanding complexities in managing the states of large applications
- State management and the global state
- Getting started and setting up NgRx
- Writing an action
- Writing an effect
- Writing a reducer
- Writing a selector and using a selector and dispatching it in a component
- Configuring the store

Technical requirements

The following link will take you to the finished version of code for this chapter: `https://github.com/PacktPublishing/Spring-Boot-and-Angular/tree/main/Chapter-12/superheroes`.

Understanding complexities in managing the states of large applications

Data management in frontend applications is very important, just like how essential data management is in backend applications and databases. As we add more features to our application, we know that the number of components, modules, and services working inside our Angular project is also growing.

This also means that the data flow in the application is growing and becoming complex. A complex data flow can lead to an unmaintainable application, inconsistent and scattered states in different components, and nested input and output bindings that result in complex code structures. Due to these possible issues when it comes to managing data in Angular, a solution called **state management** was introduced as a standard solution for maintaining data in frontend applications.

State management is an extension or library that is mainly used for managing and handling data in frontend applications. It introduces a pattern where all data being used is stored in one big object that acts as the state of the whole application. This concept is also known as a **single source of truth**. In this case, no matter how many components or how many services are added to our application, there is always a single object where we can retrieve the data we need. You can compare this state to an acting database for the frontend application.

Before proceeding with state management, let's compare the flow of data without and with state management.

The flow of data without state management

Data flow in Angular starts on the services. We call endpoints in the services to retrieve and manage the data that we need for our application. As the number of features increases, the number of services added and called increases, resulting in a more complex data flow. Let's look at a graphical illustration of the flow of data without state management:

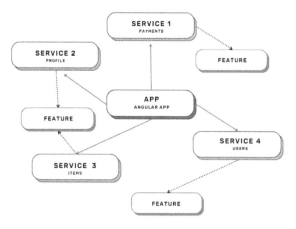

Figure 12.1 – The flow of data without state management

In the preceding graphical illustration, we can see that we have four different services that are responsible for managing different kinds of data; each feature retrieves the data it needs from these services.

As we can see, the retrieval that occurs is scattered as the features are retrieving the data on different sources or services. This results in multiple data flows, and they can get larger as more services and features are required.

This can also lead to inconsistencies in data being held by each component as the source is coming from different services, leading to some unexpected bugs in the application. Now, let's look at the flow of data with state management.

The flow of data with state management

In the previous data flow, we saw that the flow of data is not optimized, which can result in several problems in our application as the data flow's direction is very complex. When implementing state management in our Angular application, we will have the following data flow:

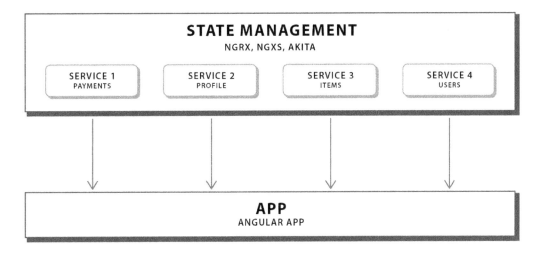

Figure 12.2 – The flow of data with state management

In the preceding graphical illustration, we can see that all of the services of our application are handled by state management. We are still using services to retrieve data in our database. The significant difference here is that our features are now accessing all the retrieved data in the state instead of directly accessing it in the services.

This allows the data to flow in one direction and has a single origin for all the data being used in the application. With this approach, inconsistency in the states, possible bugs, and multiple API calls can be avoided.

With that, we have learned about the importance of state management in developing applications, especially enterprise-level apps.

Now, let's discuss more state management concepts and global states.

State management and the global state

State management, as discussed in the previous section, is an extension or library that allows us to manage the flow of our data in the application in just one direction.

This is possible due to global states, which will contain all of the data. To understand how state management works, let's discuss each of the building blocks of state management.

Global state/store

The **global state**, also known as the **store**, is the most crucial element in state management. The primary responsibility of a global state is to store all the data retrieved by the API or simply data being used in the application.

This means that all components in an Angular application will retrieve the data in the global state. Think of it as a database of the Angular application but in the form of a JSON object where we can get each property as slices.

Actions

Actions express unique events in your application. They are directly called in our components using the dispatch() function, which helps identify what events should be performed, such as modifying the state or calling APIs to retrieve data.

Actions are just simple interfaces; the type property identifies what action is dispatched. This simple string is just a definition of the action, and we can add properties to the actions for the data we require in the API or state.

Let's have a look at an example of an action interface:

```
{
type: '[Blog] Add Blog',
title: string;
author: string;
content: string;
}
```

The preceding example action is dispatched when a new blog is created. This is called when the **Submit** button is clicked, and information such as `title`, `author`, and `content` is added as additional metadata to be passed on to the effect or reducer.

Reducers

Reducers are the decision-makers of state management. They are the ones that decide which actions to handle based on the action type. Reducers are also the ones that can change the value of the state.

Reducers are pure functions and handle state transitions synchronously; let's have a look at an example of a reducer:

```
export const blogReducer = createReducer( initialState,
  on(BlogActions.addBlog, (state, {blog})=> ({ ...state,
    blogs: [...state.blogs, blog]}))
);
```

In the preceding example, we have created a reducer for the `addBlog()` action. This allows us to add a new blog object in the blog's state once we have dispatched the `addBlog()` action.

We will discuss reducers in more detail later in the *Writing a reducer* section of this chapter.

Selectors

Selectors are pure functions that allow us to retrieve slices of data in our store. It is a change detection mechanism where, when the value of the state changes, it compares the parts of the state and only sends the state if the changes are detected. This is a practice called **memorization**.

Selectors are used in components to get the data used in the UI. It is returned as an Observable that listens to the state changes.

Let's look at an example of a selector:

```
// selector for list of blogs
// blog.selector.ts
export const selectBlogList = (state: AppState) => state.blogs;

// blog component
// blog.component.ts
blogs$ = this.store.select<Array<Blog>(selectBlogList);
    this.blogs$.subscribe(data => {
```

```
        console.log(data) // list of blogs from the state;
    });
```

In the preceding example, we have created a selector for the blog slice, as well as a function that returns the *blogs* metadata, called `selectBlogList()`. We used this function in our `blog` component as a parameter for the `select` function to retrieve the data by subscribing to the selector. The subscription will emit once the value of the blog's slice changes. We will discuss selectors in more detail in the next section of this chapter.

Effects

Effects are specific elements that the NgRx library uses; this is an *RxJs-powered* side effect model that handles external interactions such as API calls, web socket messages, and time-based events. Using effects, we can isolate our components from interacting with external sources and reduce their responsibilities. Let's look at a comparison between an application with and without side effects.

Application without side effects

The following is an application without side effects:

```
export class BlogPageComponent {
    movies: Blog[];
    constructor(private blogService: MoviService) {}
    ngOnInit() {
        this.blogService
            .getAll()
            .subscribe(blogs => this.blogs = blogs);
    }
}
```

In the preceding code example, we have a component that has several responsibilities, as follows:

- Managing the state of the blogs (the component has its blog state)
- Using the blog service to call an external API to get the list of blogs
- Modifying the state of the blog inside the component

This means that every component with a service dependency also has its state of data. Now, let's look at an example of an application with side effects.

Application with side effects

The following is an application with side effects:

```
export class BlogsPageComponent {
  blogs$: Observable<Blog[]> = this.store.select(state =>
    state.blog);

  constructor(private store: Store<{ blogs: Blog[] }>) {}

  ngOnInit() {
    this.store.dispatch({ type: '[Blog Page] Load Blog'});
  }
}
```

In the preceding code example, we can see that the code for our blog page component has been reduced, and, at the same time, its responsibility is also less complex. Now, the component's responsibility is to dispatch an action that will allow effects to identify what service needs to be called to retrieve the data.

Let's look at an example effect for the blog state:

```
@Injectable()
export class BlogEffects {
  loadBlogs$ = createEffect(() => this.actions$.pipe(
ofType('[Blog Page] Load Blog'),
  mergeMap(() => this.blogService
      .getAll().pipe(
        map(blogs => ({ type: '[Blogs API] Blogs Loaded
                      Success', payload: blogs })),
        catchError(() => EMPTY)
      ))
    )
);
  constructor(private actions$: Actions,
              private blogService: BlogService) {}
}
```

In the preceding code example, we created a new effect named `loadBlogs$`. This effect is responsible for calling the `getAll()` method from the blog service to retrieve the list of blogs from the external endpoint. At the same time, it is also responsible for dispatching a new action that passes the retrieved blog list into the reducer to modify the store. We will discuss how to write effects in the next section of this chapter.

With that, we've seen all of the building blocks that make up state management. Let's look at a detailed graphical illustration of how data flows in state management:

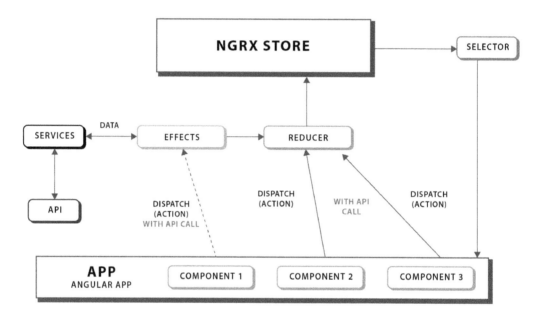

Figure 12.3 – How data flows when using NgRx state management

In the preceding graphical illustration, we can see that our UI components have only one responsibility, and this is to dispatch actions. If the action needs to call an API, an effect will be called to invoke an API using a service, and after getting the response data, the effect will also dispatch an action to call a reducer to modify the store.

On the other hand, if the action that's sent from the component will alter the state, it will not need any side effects and call the reducer that matches the type of the action. All of the changes in the store will be detected by the selectors and emit the latest state to be used in the UI components.

With that, we have learned about the necessary concepts surrounding state management and how data flows together with the building blocks of state management. In the next section, we will learn how to set up and configure one of the most famous state management libraries in Angular: **NgRx**.

Getting started and setting up NgRx

To use NgRx state management, we must install the `@ngrx/store` library; this will contain all of the functions that will allow us to configure the store and create reducers and actions.

To install the `@ngrx/store` library, we must execute the following command:

ng add @ngrx/store

The preceding command will perform the following steps:

1. Update `package.json` by adding `@ngrx/store` to the dependencies.
2. Run `npm install` to install the dependencies.
3. Update `src/app/app.module.ts` by adding `StoreModule.forRoot(reducers, {})` to the `imports` array.

Before executing this command, make sure that the version of `@ngrx/store` is aligned with the version of your Angular; in our project, our Angular version is version `13.3.0`, which means that we need to use version 13 of `@ngrx/store`.

Flags are also available that allow us to install `@ngrx/store` with customizations. The following is the list of flags we can use:

*   `--path`: Specifies the path to the module where you want to import `StoreModule`.
*   `--project`: The name of the project that is defined in `angular.json`.
*   `--module`: The name of the file containing the module where you want to import `StoreModule`.
*   `--minimal`: This provides the minimal setup for the root state management if set to `true`. It imports `StoreModule.forRoot()` in the module with an empty object.
*   `--statePath`: This is the path where the state will be created.
*   `--stateInterface`: The interface that defines the state.

Adding NgRx to our Angular project

Now, let's add this to our Angular project. We only want to use the minimal setup as we will add the reducers and store step by step. After successfully executing the `ng add @ngrx/store` command, we will have the following changes in our project:

```
// app.module.ts
 imports: [
    … other modules
    StoreModule.forRoot({}, {}),
```

```
    ],
    // package.json
    "dependencies": {
        … other dependencies
        "@ngrx/store": "^13.2.0",
    },
```

In the preceding code example, we can see that StoreModule.forRoot() has been added without any objects; this means that we initially imported the store without reducers.

With that, we have successfully installed @ngrx/store in our Angular project. Now, we will install another extension to help us debug the state.

Installing NgRx DevTools

NgRx DevTools is a valuable extension that provides developer tools and instrumentation for the store. It allows us to check the values of the state, implement time travel debugging, and have a visual representation of the previous and current values of the data in our store.

We must execute the following command to install NgRx DevTools in our Angular project:

ng add @ngrx/store-devtools

After successfully executing this command, the following changes will be implemented in our project:

```
// app.module.ts
imports: [
… other modules
// Instrumentation must be imported after importing
// StoreModule (config is optional)
StoreDevtoolsModule.instrument({
  maxAge: 25, // Retains last 25 states
  logOnly: environment.production, // Restrict extension to
                                   // log-only mode
  autoPause: true, // Pauses recording actions and state
                   // changes when the extension window is
                   //not open
}),
],
```

In the preceding code example, we can see that a new module called `StoreDevtoolsModule` has been added; this will allow DevTools to be used once we run our application locally.

The next step to using DevTools is to add the Redux extension to our browser. To add this extension, go to one of the following links for your respective browser:

- **Google Chrome**: `https://chrome.google.com/webstore/detail/redux-devtools/lmhkpmbekcpmknklioeibfkpmmfibljd`

- **Mozilla Firefox**: `https://addons.mozilla.org/en-US/firefox/addon/reduxdevtools/`

After adding this extension to your preferred browser, running your Angular project with the imported `StoreDevToolModule` module will be automatically detected by this extension. It will provide an interface for viewing the state:

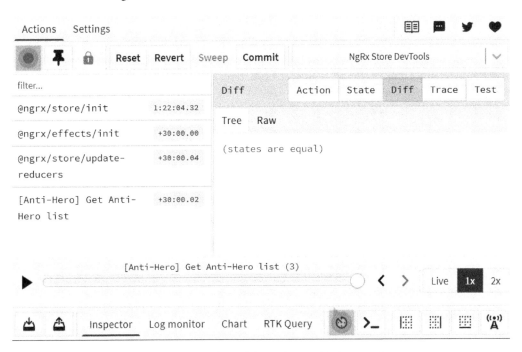

Figure 12.4 – Interface of the Redux DevTools extension

The preceding screenshot shows that our Redux DevTools extension has been activated; once we open our Angular project in our browser tab, we will see more Redux DevTools in action as we write our code.

Now that we have configured our store and installed NgRx DevTools in our application, we are ready to write the building blocks for our state management.

Writing an action

The first building block of state management is that we will write our actions. When writing actions, we have several rules we can follow so that we have good actions in our application:

- **Upfront**: Writing actions should always come first before developing the features. This gives us an overview of what should be implemented in the application.
- **Divide**: We should always categorize the actions based on the event source and the associated data.
- **Many**: Writing more number actions is not an issue. It is more beneficial as more actions create a better overview of the flow of your application.
- **Event-Driven**: Capture *events* as you separate the description of an event and how it's handled.
- **Descriptive**: Always provide meaningful information using type metadata. This helps debug the state.

Let's look at an example action that will set the list of blogs in our state:

```
import { createAction, props } from '@ngrx/store';
export const setBlogList = createAction(
  '[Blog] Set Blog List',
    props<{ blogs: ReadonlyArray<Blog> }>(),
);
```

In the preceding code example, we used the `createAction()` function to create our action. The `createAction()` function also returns a function that returns an object of the action interface; in this case, it will return "`[Blog] Set blog list`" as the action type and the array of blogs as the additional properties.

To dispatch the action, we will use the `dispatch()` function and use `setBlogList` as a parameter:

```
ngOnInit() {
      store.dispatch(setBlogList ({ blogs: this.blogs}));
}
```

Implementing actions in the project

Our primary goal for our project is to create the entire cycle to get the list of anti-heroes in our API and place it in our store. The first step is to take the actions we need; let's look at the two actions that we should make for this feature:

- `getAntiHeroList`: This action will retrieve the list of blogs from the external API provided by our Spring project.
- `setAntiHeroList`: This action will place the retrieved list of blogs in our store.

Now that we have identified the list of actions we will create, in the `anti-heroes` folder, we will create a `state/anti-hero.actions.ts` file where we will place all of our actions.

Let's place the following code in the `anti-hero.actions.ts` file:

```
import { createAction, props } from '@ngrx/store';
import { AntiHero } from '../models/anti-hero.interface';
export enum AntiHeroActions {
  GET_ANTI_HERO_LIST = '[Anti-Hero] Get Anti-Hero list',
  SET_ANTI_HERO_LIST = '[Anti-Hero] Set Anti-Hero list',
}
export const getAntiHeroList = createAction(
    AntiHeroActions.GET_ANTI_HERO_LIST,
);
export const setAntiHeroList = createAction(
  AntiHeroActions.SET_ANTI_HERO_LIST,
  props<{ antiHeroes: ReadonlyArray<AntiHero> }>(),
);
```

In the preceding code example, we have created two actions for getting and setting the anti-hero list. The first action, `getAntiHeroList`, has a single parameter, which is the type. This does not need any additional properties as this will only call the API to retrieve the list of anti-heroes through the use of effects.

On the other hand, the second action, `setAntiHeroList`, has two parameters: the type and an additional property called `antiHero`. This will set the value of the store with the retrieved list of anti-heroes through the use of reducers.

It is also excellent practice to make our action definitions enums in our code as this will help us avoid typographical errors when using the definition in other parts of the application.

With that, we have successfully created the required action for our anti-heroes list feature. Now, we will discuss how to write effects that will be used to call the API and retrieve the anti-hero list.

Writing an effect

We successfully created our actions in the previous section. Now, we will make the effects that will be responsible for calling our external API.

Effects are not included in the `@ngrx/store` library; we will install a separate library that will allow us to use the functions for effects.

To install effects in our application, we must execute the following command:

ng add @ngrx/effects

The preceding command will perform the following steps:

1. Update the package.json file with the @ngrx/effects dependency.
2. Run npm install to install the added dependency.
3. Add EffectsModule.forRoot() to the imports array of your app.module.ts file.

Some flags are available that allow us to install @ngrx/effects with customizations; the following is the list of flags we can use:

- --path: Specifies the path to the module where you want to import EffectsModule.
- --project: The name of the project defined in angular.json.
- --skipTests: This creates a test file when it is set to false.
- --module: The name of the file containing the module where you want to import EffectsModule.
- --minimal: This provides the minimal setup for the root effects if set to true. It imports EffectsModule.forRoot() in the module with an empty object.
- --group: Group the effects files within the effects folder.

After successfully adding the dependency of the effect to our application, we can create our effects. Under the anti-heroes/state folder, we must create a new file named anti-hero.effects.ts. The first thing we need to do is create a class that has an @Injectable annotation:

```
@Injectable()
export class AntiHeroEffects {
  constructor(
    private actions$: Actions,
    private antiHeroService: AntiHeroService,
    private router: Router
  ) {}
}
```

In the preceding code example, we can see that effects are also service classes and can be injected by other services; we have injected the following services into AntiHeroEffects:

- Actions: A service from @ngrx/effects that returns an observable that we can assign a type to. This will act as the identifier when an action is dispatched.

- `AntiHeroService`: Our created service that contains the external APIs for our anti-heroes, found under `anti-hero/services/anti-hero.service.ts`.

- `Router`: Used for redirection once an API call is made.

After creating our `AntiHeroEffect` class and injecting our services, we can begin making our effects. The first thing we need to think of is what kind of effect we need to get the anti-heroes since we have the `GET_ANTI_HERO LIST` and `SET_ANTI_HERO_LIST` actions.

We should create an effect that has a type of `GET_ANTI_HERO_LIST` and can call the `getAntiHeroes()` function from `AntiHeroService`.

To create this API, we can write the following code:

```
import { Actions, createEffect, ofType } from '@ngrx/effects';
getAntiHeroes$ = createEffect(() => {
    return this.actions$.pipe(
        ofType(AntiHeroActions.GET_ANTI_HERO_LIST),
        mergeMap(() => this.antiHeroService.getAntiHeroes()
        )
    }, {dispatch: true}
    );
```

In the preceding code example, we used the `createEffect()` function to create our effects; this returns an action that has two parameters:

- `ofType(AntiHeroActions.GET_ANTI_HERO_LIST)`: The first parameter uses the `ofType` operator, which defines the action type of the effect. This means that if the `GET_ANTI_HERO_LIST` action is dispatched, this effect will be called.

- `mergeMap(() => this.antiHeroService.getAntiHeroes()`: The second parameter uses the `mergeMap` operator, which will allow us to invoke the `getAntiHeroes()` function to call the endpoint.

With that, we have our effect for the `GET_ANTI_HERO_LIST` actions, but this is not complete yet. After getting the list of anti-heroes, we want to dispatch another action that sets the anti-heroes list in our state. To implement this, we can use the following code:

```
mergeMap(() => this.antiHeroService.getAntiHeroes()
            .pipe(
              map(antiHeroes => ({ type: AntiHeroActions.SET_
ANTI_HERO_LIST, antiHeroes })),
              catchError(() => EMPTY)
            ));
```

In the preceding code, we have added a pipe to our `mergeMap` operator; this calls a `map` operator that returns (`{ type: AntiHeroActions.SET_ANTI_HERO_LIST, antiHeroes })`). This will dispatch another action that has a type of `SET_ANTI_HERO_LIST` and has additional `antiHeroes` objects coming from the list of anti-heroes retrieved from the API.

Our effects for getting the list of anti-heroes feature is complete. The last step is to add `AntiHeroEffects` to our `effects` module. As we may recall, our `anti-heroes` module is lazy loaded, which means that we will not add `AntiHeroEffects` to `EffectsModule.forRoot([])` located in the `app.module.ts` file; otherwise, we would need to add `EffectsModule.forFeature([AntiHeroEffects])` in the imports of the `anti-hero.module.ts` file. This means that this `effects` class is only used under this module.

With that, we have successfully configured and created our effects for the anti-hero list feature. In the next section, we will write the reducers that will modify our state.

Writing a reducer

NgRx states are immutable objects; we cannot modify their values through direct assignment, and the only way we can change their states is through reducers.

Reducers have different parts that we should implement, as follows:

- The interface or type that defines the properties of the state
- The arguments, which consist of the initial state and the current action
- The list of functions that handle that state changes based on the dispatched actions

We will create these reducer parts under the `anti-heroes/state/anti-hero.reducers.ts` file.

The state interface

The state interface defines the shape of the state; this contains the properties or the slices of the state. In our application, we need a property that will hold the list of anti-heroes.

To implement the interface, we can use the following code:

```
export interface AntiHeroState {
    antiHeroes: ReadonlyArray<AntiHero>;
}
```

The initial state

The next part we need to implement is the initial state; this defines what the initial values of the state slices are. In our anti-hero state, we will set the `antiHeroes` slice to an empty array.

To implement this, we can use the following code:

```
export const initialState: AntiHeroState = {
    antiHeroes: []
}
```

The reducer function

After creating our initial state, we can implement our reducer function; this will hold the list of functions that will be called, depending on the type of action that is dispatched.

To implement the reducer function, we can use the following code:

```
export const antiHeroReducer = createReducer(
  initialState,
  on(setAntiHeroList, (state, { antiHeroes }) => { return {...
state, antiHeroes}}),

  );
```

In the preceding code example, we can see that we have used a `createReducer()` function from the `@ngrx/store` library; this will contain all the functions that will modify our anti-hero state. The first parameter is our initial state, while the second parameter is a function that will be called when an action of `SET_ANTI_HERO_LIST` is dispatched.

This means that the effect we created earlier will call this once the API has retrieved the anti-hero list successfully; this function contains two parameters – one that holds the current state and another that holds the list of anti-heroes objects from the API. To modify the `antiHeroes` state with the retrieved list, we have returned `{...state, antiHeroes}`.

Now that we have finished writing the reducers for our state, the last step is to register our reducers in the store. We will apply the same rules that we applied for the effects; since our anti-heroes module is lazy loaded, we will register our anti-hero reducer in our `anti-hero.module.ts` file by adding `StoreModule.forFeature('antiHeroState,' antiHeroReducer)`. The first parameter is the key for our anti-hero state, while the second is the function returned from the `createReducer()` function.

With that, we have successfully created and registered our reducer for the anti-hero list feature. Now, let's discuss the NgRx selectors to get the state and how to dispatch actions in components.

Writing a selector and using a selector and dispatching it in a component

In the previous section, we successfully implemented reducers that can mutate the values of our state. This means that our state contains valuable data that we can get from the Angular components; we can use selectors to do this.

Selectors are pure functions that allow us to retrieve slices of state; we can use several helper functions, such as `createSelector()` and `createFeatureSelector()`, to create our selectors for the store.

Selecting root states

While selecting the root states, we will be using a pure function to create our selector. Let's look at an example of a selector selecting the list of blogs under the root state (`AppState`):

```
// blogs.selectors.ts
export const selectBlogs = (state: AppState) => state.blogs
```

In the preceding code example, we have only created a function that returns the `blogs` slice; this is feasible when we select slices under the project's root state. To use the created selector in our component, we can use the following code:

```
//blogs.page.ts
blogs$ = this.store.select(selectBlogs())
constructor(private store: Store<AppState>,){
    this.blogs$.subscribe((data) => {
        this.blogs = data;
    });
}
```

In the preceding code example, we injected `Store` from the `@ngrx/store` library. `Store` provides a `select` function that accepts selectors as a parameter and returns an observable that returns the slice of state that is defined by the selector.

In this case, we have subscribed to the `blogs$` observable from the `select(selectBlogs()` function to retrieve the `blogs` slice that holds the list of blogs.

Selecting feature states

While selecting feature states, we will use the `createSelector()` and `createFeatureSelector()` functions to create the selector. Let's look at an example of a selector selecting the list of blogs found under the feature state (`BlogState`):

```
// blogs.selectors.ts
import { createSelector, createFeatureSelector } from '@ngrx/
store';

export const selectBlogsState =
createFeatureSelector<BlogsState>('blogsState')

export const selectBlogs = () => createSelector
    selectBlogsState,
    (state: BlogsState) => state.blogs
)
```

In the preceding code example, the first step is to create the feature selector that will return the whole `BlogState`. Here, we have used `createFeatureSelector()` and the state's key to identify the feature state we want to select.

The second step is to create the main selector of the blog slice; `createSelector()` has two parameters, where the first one is the `BlogState` feature selector, and the second one is a function where the returned `BlogState` from the feature selector is the parameter. The returned value is the blog slice.

Implementing selectors in our project

So far, we have learned how to create selectors using the `createFeatureSelector()` and `createSelector()` functions. Now, let's implement them in our project. The first thing we need to identify is the states or slices. The first slice that needs a selector is a blog slice located under `AnitHeroState`. Remember that `AntiHeroState` is not our root state; this means that we will have a feature selector for the following state.

The second selector we need is the selector for the `antiHeroes` slice, which contains the array of anti-heroes retrieved in the API. Finally, the third selector we want will need to select specific `antiHero` data from the list based on the `id` parameter.

To create all of these selectors, place the following code in the `anti-hero/state/anti-hero.selectors.ts` file:

```
// select the AntiHeroState
export const selectAntiHeroState =
createFeatureSelector<AntiHeroState>('antiHeroState')

// selecting all antiheroes
export const selectAntiHeroes = () => createSelector(
    selectAntiHeroState,
    (state: AntiHeroState) => state.antiHeroes
)
// selecting an antihero base on id
export const selectAntiHero = (id: string) => createSelector(
    selectAntiHeroState,
    (state: AntiHeroState) => state.antiHeroes.find(d =>
        d.id === id)
)
```

After successfully creating all of the selectors, we can use the on `anti-hero/pages/list.component.ts` file by adding the following code:

```
antiHeroes$ = this.store.select(selectAntiHeroes());
constructor(
    private router: Router,
    private store: Store<AppState>,
    ) { }
  ngOnInit(): void {
    this.assignAntiHeroes();
  }
  assignAntiHeroes() {
    this.antiHeroes$.subscribe((data) => {
      this.antiHeroes = data;
    });
  }
```

In the preceding code example, we used the `selectAntiHeroes()` selector to get the array of anti-heroes from the state. `antiHeroes$` is an Observable that returns the current state of the `antiHero` slice once subscribed.

Finally, we must get the anti-heroes list feature. We can do this by dispatching the GET_ANTI_HERO_LIST action in the list component in the ngOnInit() hook. This will call the effect that we created earlier, which invokes the endpoint for getting the list of anti-heroes:

```
  ngOnInit(): void {
 this. store.dispatch({type:    AntiHeroActions.GET_ANTI_HERO_
 LIST});
    this.assignAntiHeroes();
 }
```

With that, we have successfully created selectors for the components to retrieve data from the state. In the next section, we will discuss the available configurations we can implement for the store.

Configuring the store

In the previous sections, we created all of the building blocks of NgRx that complete a fully functional store for the application. In this section, we will learn how to configure the NgRx store using runtime checks.

Runtime checks

Runtime checks are used to configure the NgRx store to allow developers to follow the NgRx and Redux core concepts and best practices. This is very useful, especially for developers new to NgRx; they display errors regarding development based on the activated runtime checks.

@ngrx/store provides six built-in runtime checks:

- strictStateImmutability: Checks if the state isn't mutated (default: *On*)

- strictActionImmutability: Checks if the actions aren't mutated (default: *On*)

- strictStateSerializability: Checks if the state is serializable (default: *On*)

- strictActionSerializability: Checks if the actions are serializable (default: *Off*)

- strictActionWithinNgZone: Checks if actions are dispatched within NgZone (default: *Off*)

- strictActionTypeUniqueness: Checks if the registered action types are unique (default: *Off*)

To change the default configuration of the runtime checks, we will use the runtimeChecks property on the root store's config object. The value of each runtime check can be assigned with true to activate the check or false to deactivate the check:

```
@NgModule({
 imports: [
  StoreModule.forRoot(reducers, {
```

```
                runtimeChecks: {
                        strictStateImmutability: true,
                        strictActionImmutability: true,
                        strictStateSerializability: true,
                        strictActionSerializability: true,
                        strictActionWithinNgZone: true,
                        strictActionTypeUniqueness: true,
                            },
                }),
            ],
    })
```

strictStateImmutability

This is the number one rule of NgRx. It is activated by default, and the runtime checks verify if the developer modifies the state object.

Example violation of this rule:

```
export const reducer = createReducer(initialState, on(addBlog,
(state, { blog }) => ({
// Violation 1: we assign a new value to loading
state.loading = false,
 // Violation 2: `push` modifies the array
 // state.blogs.push(blog) })) );
```

Fix for this violation:

```
export const reducer = createReducer( initialState, on(addBlog,
(state, { blog }) =>
// Fix: We are returning the state as a whole object with
// the new values
   ({ ...state,
    loading: false,
    blogs: [...state.blogs, blog],
})) );
```

strictActionImmutability

This runtime check is similar to `strictStateImmutability` but is for actions. This runtime check verifies if the developer modifies the action. This check is activated by default.

Example violation of this rule:

```
export const reducer = createReducer(initialState, on(addBlog,
(state, { blog }) => ({
// Violation: it's not allowed to modify an action
blog.id = uniqueID();
return { ...state, blogs: [...state.blogs, blog]
} })) );
```

Fix for this violation:

```
//blog.actions.ts
export const addBlog = createAction( '[Blog List] Add Blog',
// Fix: we will return the object in the action with the
// new value
(description: string) =>
({ id: uniqueID(), description }) );


//blog.reducer.ts
export const reducer = createReducer(
initialState,
on(addBlog, (state, { blog }) => ({
...state,
blogs: [...state.blogs, blog],
})) );
```

strictStateSerializability

This runtime check verifies if the values placed in the state are serializable. This is essential for persisting the state so that it can be rehydrated in the future. This is deactivated by default.

Example violation of this rule:

```
export const reducer = createReducer(
initialState,
on(addBlog, (state, { blog }) => ({
...state,
blogs: [...state.blogs, blog],
// Violation: a Date type is not a serializable value.
```

```
createdOn: new Date()
})) );
```

Fix for this violation:

```
export const reducer = createReducer(
initialState,
on(addBlog, (state, { blog }) => ({
...state,
blogs: [...state.blogs, blog],
// Fix: We should convert the date into a JSON Object.
createdOn: new Date().toJSON()
})) );
```

strictActionSerializability

This runtime check is similar to strictStateSerializability, but for actions. It checks if the states are serializable. This is done by Redux DevTools to debug errors.

Example violation of this rule:

```
const createBlog = createAction(
'[Blog List] Add Blog,
blog => ({ blog,
// Violation, a function is not serializable
logBlog: () => { console.log(blog); }, }));
```

Fix for this violation:

```
const createBlog = createAction(
'[Blog List] Add Blog,
// Fix: we should use props to receive parameters
 props<{blog: Blog}>()
);
```

strictActionWithinNgZone

This runtime check verifies if the actions are dispatched by asynchronous tasks within NgZone. This check is deactivated by default.

Example violation of this rule:

```
// Callback outside NgZone
// Violation: the createBlog actions is invoked outside the
// ngZone
callbackOutsideNgZone() {
        this.store.dispatch(createBlog ());
}
```

Fix for this violation:

```
import { NgZone } from '@angular/core';
constructor(private ngZone: NgZone){}
 // use run() function to call the dispatch inside the
 // NgZone
function callbackOutsideNgZone(){
  this.ngZone.run(
    () => {  this.store.dispatch(createBlog());
  }
}
```

strictActionTypeUniqueness

This runtime check prevents developers from registering the same action type more than once. This check is deactivated by default.

Example violation of this rule:

```
//Violation: two actions have the same type
export const addBlog = createAction('[Blog] Add Blog'); export
const modifyBlog = createAction('[Blog] Add Blog');
```

Fix for this violation:

```
//Violation: two actions have the same type
export const addBlog = createAction('[Blog] Add Blog'); export
const modifyBlog = createAction('[Blog] Modify Blog');
```

Summary

With that, we have reached the end of this chapter. Let's revisit the valuable things you have learned regarding the concepts and importance of having state management in applications.

A store serves as a single source of truth that provides a unidirectional flow of data to prevent inconsistency and mishandled subscriptions.

You also learned how to install and configure the NgRx store and NgRx DevTools library with parameters for custom configuration. Lastly, you learned about the concepts surrounding state management and how to write the different blocks of NgRx, such as actions, reducers, effects, and selectors.

In the next chapter, we will complete the CRUD functionality of our application by using the building blocks of NgRx. We will add, remove, and update items using actions, effects, and reducers.

13

Saving, Deleting, and Updating with NgRx

In the previous chapter, we learned about the concepts and features of NgRx. We learned the importance of state management as it provides a single source for the application to have a unidirectional data flow and reduces the responsibility of components. We also learned the building blocks of NgRx, which are actions, effects, reducers, and selectors. Lastly, we implemented the getting and displaying of the anti-heroes list feature using NgRx in our application.

In this chapter, we will now complete our application's missing features – saving, deleting, and updating data by still using NgRx.

In this chapter, we will cover the following topics:

- Removing an item without side effects using NgRx
- Removing an item with side effects using NgRx
- Adding an item with side effects using NgRx
- Updating an item with side effects using NgRx

Technical requirements

The link to the finished version of the code is `https://github.com/PacktPublishing/Spring-Boot-and-Angular/tree/main/Chapter-13/superheroes`.

Removing an item without a side effect using NgRx

In this section, we will first see how to delete items without using side effects in NgRx. As we learned in the previous chapter, side effects are used to call external APIs to retrieve data. This means that without using effects, we will delete the data by dispatching an action to invoke a reducer base on the dispatched type. This section will help us see the difference in the flow and behavior of using effects in the application.

Creating the delete action

The first step is to create the action for the delete feature. In our project, in the `anti-hero/state/anti-hero.actions.ts` file, we will add a new action interface and a new function for deletion.

Let's have a look at the implementation of the following code:

```
export enum AntiHeroActions {
  GET_ANTI_HERO_LIST = '[Anti-Hero] Get Anti-Hero list',
  SET_ANTI_HERO_LIST = '[Anti-Hero] Set Anti-Hero list',
  REMOVE_ANTI_HERO_STATE =
    '[Anti-Hero] Remove ALL Anti-Hero (STATE)',
}
export const removeAntiHeroState = createAction(
    AntiHeroActions.REMOVE_ANTI_HERO_STATE,
  props<{ antiHeroId: string }>()
);
```

In the preceding code example, we can see that we have added a new action named REMOVE_ANTI_HERO_STATE. We have also created an action with the newly created type, which has a `props` parameter that accepts an anti-hero ID. The ID is needed for the reducer to identify what data we should delete from our store.

Creating the delete reducer

Now, let's create the reducer for deleting data from our store. The first thing we need to think of is what our reducer would look like if it could remove a single piece of data from an array using the provided ID. One way we can implement this is by using the `filter()` function to extract the data in the array.

Let's add the following code in the `anti-hero/state/anti-hero.reducers.ts` file:

```
export const antiHeroReducer = createReducer(
  initialState,
  on(setAntiHeroList, (state, { antiHeroes }) => { return
    {...state, antiHeroes}}),
  on(removeAntiHeroState, (state, { antiHeroId }) => {
    return {...state, antiHeroes:
      state.antiHeroes.filter(data => data.id !=
```

```
                                    antiHeroId) }
    }),
  );
```

In the preceding code example, we can see that we have added a new reducer for our delete feature. This accepts the anti-hero ID coming from the `removeAntiHeroState` action and returns the new state with the modified `antiHeroes` value where the anti-hero data that has the given ID is already filtered. If the reducer successfully modifies the value of the `antiHeroes` state, any selectors subscribed to the changes of this state will emit the new value in the component.

Dispatching the action

The last step we need to do is to dispatch the action in our component. To implement this step, we need to call a dispatch when the **Delete** button for each piece of anti-hero data is clicked.

In the `anti-hero/components/anti-hero-list.component.ts` file, we have added `emittethatch`, which passes the selected anti-hero object and `TableAction`, based on the button clicked by the user.

Let's have a recap of the code we have implemented for this feature in the following files:

anti-hero-list.component.ts

```
// See full code on https://github.com/PacktPublishing/Spring-
Boot-and-Angular/tree/main/Chapter-13 /


export class AntiHeroListComponent implements OnInit {
    // other code for component not displayed
  @Output() antiHero = new EventEmitter<{antiHero:    AntiHero,
action :TableActions}>();
    selectAntiHero(antiHero: AntiHero, action: TableActions)   {
      this.antiHero.emit({antiHero, action});
  }
}
```

anti-hero-list.component.html

```
// See full code on https://github.com/PacktPublishing/Spring-
Boot-and-Angular/tree/main/Chapter-13
```

```
<button (click)="selectAntiHero(element, 1)" mat-raised-button
color="warn">
          <mat-icon>delete</mat-icon> Delete
</button>
```

table-actions.enum.ts

```
export enum TableActions {
  View,
    Delete
}
```

In the preceding code example, we can see that if the **Delete** button is clicked, this will emit the whole anti-hero object and the value 1, which represents the value for **Delete enum**.

Now, we need to dispatch the REMOVE_ANTI_HERO_STATE action in the list component when the **Delete** button has emitted an event. To implement this part, we will add the following code in the following files:

list.component.ts

```
selectAntiHero(data: {antiHero: AntiHero, action:
  TableActions}) {
  switch(data.action) {
    case TableActions.Delete: {
      this.store.dispatch({type:
        AntiHeroActions. REMOVE_ANTI_HERO_STATE,
        antiHeroId: data.antiHero.id});
      return;
    }
    default: ""
  }
}
```

list.component.html

```
// See full code on https://github.com/PacktPublishing/Spring-
Boot-and-Angular/tree/main/Chapter-13
<!-- Dumb component anti hero list -->
```

```
<app-anti-hero-list [antiHeroes]="antiHeroes"
(antiHero)="selectAntiHero($event)" [headers]="headers"></app-
anti-hero-list>
```

In the preceding code example, we created a function that checks the action triggered by the user with the `TableActions` value. If `TableActions` has a delete value, we will dispatch `REMOVE_ANTI_HERO_STATE` and pass the ID of the anti-hero object that will be used by the reducer we have created.

We have now successfully implemented the delete feature of our application with NgRx, but in this case, we are only deleting the items in our UI, and we are not syncing the changes in the database.

In the next section, we will implement the use of side effects in the deleting of data.

Removing an item with side effects using NgRx

In this section, we will improve the delete functionality by adding effects in our state. Our current delete feature only removes the data in the store but does not sync the changes in the database. This means that if we refresh our application, the data that we have deleted will be available again.

To sync the changes in the database, what we should do is create an effect that will invoke the delete API. Let's have a look at the step-by-step changes in our code in the following sections.

Creating a new action type

The first step we need to do is create a new action type. The effects in NgRx will use the new action type for deleting feature later.

We will add `REMOVE_ANTI_HERO_API` in the `AntiHeroActions` enum under the `anti-hero/state/anti-hero.actions.ts` file.

Let's have a look at the added action in the following code:

```
export enum AntiHeroActions {
  GET_ANTI_HERO_LIST = '[Anti-Hero] Get Anti-Hero list',
  SET_ANTI_HERO_LIST = '[Anti-Hero] Set Anti-Hero list',
  REMOVE_ANTI_HERO_API =
    '[Anti-Hero] Remove Anti-Hero (API)',
  REMOVE_ANTI_HERO_STATE =
    '[Anti-Hero] Remove Anti-Hero (STATE)',
}
```

We can see in the preceding code example that a new action type was added for our actions. Take note that we do not need to create a new action for this type as we will be calling an effect instead of an action once this action type is dispatched.

Creating the delete effect

The next step we need to do is to create the effect for the delete feature. In the `anti-hero/state/anti-hero.effect.ts` file, we will add the following code:

```
// See full code on https://github.com/PacktPublishing/Spring-
Boot-and-Angular/tree/main/Chapter-13
removeAntiHero$ = createEffect(() => {
    return this.actions$.pipe(
        ofType(AntiHeroActions.REMOVE_ANTI_HERO_API),
        mergeMap((data: { payload: string}) =>
            this.antiHeroService.deleteAntiHero(data.payload)
            .pipe(
              map(() => ({ type:
                AntiHeroActions.REMOVE_ANTI_HERO_STATE,
                antiHeroId: data.payload })),
              catchError(() => EMPTY)
            ))
        )
    }, {dispatch: true}
    );
```

In the preceding code example, we can see that we have created a new effect for our delete action; this has a type of REMOVE_ANTI_HERO_API, which calls the `deleteAntiHero()` function in `AntiHeroService` for the data deletion based on the passed ID, and once the API is successful.

The effect will dispatch another action, REMOVE_ANTI_HERO_STATE, which we created in the previous section, which removes the anti-hero from the store. This means that the data we delete from the database will also be deleted from our NgRx store.

Modifying the dispatch

The last step for this feature is to modify the action being dispatched in the `list.component.ts` file. In the previous section, we call the REMOVE_ANTI_HERO_STATE action directly in our component; we will change this into REMOVE_ANTI_HERO_API as we should now call the effect, which will invoke the API and at the same time will call the REMOVE_ANTI_HERO_STATE action.

Let's have a look at the following code example:

```
selectAntiHero(data: {antiHero: AntiHero, action:
TableActions}) {
    switch(data.action) {
      case TableActions.Delete: {
        this. store.dispatch({type:
          AntiHeroActions.REMOVE_ANTI_HERO_API,
          payload: data.antiHero.id});
        return;
      }
      default: ""
    }
  }
```

In the preceding code example, we are now dispatching the effect in our list component. This will call the API first before updating our store in the application; the changes in our store and database are synced.

In the next section, we will implement the addition of data with side effects to our application.

Adding an item with side effects using NgRx

In this section, we will implement the *add* functionality with side effects in NgRx. The steps are similar to how we implemented the delete feature. We will create the building blocks step by step and create the dispatch logic in our component.

Creating the actions

The first step we need to do is create the required action types and actions for our add feature. To implement the actions, we can think of how we created the actions for the delete feature.

The concept is the same. There are two action types that we need to create, and these are ADD_ANTI_ HERO_API and ADD_ANTI_HERO_STATE. The first type will be used by the effect that will call the API, and the second type will be used by the reducer that will modify the state by adding the newly created data.

After creating the two action types, we also need to create an action using the createAction() function for the ADD_ANTI_HERO_STATE type. The effect will dispatch this once the API has been successfully called.

Let's have a look at the following code implementation:

```
// See full code on https://github.com/PacktPublishing/Spring-
Boot-and-Angular/tree/main/Chapter-13

export enum AntiHeroActions {
  GET_ANTI_HERO_LIST = '[Anti-Hero] Get Anti-Hero list',
  SET_ANTI_HERO_LIST = '[Anti-Hero] Set Anti-Hero list',
  ADD_ANTI_HERO_API = '[Anti-Hero] Add Anti-Hero (API',
  ADD_ANTI_HERO_STATE = '[Ant
    i-Hero] Add Anti-Hero (STATE)',
  REMOVE_ANTI_HERO_API =
    '[Anti-Hero] Remove Anti-Hero (API)',
  REMOVE_ANTI_HERO_STATE =
    '[Anti-Hero] Remove Anti-Hero (STATE)',
}

export const addAntiHeroState = createAction(
  AntiHeroActions.ADD_ANTI_HERO_STATE,
  props<{ antiHero: AntiHero }>()
)
```

In the preceding code example, we can see that we have added the two new types in AntiHeroActions. We have also created a new action with the ADD_ANTI_HERO_STATE type, which accepts an antiHero property that will be pushed as a new item in the anti-hero state.

Creating the effect

The next step we need to do is to create the effect for the *add* feature. In the anti-hero/state/ anti-hero.effect.ts file, we will add the following code:

```
// add anti-heroes to the database
  addAntiHero$ = createEffect(() =>{
    return this.actions$.pipe(
        ofType(AntiHeroActions.ADD_ANTI_HERO_API),
        mergeMap((data: {type: string, payload: AntiHero})
          => this.antiHeroService.addAntiHero(data.payload)
          .pipe(
```

```
        map(antiHeroes => ({ type:
          AntiHeroActions.ADD_ANTI_HERO_STATE,
          antiHero: data.payload })),
        tap(() =>
          this.router.navigate(["anti-heroes"])),
        catchError(() => EMPTY)
      ))
    )
  }, {dispatch: true})
```

In the preceding code example, we can see that we have created an effect similar to the effect for the delete feature. This effect uses the ADD_ANTI_HERO_API type and invokes the addAntiHero() function from antiHeroService to call the POST API to add new data to the database.

After successfully calling the POST API, the effect will dispatch the ADD_ANTI_HERO_STATE action and pass the new anti-hero data coming from the API response to be added by the reducer. We have also added a tap operator, which calls a navigate function that will navigate to the list page after creating the new anti-hero.

Creating the reducer

After creating the effects, we need to sync the changes implemented in the database with our store, and the reducer will do this.

Let's have a look at the following code implementation:

```
export const antiHeroReducer = createReducer(
  initialState,
  on(setAntiHeroList, (state, { antiHeroes }) => { return
    {...state, antiHeroes}}),
  on(removeAntiHeroState, (state, { antiHeroId }) => {
    return {...state, antiHeroes:
      state.antiHeroes.filter(data => data.id !=
        antiHeroId)}
  }),
  on(addAntiHeroState, (state, {antiHero}) => {
    return {...state, antiHeroes: [...state.antiHeroes,
            antiHero]}
  }),
);
```

In the preceding code example, we can see that we have added a new reducer for our *add* feature. This accepts the new anti-hero data coming from the addAntiHeroState action and returns the new state with the modified antiHeroes value where the new anti-hero is already added in the array.

If the reducer successfully modifies the value of the antiHeroes state, any selectors subscribed to the changes of this state will emit the new value in the component.

Dispatching the action

The last step we need to do is to dispatch the action in our component. To implement this step, we will invoke the dispatch action once the **Create** button in the anti-hero form is clicked. In the anti-hero/components/anti-hero-form.component.ts file, we have added an emitter that passes the value of the form and the button label to identify if the action is created or updated.

Let's have a recap of the code we have implemented for this anti-hero form:

```
export class AntiHeroFormComponent implements OnInit {
  @Input() actionButtonLabel: string = 'Create';
  @Output() action = new EventEmitter();
  form: FormGroup;
  constructor(private fb: FormBuilder) {
    this.form = this.fb.group({
      id: [''],
      firstName: [''],
      lastName: [''],
      house: [''],
      knownAs: ['']
    })
  }
  emitAction() {
    this.action.emit({value: this.form.value,
                      action: this.actionButtonLabel})
  }
}
```

In the preceding code example, we can see that the anti-hero form emits the form value as an anti-hero object that will be passed to the effect.

This also gives the current action, as we will also be using this anti-hero form component for the update. Once the button is clicked, we need to have a function in the form.component.ts file that will dispatch the effect.

Let's have a look at the following code example:

```
// form.component.html
<app-anti-hero-form [selectedAntiHero]="antiHero"
(action)="formAction($event)"></app-anti-hero-form>

// form.component.ts
 formAction(data: {value: AntiHero, action: string}) {
    switch(data.action) {
      case "Create" : {
        this.store.dispatch({type:
          AntiHeroActions.ADD_ANTI_HERO_API,
          payload: data.value});
        return;
      }
      default: ""
    }
  }
```

In the preceding code example, we can see that we have created the `formAction()` function, which dispatches an action based on the passed value from the anti-hero form component.

This uses a `switch` statement, as this will also be called when the action is `update`. We have now successfully created the *add* feature for our application using the building blocks of NgRx.

In the next section, we will implement the modification of data with side effects.

Updating an item with a side effect using NgRx

In this last section, we will implement the final missing feature, which is the *update* functionality, where we will create the building blocks step by step and the dispatch logic in our component as we did for the *add* and *delete* features.

Creating the actions

The first step we need to do is to create the required action types and actions for our update feature. We will first create the two action types we need, which are `MODIFY_ANTI_HERO_API` and `MODIFY_ANTI_HERO_STATE`. The first type will be used by the effect that will call the API, and the second type will be used by the reducer that will modify the state by changing the data based on the new anti-hero object.

After creating the two action types, we also need to create an action using the `createAction()` function for the `MODIFY_ANTI_HERO_STATE` type. The effect will dispatch this once the API has been successfully called.

Let's have a look at the following code implementation:

```
// See full code on https://github.com/PacktPublishing/Spring-
Boot-and-Angular/tree/main/Chapter-13

export enum AntiHeroActions {
  GET_ANTI_HERO_LIST = '[Anti-Hero] Get Anti-Hero list',
  SET_ANTI_HERO_LIST = '[Anti-Hero] Set Anti-Hero list',
  ADD_ANTI_HERO_API = '[Anti-Hero] Add Anti-Hero (API',
  ADD_ANTI_HERO_STATE =
    '[Anti-Hero] Add Anti-Hero (STATE)',
  REMOVE_ANTI_HERO_API =
    '[Anti-Hero] Remove Anti-Hero (API)',
  REMOVE_ANTI_HERO_STATE =
    '[Anti-Hero] Remove Anti-Hero (STATE)',
  MODIFY_ANTI_HERO_API =
    '[Anti-Hero] Modify Anti-Hero (API)',
  MODIFY_ANTI_HERO_STATE =
    '[Anti-Hero] Modify Anti-Hero (STATE)',
}
export const modifyAntiHeroState = createAction(
    AntiHeroActions.MODIFY_ANTI_HERO_STATE,
    props<{ antiHero: AntiHero }>()
);
```

In the preceding code example, we can see that we have added the two new types in `AntiHeroActions`. We have also created a new action with the `MODIFY_ANTI_HERO_STATE` type, which accepts an `antiHero` property that will be used to modify the current values in the store.

Creating the effect

The next step we need to do is to create the effect for the *add* feature. In the `anti-hero/state/anti-hero.effect.ts` file, we will add the following code:

```
// modify anti-heroes in the database
    modifyAntiHero$ = createEffect(() =>{
```

```
    return this.actions$.pipe(
        ofType(AntiHeroActions.MODIFY_ANTI_HERO_API),
        mergeMap((data: {type: string, payload: AntiHero})
          => this.antiHeroService.updateAntiHero(
          data.payload.id, data.payload)
          .pipe(
            map(antiHeroes => ({ type:
                AntiHeroActions.MODIFY_ANTI_HERO_STATE,
                antiHero: data.payload })),
            tap(() =>
              this.router.navigate(["anti-heroes"])),
            catchError(() => EMPTY)
          ))
        )
    }, {dispatch: true})
```

In the preceding code example, we can see that we have created an effect similar to the effect for the *add* and *delete* features. This effect uses the MODIFY_ANTI_HERO_API type and invokes the updateAntiHero() function from antiHeroService to call the PUT API to modify the anti-hero with the ID parameter in the database.

After successfully calling the PUT API, the effect will dispatch the MODIFY_ANTI_HERO_STATE action and pass the modified anti-hero data coming from the API response to be added by the reducer, and the same as with the *add* effect, we have also added a tap operator, which calls a navigate function that will navigate to the list page after modifying the anti-hero.

Creating the reducer

After creating the effects, we need to sync the changes implemented in the database with our store, and the reducer will do this.

Let's have a look at the following code implementation:

```
export const antiHeroReducer = createReducer(
  initialState,
  on(setAntiHeroList, (state, { antiHeroes }) => {
    return {...state, antiHeroes}}),
  on(removeAntiHeroState, (state, { antiHeroId }) => {
    return {...state, antiHeroes:
      state.antiHeroes.filter(data => data.id !=
```

```
                                         antiHeroId) }
    }),
    on(addAntiHeroState, (state, {antiHero}) => {
      return {...state, antiHeroes: [...state.antiHeroes,
                                     antiHero] }
    }),
    on(modifyAntiHeroState, (state, {antiHero}) => {
      return {...state, antiHeroes: state.antiHeroes.map(data
        => data.id === antiHero.id ? antiHero : data)}
    }),


  );
```

In the preceding code example, we can see that we have added a new reducer for our update feature. This accepts the modified anti-hero data coming from the `addAntiHeroState` action and returns the new state with the modified `antiHeroes` value, where we replace the anti-hero with the given ID with the new object using the `map()` operator.

If the reducer successfully modifies the value of the `antiHeroes` state, any selectors subscribed to the changes of this state will emit the new value in the component.

Dispatching the action

The last step we need to do is to dispatch the action to our component. To implement this step, we will do the same steps as we did for the *add* feature. We will still use the `anti-hero/components/anti-hero-form.component.ts` file for updating the data.

The only difference here is that we will bind the selected anti-hero value in our form; the anti-hero form component should accept an anti-hero object and should patch the value in the form group.

Let's have a look at the following code example:

```
export class AntiHeroFormComponent implements OnInit {
  @Input() actionButtonLabel: string = 'Create';
  @Input() selectedAntiHero: AntiHero | null = null;
  @Output() action = new EventEmitter();
  form: FormGroup;
  constructor(private fb: FormBuilder) {
    this.form = this.fb.group({
      id: [''],
      firstName: [''],
```

```
      lastName: [''],
      house: [''],
      knownAs: ['']
    })
  }
  ngOnInit(): void {
    this.checkAction();
  }

  checkAction() {
    if(this.selectedAntiHero) {
      this.actionButtonLabel = "Update";
      this.patchDataValues()
    }
  }
  emitAction() {
    this.action.emit({value: this.form.value,
      action: this.actionButtonLabel})
  }
}
```

In the preceding code example, we can see that we have added the checkAction() function, which checks whether we have passed an anti-hero object in the anti-hero form component.

This indicates that if the object is not null, this will be an *Update* action, and we must display the selected anti-hero details in each field by binding the form using the patchValue() method.

Now let's have the code implementation for the form component:

```
// form.component.html
<app-anti-hero-form [selectedAntiHero]="antiHero"
(action)="formAction($event)"></app-anti-hero-form>

// form.component.ts
antiHero$: Observable<AntiHero | undefined>;
  antiHero: AntiHero | null = null;

  constructor(private router: ActivatedRoute,
    private store: Store<AppState>) {
    const id = this.router.snapshot.params['id'];
```

```
      this.antiHero$ = this.store.select(selectAntiHero(id));
      this.antiHero$.subscribe(d => {
        if(d) this.antiHero = d;
      });


    }
  formAction(data: {value: AntiHero, action: string}) {
    switch(data.action) {
      case "Create" : {
        this.store.dispatch({type:
          AntiHeroActions.ADD_ANTI_HERO_API,
          payload: data.value});
        return;
      }
      case "Update" : {
        this.store.dispatch({type:
          AntiHeroActions.MODIFY_ANTI_HERO_API,
          payload: data.value});
        return;
      }
      default: ""
    }
  }
```

In the preceding code example, we can see that we have added a new case in the `formAction()` function, which also dispatches an action but of type `MODIFY_ANTI_HERO_API`.

We have also used the `selectAntiHero()` selector to select the anti-hero using the ID in our URL route that will be passed in our `anti-hero-form.component.ts` file.

Summary

With this, we have reached the end of this chapter. Let's have a recap of the valuable things we have learned; we have completed the CRUD features of applications using the building blocks of NgRx, and we have learned the difference between using and not using side effects in state management. Side effects are essential for our changes in the store to be synced with the database.

We have also learned, step by step, how to create the building blocks of NgRx with the different actions we need for our application.

In the next chapter, we will learn how to apply security features in Angular, such as adding user login and logout, retrieving user profile information, protecting application routes, and calling an API with protected endpoints.

14

Adding Authentication in Angular

In the previous chapter, we completed the CRUD features of our Angular application using the building blocks of NgRx. We also learned the step-by-step process of writing the actions, reducers, and effects in our application that will be used to modify the value of states. We also learned the difference between using and not using effects in the application. Effects are essential for us to communicate with the external APIs that allow the database changes to be synced in the NgRx store.

In this chapter, we will learn how to add authentication in our Angular application; we will implement a login page that will provide a valid JWT, protect routes, and apply API authentication with the use of NgRx.

In this chapter, we will cover the following topics:

- Adding user authentication
- Protecting routes
- Calling an API

Technical requirements

The complete code for this chapter can be found at: `https://github.com/PacktPublishing/Spring-Boot-and-Angular/tree/main/Chapter-14`.

Adding user authentication

Adding user authentication is one of the main requirements in developing an application. This feature allows us to restrict pages and features from unauthorized users. We can achieve user authentication in different ways, and one way to implement this is by providing a login page that will ask for credentials.

Let's have a look at the step-by-step process of implementing the authentication feature.

The authentication API

Let us first recap the authentication API we created in our Spring Boot project. The endpoints for authentication are as follows:

- {BASE_URL}/authenticate: The main endpoint for authentication accepts an object with email and password fields and returns a valid JWT that will be used for calling endpoints. The following is an example response object of the endpoint:

```
// valid JWT
{
    "token": "eyJhbGciOiJIUzI1NiJ9.eyJzdWIiOiJ0ZXN0QGdtYWl
sLmNvbSIsImlhdCI6MTY1OTQyODk2MSwiZXhwIjoxNjU5NDY0OTYxfQ.
WU_aZjmlfw--LCovx4cZ4_hcOTGiAgPnSaM0bjdv018"
}
```

- {BASE_URL}/register: The endpoint for creating new valid credentials for login. JWT, as stated in *Chapter 7*, *Adding Spring Boot Security with JWT*, is used chiefly on RESTful web services that cannot maintain a client state since JWT holds some information connected to the user. This will be used primarily in the headers of endpoints that we will request.

In our project, let's create a service named AuthenticateService under the core/services folder by executing the following command:

ng g core/services/authenticate

After successfully creating the service, we will place the following code in the service:

```
export class AuthenticateService {

  constructor(private http: HttpClient) { }
  // for login endpoint
  login(data: {email: string, password: string}):
    Observable<any> {
    return this.http.post<any>(
     `${environment.authURL}/authenticate`,
      data).pipe(
      tap((data: any) => data),
      catchError(err => throwError(() => err))
   )
  }
  // for register endpoint
  register(data: {email: string, password: string}):
```

```
        Observable<any> {
        return this.http.post<any>(
          `${environment.authURL}/register`, data).pipe(
          tap((data: any) => data),
          catchError(err => throwError(() => err))
        )
      }
    }
```

`AuthenticateService` will hold the two endpoints we will use for our login page. Now, let's create the interceptor for our application.

The HTTP interceptor

HTTP interceptors are features of Angular that allow us to intercept HTTP requests to transform their headers, the body, or the response. This provides the `intercept()` function, which will enable us to get the outgoing request and call the next interceptor or the backend.

We will mainly use the interceptor to modify the headers of our endpoint requests, which will be responsible for adding the `Authorization: Bearer {JWT}` header for each invoked request.

To implement the interceptor, we will create the `core/interceptors/header.interceptor.ts` file, and we will place the following code within it:

```
@Injectable()
export class HeaderInterceptor implements HttpInterceptor {
  intercept(httpRequest: HttpRequest<any>, next:
    HttpHandler): Observable<HttpEvent<any>> {
    const Authorization = localStorage.getItem('token') ?
      `Bearer ${localStorage.getItem('token')}` : '';
    if(httpRequest.url.includes('api/v1'))
    return next.handle(httpRequest.clone({ setHeaders: {
      Authorization } }));
    else
    return next.handle(httpRequest);
  }
}
```

In the preceding code example, we have added a new implementation for the `intercept()` function. The first step is to retrieve the valid JWT in our local storage that will be used in the HTTP headers. We will only use the JWT if the request endpoint has an `api/v1` substring, as these are the endpoints that are protected.

The next step is to clone the request and add the `Authorization: Bearer {JWT}` header in the cloned request and call the `next()` function to call the API with the added header.

We have now created our interceptor; the last step is to add the interceptor in `AppModule`.

Let's have a look at the following code:

```
providers: [
   { provide: HTTP_INTERCEPTORS, useClass:
            HeaderInterceptor, multi: true }
],
```

In the preceding code example, we will now intercept every HTTP call on the anti-heroes endpoint and will add the generated JWT in the request headers.

The authentication module

The next step is to create an authentication module; this module will be responsible for holding the login and registration page that will accept the users and credentials and call the authenticate and register endpoints.

To create the authentication module, we will execute the following command:

ng g m auth

After successfully creating the authentication module, we will import several modules we need for our authentication module:

```
@NgModule({
  declarations: [
  ],
  imports: [
    CommonModule,
    MaterialModule,
    FormsModule,
    ReactiveFormsModule,
    CoreModule,
  ]
});
```

Now, we will create the different parts of our module.

The authentication form

We will create the main form for our authentication module; this is considered the dumb component of our module as it will accept and emit the values of the form to the login and registration page.

To create the authentication form component, we will execute the following command:

```
ng g c auth/components/auth-form
```

After successfully creating the component, we will now implement the form's code. In the TypeScript file of the auth-form component, we will place the following code:

```
export class AuthFormComponent {
  @Input() error: string = "";
  @Input() title: string = "Login"
  @Output() submitEmitter = new EventEmitter();
  form: FormGroup;
  constructor(private fb: FormBuilder) {
    this.form = this.fb.group({
      email: [''],
      password: ['']
    })

  }
  submit() {
    this.submitEmitter.emit(this.form.value);
  }
}
```

In the preceding code example, we can see that we have created a reactive form with an email and password form control. We have also created an emitter that will pass the values of the form into the parent component, as this component will be used by both the login and the register page. Now, we will implement the HTML code and the CSS of the auth-form component.

> **Note**
>
> Please refer to the link provided for the entire code implementation:
>
> https://github.com/PacktPublishing/Spring-Boot-and-Angular/tree/main/Chapter-14/superheroes/src/app/auth/components/auth-form

In the implemented code, we have bound the reactive form with the email and password input. We have also created a condition where the button changes if the page is currently on login or register.

We have successfully created our authentication form; now, we will create our login and registration page.

The login and registration page

The login and registration pages are considered to be the smart components of our application, as these are the components that will dispatch the action for calling the authentication API.

To create the login and register page, we will execute the following command:

```
ng g c auth/page/login auth/page/register
```

After successfully creating the two pages, we will run the code for the login and register components:

Login Page

```
//TS File
export class LoginComponent{
  constructor(private authService: AuthenticateService,
    private router: Router) {
  }
  submit(data:{email:string, password:string}) {
    this.authService.login(data).subscribe((data) => {
      this.router.navigate(['/anti-heroes']);
      localStorage.setItem('token', data.token);
    });
  }
}
// HTML File
<app-auth-form (submitEmitter)="submit($event)"></app-auth-form>
```

Register Page

```
// TS File
export class RegisterComponent {
  error: string = "";
```

```
  constructor(private authService: AuthenticateService) {
  }
  submit(data: User) {
    this.authService.register(data).subscribe((data) => {
      this.router.navigate(['/']);
    });
  }
}
// HTML File
<app-auth-form title="Register"
(submitEmitter)="submit($event)"></app-auth-form>
```

In the preceding code example, we can see that the login page and registration pages are using the same authentication form component. Once the form is submitted, it will pass the form value into the `login()` or `register()` functions to authenticate or create the user, respectively. If the login is successful, we will redirect the user to the anti-heroes list page and place the generated token from the API in the local storage.

The routing module

The next step is to create the auth-routing module that will define the routes for the authentication module. To create the module, let's execute the following command:

ng g m auth/auth-routing --flat

After creating the routing module, we will run the following code:

```
const routes: Routes = [
  {
    path: "",
    component: LoginComponent
  },
  {
    path: "register",
    component: RegisterComponent
  }
];
@NgModule({
  declarations: [],
```

```
    imports: [RouterModule.forChild(routes)],
    exports: [RouterModule],
})
export class AuthRoutingModule {}
```

We also need to modify our app-routing module, as we need our base path to redirect to the login page; let's implement the following modification:

```
const routes: Routes = [
    {
        path: "",
        redirectTo: "login",
        pathMatch: "full",
    },
    {
        path: "login",
        loadChildren: () =>
        import("./auth/auth.module").then((m) => m.AuthModule),
    },
    {
        path: "anti-heroes",
        loadChildren: () =>
          import("./anti-hero/anti-hero.module").then((m) =>
                m.AntiHeroModule),
    }
];
```

In the preceding implemented code, we can see that once we go to the base path, this will now load the AuthModule and redirect us to the login page, as shown in *Figure 14.1*.

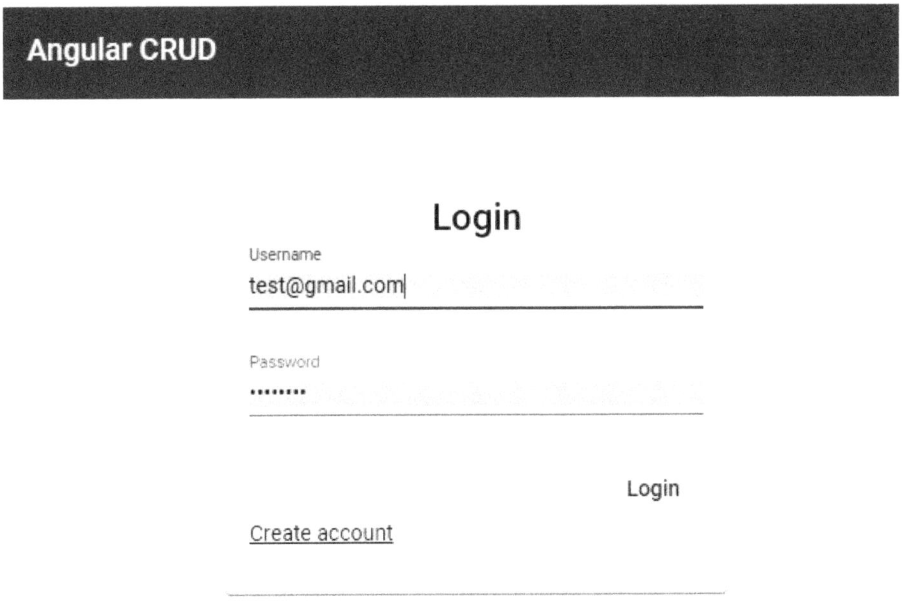

Angular CRUD

Login

Username

test@gmail.com|

Password

....

Login

Create account

Figure 14.1 – The Login page

We should now be able to log in with our user in the database. If no user has been created, we can create a new one using the registration page, and once the login is successful, we will be redirected to the anti-hero list page, as shown in *Figure 14.2*.

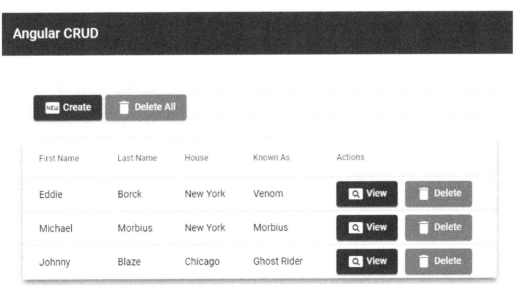

Figure 14.2 – The anti-hero list page

We can also observe that our valid JWT is already placed in our local storage as the HTTP interceptor is using the JWT. As we open a request made by our application, we can see that the headers have the generated JWT:

```
Accept:
application/json, text/plain, */*
Accept-Encoding:
gzip, deflate, br
Accept-Language:
en-AU,en-US;q=0.9,en;q=0.8,bs;q=0.7,fr-
CA;q=0.6,fr;q=0.5,tl;q=0.4
Authorization:
Bearer eyJhbGciOiJIUzI1NiJ9.eyJzdWIiOiJ0ZXN0QGdtYWlsLmNvbSIsIm
lhdCI6MTY1OTY5ODM2NSwiZXhwIjoxNjU5NzM0MzY1fQ.2SDLmvQcME5Be9Xj-
zTeRlc6kGfQVNCMIWUBOBS5afg
```

In the preceding example headers, we can see that the `Authorization` header contains the valid JWT for every API request the application calls. The placement of the JWT in the header is done when our login is successful and we are redirected to the `AntiHeromodule`.

Token validation

The next step we need to do is to add token validation to check whether our token already expired. To implement this feature, we add the `@auth0/angular-jwt` library by executing the following command:

npm install @auth0/angular-jwt --save

The `@auth0/angular-jwt` library provides useful functions, such as `isTokenExpired()`, which checks whether the JWT is expired, and `decodeToken()`, which retrieves the information from the JWT.

After successfully installing the library, we will add the following code to our authenticate service:

```
isAuthenticated(): boolean {
    const token = localStorage.getItem('token') ?? '';
    // Check whether the token is expired and return
    // true or false
    return !this.jwtHelper.isTokenExpired(token);
}
```

We also need to import the JWT module into our `app.module.ts` file:

```
imports: [
   JwtModule.forRoot({})
 ],
```

We will use the `isAuthenticated()` function on our login and register pages to check whether a JWT is present in our local storage. If there is a valid JWT, we will redirect the application to the anti-hero list page.

Let's have a look at the following implementation:

```
//login page (TS File)
constructor(private authService: AuthenticateService, private
router: Router,) {
    this.checkJWT();
  }
checkJWT() {
    if(this.authService.isAuthenticated()) {
      this.router.navigate(['/anti-heroes'])
    }
  }
}
```

Logout implementation

The last feature we need to implement is the logout function. To add this feature, the only function we need to add is a function that will remove the token from our storage. Let's have the code implementation as follows:

authenticate.service.ts

```
export class AuthenticateService {
… other functions
doLogout() {
    let removeToken = localStorage.removeItem('token');
    if (removeToken == null) {
      this.router.navigate(['login']);
    }
  }
}
```

In the preceding code example, we have added a `doLogout()` function that removes the token in the storage and redirects the application to the login page. Now, let's edit our `navbar` component to have a logout button:

navbar.component.html

```html
<p>
    <mat-toolbar color="primary">
      <span>Angular CRUD</span>
      <span class="example-spacer"></span>
      <button *ngIf="loggedIn" (click)="submit('logout')"
        mat-icon-button>
        <mat-icon>logout</mat-icon>
      </button>
    </mat-toolbar>
</p>
```

navbar.component.css

```css
.example-spacer {
    flex: 1 1 auto;
}
```

navbar.component.ts

```typescript
export class NavbarComponent implements OnInit{
  @Output() actionEmitter = new EventEmitter();
  @Input() loggedIn = false;
  submit(action: string) {
    this.actionEmitter.emit(action);
  }
}
```

In the preceding code implementation, we created an emitter for our navbar component. This will emit the action we have triggered in our navbar, and it will be passed into our app component.

The last step is to call the doLogout () function in our app component when the logout button is clicked. Let's have a look at the code implementation, as follows:

app.component.html

```html
<app-navbar [loggedIn]="url != '/' && !url.includes('login')"
(actionEmitter)="submit($event)"></app-navbar>
<div class="container">
    <router-outlet></router-outlet>
</div>
```

app.component.ts

```typescript
export class AppComponent {
  title = 'superheroes';
  url: string = "";
  constructor(private authService: AuthenticateService,
              private router: Router){
    this.getRoute();
  }
  submit(action: string) {
    switch (action) {
      case 'logout':
        this.authService.doLogout();
        break;
      default:
        break;
    }
  }
  getRoute() {
    this.router.events.subscribe(data => {
    if(data instanceof NavigationEnd) {
      this.url = data.url;
    }
  });
  }
}
```

In the preceding code implementation, we injected the authenticate service into our app component and called the doLogout() function. If the action is logout, we have also added a listener to the router change to check if our route is currently on login or register, and if it is, we will remove the logout button on the navbar component.

We have successfully implemented user authentication with our application, but we will still improve this implementation as we go on through this chapter. In the next section, we will discuss how to protect routes in our Angular application.

Protecting routes

One of the essential features of Angular is router guards. Guards are helpful if we want to protect our routes from being accessed directly without authentication or prevent the user from losing changes when navigating accidentally from the route.

Guards are interfaces provided by Angular that allow us to control the accessibility of a route with a provided condition. These are applied directly to the routes we want to protect.

Let's have a look at some of the guards provided by Angular:

- CanActivate: This is implemented on a route we want to prevent access to.

  - **Method signature**:

    ```
    canActivate(route:ActivatedRouteSnapshot,
    state:RouterStateSnapshot):Observable<boolean | UrlTree>
    | Promise<boolean | UrlTree> | boolean | UrlTree
    ```

    The preceding code defines the signature of the CanActivate guard. The function accepts the ActivatedRouteSnapshot and RouterStateSnapshot parameters and returns an Observable or Promise that can be of type Boolean or UrlTree.

  - **Creating the guard**:

    ```
    export class AuthGuard implements CanActivate {,
    constructor(priavte auth: AuthService, private router:
    Router) {}
    canActivate(route: ActivatedRouteSnapshot,
    state:RouterStateSnapshot): Observable<boolean> |
    Promise<boolean> | boolean {
      // return true permitted in the route, else return
      // false
    }
    }
    ```

In the preceding code example, we have created a new class named AuthGuard; we have also implemented it with the CanActivate guard and added the canActivate() function for the required logic.

- **Using the guard**:

```
// route-module file
{ path: 'hero',
  component: HeroComponent,
  canActivate: [AuthGuard]
}
```

In the preceding code example, we have used the newly created AuthGuard class in our hero route to protect it from users without a valid JWT.

- CanActivateChild: This is similar to CanActivateGuard, but this guard is applied to prevent access to child routes. Once this is added to the parent route, the guard will protect all child routes.

  - **Method signature**:

```
canActivateChild(route:ActivatedRouteSnapshot,
state:RouterStateSnapshot):Observable<boolean | UrlTree>
| Promise<boolean | UrlTree> | boolean | UrlTree
```

The preceding code example defines the signature of the CanActivateChild guard. The function accepts the ActivatedRouteSnapshot and RouterStateSnapshot parameters and returns an Observable or Promise that can be of type Boolean or UrlTree.

  - **Creating the guard**:

```
export class AuthGuard implements CanActivateChild {
constructor(private auth: AuthService, private router:
Router) {}
canActivateChild(route: ActivatedRouteSnapshot,
state:RouterStateSnapshot): Observable<boolean> |
Promise<boolean> | boolean {
  // return true permitted in the route, else return
  // false
}}
```

In the preceding code example, we have created a new class named `AuthGuard`. We have also implemented it with the `CanActivateChild` guard and added the `canActivateChild()` function for the required logic.

- **Using the guard**:

```
{
  path: user',

  canActivateChild: [AuthGuard],
  component: UserComponent,
  children: [
    { path: ':id', component: ProfileComponent},
    { path: ':id/edit', component: SettingsComponent}]
}
```

In the preceding code example, we have used the newly created `AuthGuard` class in our user path to protect its child routes that navigate to the `ProfileComponent` and `SettingsComponent` components from users without a valid JWT.

- `CanLoad`: This guard is used for lazy-loaded modules. The `CanActivate` guard can only prevent users from navigating through a route; the `CanLoad` guard prevents both navigating to and downloading the lazy-loaded module.

- **Method signature**:

```
canLoad(route:Route,segments:UrlSegment[]):
Observable<boolean>|Promise<boolean>|boolean
```

The preceding code example defines the signature of the `CanLoad` guard. The function accepts the `Route` and `UrlSegment[]` parameters and returns an `Observable` or `Promise` that can be of type `Boolean`.

- **Creating the guard**:

```
import { CanLoad, Route, Router } from '@angular/router';
export class AuthGuard implements CanLoad {
constructor(private router: Router) {}
canLoad(route:Route,segments:UrlSegment[]):Observable
<boolean>|Promise<boolean>|boolean {
  // return true or false based on a condition to load
  // a module or not
}}
```

In the preceding code example, we have created a new class named AuthGuard. We have also implemented it with the CanLoad guard and added the canLoad() function for the required logic.

- **Using the guard**:

```
{
    path: "hero",
    loadChildren: () =>
        import("./hero/hero.module").then((m) =>
                m.AntiHeroModule),
    canLoad: [AuthGuard]
}
```

In the preceding code example, we have used the newly created AuthGuard class in our hero route to protect it from users accessing and downloading the resources without a valid JWT.

- CanDeactivate: This is a guard used to prevent the user from navigating away from the current route. This is useful in scenarios such as filling out forms in the application, to avoid losing some changes on navigating out accidentally.

- **Method signature**:

```
canDeactivate(component: T, currentRoute: ActivatedRoute
Snapshot, currentState: RouterStateSnapshot,nextState?:
RouterStateSnapshot): Observable<boolean|UrlTree>|Promise<
boolean|UrlTree>|boolean |UrlTree;
```

The preceding code example defines the signature of the CanDeactivate guard. The function accepts a generic component, the ActivatedRouteSnapshot and RouterStateSnapshot parameters, and returns an Observable or Promise that can be of type Boolean or UrlTree.

- **Creating the guard**:

```
// CanDeactivateGuard service
import { Observable } from 'rxjs/Observable';
import { CanDeactivate, ActivatedRouteSnapshot,
RouterStateSnapshot } from '@angular/router';
export interface CanComponentDeactivate {
canDeactivate: () => Observable<boolean> |
Promise<boolean> | boolean;
}
```

```
export class CanDeactivateGuard implements
CanDeactivate<CanComponentDeactivate> {
    canDeactivate(component:CanComponentDeactivate,current
Route:ActivatedRouteSnapshot, currentState:RouterState
Snapshot, nextState?: RouterStateSnapshot): Observable
<boolean> | Promise<boolean> | boolean {
    return component.canDeactivate();
}
}
```

In the preceding implementation, we have created an interface that will be used in the component of the CanDeactivateGuard service:

```
export class FormComponent implements OnInit,
CanComponentDeactivate {


canDeactivate(): Observable<boolean> | Promise<boolean> |
boolean {
/* return true or false depends on a specific condition
if you want to navigate away from this route or not.*/
}
}
```

In the preceding code example, we have implemented the interface we have created for the component.

- **Using the guard**:

```
{ path: ':id/edit', component: FormComponent,
canDeactivate: [CanDeactivateGuard] }
```

In the preceding code example, we have used the newly created CanDeactivateGuard to prevent the user from navigating out of the FormComponent based on the applied condition on the canDeactivate() function.

We have learned about the different guards we can use in our application. Now, let's implement this in our Angular project.

Project implementation

The first guard we need to apply in our application is the CanLoad guard. This is necessary as we want to protect our anti-heroes routes from being accessed if there is no valid JWT. To create the CanLoad guard, execute the following command:

```
ng g g core/guards/auth
```

After executing the command, select the CanLoad option to generate a new AuthGuard class. The only thing we need to change here is the implementation of the canLoad() function. The condition we want to apply is to allow the route and modules to be loaded if the JWT is valid.

Let's have a look at the following implementation:

```
@Injectable({
  providedIn: 'root'
})
export class AuthGuard implements CanLoad {
  constructor(private router: Router, private auth:
    AuthenticateService) {}
  canLoad(route: Route, segments:UrlSegment[]):
    Observable<boolean | UrlTree> | Promise<boolean |
      UrlTree> | boolean | UrlTree {
      if (!this.auth.isAuthenticated()) {
        this. router.navigate(['login']);
        return false;
      }
      return true;
  }
}
```

In the preceding code example, we have used the isAuthenticated() function to check that the JWT is valid and not expired. If it is valid, this will return true and allow us to navigate the route. Otherwise, it will redirect us to the login page.

The last step is to apply the AuthGuard class in the anti-heroes route; in the app-routing. module.ts file, we will use the following:

```
const routes: Routes = [
... other routes here
  {
    path: "anti-heroes",
    loadChildren: () =>
      import("./anti-hero/anti-hero.module").then((m) =>
        m.AntiHeroModule),
      canLoad: [AuthGuard]
  }
];
```

We have now successfully applied the CanLoad guard in our anti-heroes route. To test whether this works, we can try deleting the token in our local storage, and this should redirect us to the login page having no valid JWT.

The last route guard we need is the CanDeactivate guard; we will apply this guard on our anti-hero form to prevent the user from losing changes when navigating away from the form. To create our CanDeactivate guard, we will execute the following command:

```
ng g g core/guards/form
```

After executing the command, select the CanDeactivate option, and this will generate a new FormGuard class. We will add an interface to this class that we will use in our form component.

Let's have a look at the following code:

```
export interface CanComponentDeactivate {
  canDeactivate: () => Observable<boolean> |
    Promise<boolean> | boolean;
}
@Injectable({
  providedIn: 'root'
})
export class FormGuard implements CanDeactivate<unknown> {
  canDeactivate(
    component: CanComponentDeactivate,
    currentRoute: ActivatedRouteSnapshot,
    currentState: RouterStateSnapshot,
    nextState?: RouterStateSnapshot): Observable<boolean |
      UrlTree> | Promise<boolean | UrlTree> | boolean |
      UrlTree {
      return component.canDeactivate ?
        component.canDeactivate() : true;
  }
}
```

In the preceding code example, we have created the CanComponentDeactivate interface that the form component will implement. This means that the condition will be placed in the component instead of the guard. In FormComponent, we will add the following code:

```
export class FormComponent implements OnInit,
CanComponentDeactivate {
```

```
  … other code implementation
  canDeactivate(): Observable<boolean> | Promise<boolean> |
    boolean {
    const confirmation = window.confirm('Are you sure?');
    return confirmation;
  }
    … other code implementation


}
```

In the preceding code example, we have implemented the `FormComponent` with the `CanComponentDeactivate` interface that we have created; we have added a `window.confirm()`, which will pop up a dialog box that will ask if the user wants to leave the current route. This is a simple implementation of the guard, as we can also add other conditions, such as if we only want to ask this question if there are changes in the form.

The last step is to apply the guard in the `FormComponent` route.

Let's have a look at the following code:

```
const routes: Routes = [
  … other routes
  {
    path: "form",
    children: [
      {
        path: "",
        canDeactivate: [FormGuard],
        component: FormComponent
      },
      {
        path: ":id",
        canDeactivate: [FormGuard],
        component: FormComponent
      }
    ]
  },
];
```

Once we have applied the `CanDeactivate` guard, navigating out from the anti-hero form will pop up a dialog box for the user, as shown in *Figure 14.3*.

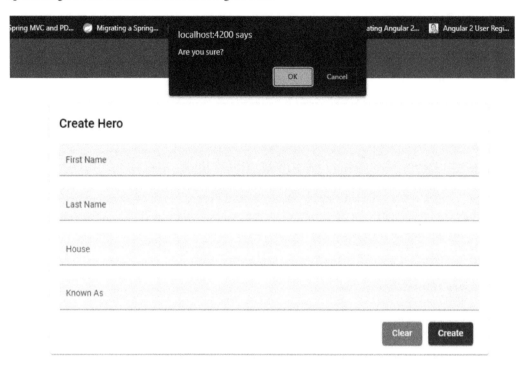

14.3 – Dialog box on navigating away from the form

We have now successfully applied guards in our Angular application; in the next section, we will directly improve our calling of API authentication with the use of NgRx state management.

Calling an API

We have already created user authentication in the previous section by calling the authentication service directly in our component. We have also stored the generated JWT in our local storage using the `setItem` function, which is also happening in our login component.

What we want to achieve is to reduce the responsibility of our components, and as we remember, we are using NgRx state management to call the APIs, and the only responsibility of our components is to dispatch the action, and NgRx will do the rest.

In this section, we will improve our API calls by using the building blocks of the NgRx state management.

Creating the actions

The first step we need is to create the actions for our authentication feature. We will create a file named auth.actions.ts in the auth/state folder, and we will have the following code:

```
import { createAction, props } from '@ngrx/store';

export enum AuthActions {
 LOGIN = '[AUTH] Login',
 SET_TOKEN = '[AUTH] Set Token',
 CREATE_USER = '[AUTH] Create User',
 AUTH_ERROR = '[AUTH] AUTH_ERROR',
}
export const setToken = createAction(
    AuthActions.SET_TOKEN,
    props<{ token: string }>(),
);
export const setError = createAction(
    AuthActions.AUTH_ERROR,
    props<{ error: any }>(),
);
```

In the preceding code, we can see that we have created four action types: the LOGIN type will be used for the effect responsible for calling the login API; the CREATE_USER type will be used for the effect accountable for calling the register API; the SET_TOKEN type will be used by a reducer that will set the generated JWT in the store after the login API has been reached; and lastly, the AUTH_ERROR type will be used to set errors in the store if the login or register API has returned an error.

Creating the effects

After creating our actions, now, we will create the effects for calling the login and register API. We will create a file named auth.effects.ts in the auth/state folder, and we will have the following implementation:

Login Effect

```
@Injectable()
  loginUser$ = createEffect(() => {
    return this.actions$.pipe(
        ofType(AuthActions.LOGIN),
```

```
            mergeMap(((data: {type: string, payload: User}) =>
              this.authService.login(data.payload)
              .pipe(
                map(data => ({ type: AuthActions.SET_TOKEN,
                                token: data.token })),
                tap(() =>
                  this.router.navigate(["anti-heroes"])),
                catchError(async (data) => ({ type:
                  AuthActions.AUTH_ERROR, error: data.error }))
            ))
          ))
        }, {dispatch: true}
```

Register Effect

```
    createUser$ = createEffect(() => {
      return this.actions$.pipe(
          ofType(AuthActions.CREATE_USER),
          mergeMap(((data: {type: string, payload: User}) =>
            this.authService.register(data.payload)
            .pipe(
              tap(() => this.router.navigate(["login"])),
              catchError(async (data) => ({ type:
                AuthActions.AUTH_ERROR, error: data.error }))
          ))
        ))
      }, {dispatch: true}
    );
```

In the preceding code, we have created effects for the login and register API. In the loginUser$ effect, once the login API is successful, it will dispatch the SET_TOKEN action and pass the generated JWT, and this will also redirect us to the anti-heroes page.

This is the same behavior we implemented in the previous section. On the other hand, the createUser$ effect, once the register API is successful, will redirect us to the login page again. This is a simple behavior, and you can customize what will happen next if the registration is successful.

We have also implemented the AUTH_ERROR action, which will be called when the login or register API fails.

Creating the reducers

The next step we need is to create the reducers. We will create a file named `auth.reducers.ts` in the `auth/state` folder, and we will have the following implementation:

```
export interface AuthState {
    token: string;
    error: any
}
export const initialState: AuthState = {
    token: "",
    error: null
}
export const authReducer = createReducer(
  initialState,
  on(setToken, (state, { token }) => { return {...state,
    token}}),
  on(setError, (state, { error }) => { return {...state,
    error}}),
  );
```

In the preceding code example, we can see that `AuthState` has two fields, which are `token` and `error`. The `token` field will contain the valid JWT once the `setToken` action is called when the authentication API is successful, and the `error` field will contain the generated error if the login or register API fails.

Creating the selectors

After creating the reducers, we will now create our selector. In this case, our selector will be simple as we only need a selector for the `error` field. We will create a file named `auth.selectors.ts` in the `auth/state` folder, and we will have the following implementation:

```
import { createSelector, createFeatureSelector } from '@ngrx/
store';
import { AppState } from 'src/app/state/app.state';
import { AuthState } from './auth.reducers';
export const selectAuthState =
createFeatureSelector<AuthState>('authState')
export const selectError = () => createSelector(
```

```
    selectAuthState,
    (state: AuthState) => state.error
)
```

In the preceding code example, we have created a selector for our `error` field; we will need this selector to display the error message in our component for the user.

Syncing in local storage

The next feature we will implement is the syncing of our state in local storage. We can achieve this by using `localStorage.setItem()` in our application. However, using this will not be maintainable, and the setting of values in the storage will be in different places.

To have a better implementation, we will use the `ngrx-store-localstorage` library. To install the library, we will execute the following command:

```
npm install ngrx-store-localstorage --save
```

After successfully installing the library, we should determine the states we want to sync with our local storage. In our case, we want the `token` field in our `auth` state to be synced. To achieve this, we make the following code changes in `auth.module.ts`:

```
import { localStorageSync } from 'ngrx-store-localstorage';
export function localStorageSyncReducer(reducer:
ActionReducer<any>): ActionReducer<any> {
  return localStorageSync({keys: ['token']})(reducer);
}
const metaReducers: Array<MetaReducer<any, any>> =
[localStorageSyncReducer];

@NgModule({
  declarations: [
   ... declared components
  ],
  imports: [
   ... other imported modules
    StoreModule.forFeature('authState', authReducer,
     {metaReducers}),
    EffectsModule.forFeature([AuthEffects]),
  ]
})
```

In the preceding code, we can see that we have created a dedicated reducer that calls the `localStorageSync` from the `ngrx-store-localstorage`, which is responsible for adding values in the local storage.

We can also specify what fields we want to sync and, in this case, we have added the token in the keys array. Once the token state changes its value, the new value will also be placed in our storage.

Dispatching and selecting a component

The last step is to dispatch the actions and use the selector for our login and register a component. Let's have a look at the following code implementation for the login and register a component:

login.component.ts

```
export class LoginComponent{
  error$ = this.store.select(selectError());
  errorSub: Subscription | undefined;

  constructor(private store: Store, private authService:
    AuthenticateService, private router: Router,
      private _snackBar: MatSnackBar) {
    this.checkJWT();
    this.getError();
  }
  submit(data: User) {
    this.store.dispatch({type: AuthActions.LOGIN,
                         payload: data})
  }
  ngOnDestroy(): void {
    this.errorSub?.unsubscribe();
  }
  getError() {
    this.error$.subscribe(data => {
      if(data) {
        this._snackBar.open(data.message, "Error");
      }
    })
```

```
    }
... other code implementation
}
```

register.component.ts

```
export class RegisterComponent implements OnInit, OnDestroy {
    error$ = this.store.select(selectError());
    errorSub: Subscription | undefined;
    constructor(private store: Store,  private _snackBar:
                MatSnackBar) {
        this.getError();
    }

    ngOnDestroy(): void {
        this.errorSub?.unsubscribe();
    }
    submit(data: User) {
        this.store.dispatch({type: AuthActions.CREATE_USER,
                             payload: data})
    }
    getError() {
        this.errorSub = this.error$.subscribe(data => {
            if(data) {
                this._snackBar.open(data.message, "Error");
            }
        })
    }
... other code implementation


}
```

We can see in the preceding code the login and register pages have almost the same implementation. We have already removed the call for the login and register service in the submit function and replaced it with the dispatching of an action. We have also used the selectError() selector to listen to see if the APIs have produced errors.

Summary

With this, we have reached the end of this chapter; let's have a recap of the valuable things you have learned.

We now know how to implement user authentication in the Angular application, and we have used an HTTP interceptor to intercept HTTP requests to transform its headers and add the valid JWT for the API calls. We have also learned about the different route guards that allow us to protect routes from unauthorized access or prevent accidental loss of data when navigating out from the route. Lastly, we have learned how to use NgRx state management by improving how to implement authentication in Angular.

The next chapter will teach us how to write end-to-end testing in Angular using the Cypress framework.

15

Writing Tests in Angular

In the previous chapter, we learned how to secure an Angular application by adding user authentication, retrieving user information, and protecting routes.

What if I told you that writing tests in the frontend could be fun and exciting? This chapter will show you how good the developer experience of Cypress E2E, short for end-to-end testing, is. Why do frontend developers love the Cypress framework?

This chapter will teach you how to write basic Cypress tests and mock HTTP requests for testing.

In this chapter, we will cover the following topics:

- Getting started with Cypress
- Writing a simple Cypress test
- Mocking HTTP responses and intercepting HTTP requests

Technical requirements

The following link will take you to the finished version of this chapter: `https://github.com/PacktPublishing/Spring-Boot-and-Angular/tree/main/Chapter-15/superheroes`.

Getting started with Cypress

In this section, you will learn what Cypress is and how to get started with it.

Cypress is an end-to-end agnostic framework for testing web applications. You can write test IDs in HTML tags and assert whether the HTML tags are rendered in the way you would expect them to be.

Let's define what **end-to-end** means. End-to-end means how a user will use your application after they land on your web application and finish tasks such as logging in, signing up, checking out, viewing a profile, logging out, filling out a form, and so on.

For instance, you can test or check the UI of your web application in different example cases or scenarios:

- The sentence of the landing page's value proposition contains the word *sale*

- The widget count of a section of your website is what you expected

- The items in the basket on the checkout page are cleared out after hitting the **Clear** button

- A login form is present when the web application's URL is `domain.com/login`

These scenarios are examples of what to test for in a web application. Cypress is a test framework where you can write and run tests that don't take much time to set up and configure.

Now, let's see how Cypress can be installed.

Installation

To start using Cypress, we must install it from the npm repository by running the following command:

```
npm i-D cypress @testing-library/cypress
```

The preceding npm command will install Cypress and the `cypress` testing library in the `dev` dependency packages. `@testing-library` is a group of common testing utilities in web development that makes the life of a developer easier

In the next section, we will learn what we must add to the npm script of our `package.json` file so that we can run the test later in this chapter.

npm script

To make it easier for us to run the Cypress test later, it's a good idea to add a new npm script to our `package.json` file to help us easily run a command. Insert the following key/value pair inside the `scripts` block of the `package.json` file:

```
"test": "npx cypress open"
```

The preceding key/value pair helps you run the test by running the `npm run test` command in your Terminal. Run the full stack application as well as the `npm run test` command in your Terminal to start Cypress.

An interactive browser app will open where you can run your test. *Figure 15.1* shows the Cypress dashboard with a welcome message after running the npm run test command. Here, we are going to use **E2E Testing**, so click that box to continue:

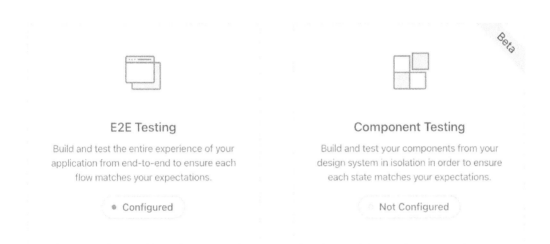

Welcome to Cypress!

Review the differences between each testing type →

E2E Testing

Build and test the entire experience of your application from end-to-end to ensure each flow matches your expectations.

● Configured

Component Testing

Build and test your components from your design system in isolation in order to ensure each state matches your expectations.

Not Configured

Figure 15.1 – The Cypress dashboard

Figure 15.2 shows the folders and files that will be automatically added to your Angular application directory. These are required for any web application that uses Cypress. We will add more to this because we are using TypeScript, but we will do that later. For now, just hit the **Continue** button; you will be taken to the following screen:

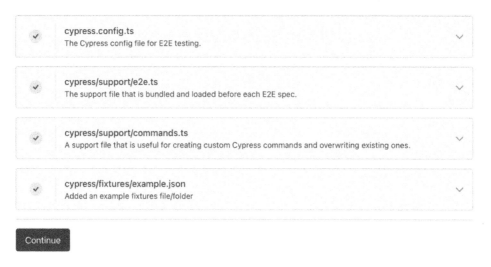

Figure 15.2 – Configuration Files

Figure 15.3 shows that you can choose different browsers to run your E2E tests. You can choose from Chrome, Microsoft Edge, and Firefox. We will stop here because we haven't written any tests yet, and we still need to help Cypress learn TypeScript. Stop Cypress from running by pressing *Ctrl + C* in your Terminal:

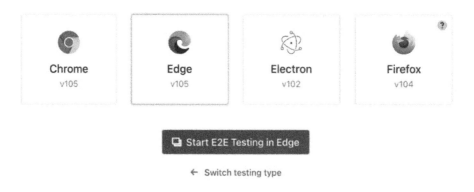

Figure 15.3 – Choose a Browser

Figure 15.4 shows the generated `cypress` folders, which contain additional folders inside them, and the `cypress.config.ts` file for editing some of Cypress's default behaviors. We will discuss the `cypress.config.ts` file later:

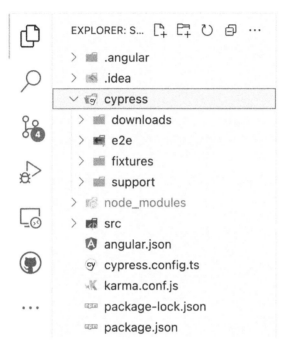

Figure 15.4 – Cypress folders and files

TypeScript for Cypress

To help Cypress understand TypeScript, we must add the `tsconfig.json` file to the root directory of the `cypress` folder. Create a new file and name it `tsconfig.json`; then, write the following configuration:

```
{
    "extends": "../tsconfig.json",
    "compilerOptions": {
        "types":["cypress", "@testing-library/cypress"],
        "isolatedModules": false,
        "allowJs": true,
        "experimentalDecorators": true,
```

```
        "skipLibCheck": true
    },
    "include": [
        "./**/*.ts",
    ],
    "exclude": []
}
```

The preceding code inherits the `tsconfig.json` file at the root of our Angular application. Then, we added `cypress` and `@testing-library/cypress` to the `tsconfig.json` file, which will help Cypress understand any TypeScript files in the Cypress directory. The array shows that we are including these TypeScript files in any level of the directory.

Now that we have set up Cypress for TypeScript, let's update the `cypress.config.ts` file in our Angular application.

Updating the Cypress config file

What is a Cypress config file? The `cypress.config.ts` file is used to store any configurations for things such as environments, timeouts, folders/files, screenshots, videos, downloads, browsers, viewports, and more that are specific to Cypress.

You are modifying the default behavior of Cypress by supplying any optional configurations you want to add. So, update the `cypress.config.ts` file with the following code:

```
import { defineConfig } from "cypress";

export default defineConfig({
  e2e: {
    setupNodeEvents(on, config) {
      // implement node event listeners here
    },
    baseUrl: "http://localhost:4200",
    video: false,
  },
});
```

The preceding code configures the base URL for Cypress where Angular runs. There is also a configuration for the video that disables the end-to-end testing recording. We are only using `baseUrl` and the video properties of the Cypress configuration.

In the next section, we will start writing some simple Cypress tests to help you gain confidence in writing tests and see how easy it is to write tests in Cypress.

Writing Cypress tests

In this section, we will start writing simple Cypress tests to see how fun and easy it is to write tests using Cypress. We will start the tests by adding a test attribute in an HTML tag in the authentication form. We are going to edit the `auth-form.component.html` file to write the `test-id` attribute. Here is what was changed in the `auth-form.component.html` line:

```
<mat-card-title data-cy="auth-title">{{title}}</mat-card-title>
```

You can see the attribute we added in the preceding code. `data-cy` is an attribute for the test ID that Cypress will use to target the HTML element we want to test.

Now that we've added our first test ID, let's go to the e2e folder inside the `cypress` directory and create a new file. The filename needs to contain *.cy*. Name the new file `anti-heroes.cy.ts` and then add the following code:

```
/// <reference types="cypress"/>

describe("Anti Heroes Page", () => {
  // basic test
  it("should display login page", () => {
    cy.visit("/");
    cy.url().should("include", "/login");
    cy.get("[data-cy=auth-title]").should("contain",
                                        "Login");
  });
});
```

The preceding code provides the first description of our test. First, we are adding a reference to the Cypress types to get extra tooling using TypeScript.

Then, we have the `describe` function, which is used for group tests. The `describe` function has two arguments. The first argument is a string, and it passes the name that the `describe` function will use. The second argument is a callback function that will contain all tests under the `describe` function.

The `it` function also accepts a string for the name of the test and a callback function for the details of the tests. The first `it` function tests whether an authenticated user can see the login page if the user visits the root domain of the Angular app's URL.

cy is an object where you can chain different types of commands. We are using the visit command, which allows us to write the URL we will use to navigate to localhost:4200 once we run the test. cy.url asserts that the URL can be found on the login subpage. We are also testing mat-card-title through the data-cy= "auth-title" attribute, which has the word *Login* in this test.

As you can see, the first test is easy to write. The setup for writing the test is also easy. But before we run our first test, let's create a user for our test:

Figure 15.5 – A user for E2E testing (Angular app login page)

In *Figure 15.5*, we are creating a user for our E2E testing. The user@cypress.com username is just a made-up email address you are not required to use. You can use whatever email address you want. We will use the user@cypress.com user to log into our app and use the web app like a real user would use our application.

Now, go to your Terminal and run the npm run test command to run Angular's E2E tests. Go to the **Specs** section of the Cypress dashboard to find the list of **E2E specs**:

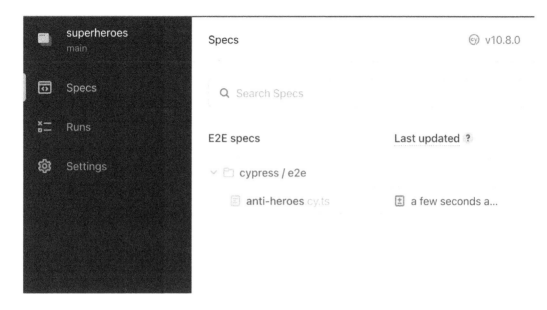

Figure 15.6 – E2E specs

Figure 15.6 shows the list of **E2E specs** files for testing. Here, there is a single spec file; this is the one we created earlier.

Click on the **anti-heroes** spec to run the test we created and see whether it is passing or failing:

Figure 15.7 – Passing test

Figure 15.7 shows that the two asserts we wrote in our test are passing. This means that the login subpage is where the unauthenticated user was directed after landing on the root domain page. The passing test also tells us that the title of the form the user saw was *Login* and not *Register*.

If you change should("contain", "Login"); to should("contain", "Register");, the test will fail, which is an indicator that the test is accurate and that it is not just passing anything we write in the test.

With that, we have finished writing a simple E2E test using Cypress and saw that our tests are passing. In the next section, we will mock HTTP responses and intercept HTTP requests that our Angular application sends so that we no longer need the backend application to run these tests.

Mocking HTTP responses and intercepting HTTP requests

Mocking tests can help us isolate and focus on tests and not on the state of external dependencies or behavior. In this section, we will mock the HTTP responses of our server and intercept the HTTP requests of our Angular application for testing. We are going to intercept the HTTP requests so that we can send fake responses to Angular and not pollute our dev database.

We will start by adding a new file to the root of the cypress directory. Name the file global.d.ts. The global.d.ts file, also known as **global libraries**, provides a way to make interfaces and types globally available in our TypeScript code.

After creating the global.d.ts file, write the following code inside it:

```
/// <reference types="cypress"/>

declare namespace Cypress {
    interface Chainable {
        getCommand(url: string, responseBody: Array<any>):
          Chainable<any>;
        deleteCommand(url: string): Chainable<any>;
        postCommand(url: string, requestBody: any):
          Chainable<any>;
    }
}
```

The preceding code allows us to use custom chainable commands, which will give us IntelliSense whenever we hit the dot after writing *cy*.

Now that we've added global.d.ts, let's install a library that can generate a unique universal ID, also known as a **UUID**, and use it as a temporary ID for a fake object we will create to respond to Angular's HTTP request.

The following npm command will install an npm library called uuid to help us generate the UUID we need:

```
npm i uuid
```

We also need the types for the uuid library we installed:

```
npm i -D @types/uuid
```

The preceding npm command will install the uuid TypeScript types.

Now, we need a file for the fixtures in our Cypress test. A **fixture** is the fixed state of an object or array that's used as a baseline for running tests:

1. Go to the fixtures folder inside the cypress directory in your application. Create two JSON files and name them anti-heroes.json and user.json.

2. Copy the content of the file from https://github.com/PacktPublishing/Spring-Boot-and-Angular/blob/main/Chapter-15/superheroes/cypress/fixtures/anti-heroes.json and paste it into the anti-heroes.json file.

3. Next, copy the content of the file from https://github.com/PacktPublishing/Spring-Boot-and-Angular/blob/main/Chapter-15/superheroes/cypress/fixtures/user.json and paste it into the user.json file.

    The preceding JSON objects are objects that we are going to use in our fixtures. We will use these as response bodies to send mock responses.

4. Now, let's update the commands.ts file in the support folder inside the cypress directory. Use the following code:

    ```
    // @ts-check
    ///<reference path="../global.d.ts" />
    /// <reference types="cypress"/>
    import { v4 as uuidv4 } from "uuid";
    Cypress.Commands.add("getCommand", (url: string,
    responseBody: Array<any>) => {
        cy.intercept("GET", url, {
            statusCode: 200,
            body: responseBody,
        });
    });
    ```

```
Cypress.Commands.add("deleteCommand", (url: string) => {
    cy.intercept("DELETE", url, {
        statusCode: 200,
    });
});
Cypress.Commands.add("postCommand", (url: string,
requestBody: any) => {
    requestBody.id = uuidv4();
    cy.intercept("POST", url, {
        statusCode: 201,
        body: requestBody,
    });
});
```

The preceding code implements the custom chainable commands we wrote inside the `global.d.ts` file. `getCommand`, `deleteCommand`, and `postCommand` require URLs as strings to intercept any HTTP requests. The custom chainable commands require a state, which will be a fixture.

5. Now, let's write more tests in `anti-heroes.cy.ts`. But first, we must add more test IDs for the tests we write.

    Go to `auth-form.component.html` and update the code with the following code:

```
<mat-card>
    <mat-card-title
      data-cy="auth-title">{{title}}</mat-card-title>
    <mat-card-content>
        <form [formGroup]="form"
          (ngSubmit)="submit()">
        <p *ngIf="error" class="error">
            {{ error }}
        </p>
        <p>
            <mat-form-field>
            <input type="text"
              matInput placeholder="Username"
              formControlName="email"
              data-cy="email">
            </mat-form-field>
```

```
        </p>
        <p>
            <mat-form-field>
            <input type="password"
              matInput placeholder="Password"
              formControlName="password"
              data-cy="password">
            </mat-form-field>
        </p>
        <div class="button">
            <button type="submit"
              mat-button data-cy="submit-login">
              {{title}}</button>
        </div>
        <p *ngIf="title == 'Login'" class="link"
          [routerLink]="['register']"
          routerLinkActive="router-link-active">
          Create account</p>
        <p *ngIf="title == 'Register'"
          class="link" [routerLink]="['']"
          routerLinkActive="router-link-active">
          Sign In</p>
        </form>
    </mat-card-content>
  </mat-card>
```

The preceding code contains four data-cy attributes that will be used as targeted selectors. You can find the data-cy selectors in the mat-card-title, inputs, and button elements.

6. The next file to update will be navbar.component.html. Use the following code to update the file:

```
<p>
  <mat-toolbar color="primary">
    <span data-cy="logo">Angular CRUD</span>
  </mat-toolbar>
</p>
```

The preceding code contains one data-cy attribute, which you can find in the span element.

7. Next, we need to update the `anti-hero-list-component.html` file:

```html
<table mat-table [dataSource]="antiHeroes" class="mat-
elevation-z8">
    <!-- Data for columns -->
    <ng-container *ngFor="let item of headers"
      [matColumnDef]="item.fieldName">
      <th mat-header-cell *matHeaderCellDef>
       {{item.headerName}} </th>
      <td mat-cell *matCellDef="let element"
        data-cy="row"> {{element[item.fieldName]}}
      </td>
    </ng-container>
    <!-- Actions for specific item -->
    <ng-container matColumnDef="actions">
        <th mat-header-cell *matHeaderCellDef>
          Actions </th>
        <td mat-cell *matCellDef="let element">
            <button (click)="selectAntiHero(element,
              0)" mat-raised-button color="primary"
              data-cy="view">
                <mat-icon>pageview</mat-icon> View
            </button>
             
            <button (click)="selectAntiHero(element,
              1)" mat-raised-button color="warn"
              data-cy="delete">
                <mat-icon>delete</mat-icon> Delete
            </button>
        </td>
    </ng-container>
    <tr mat-header-row
      *matHeaderRowDef="headerFields"></tr>
    <tr mat-row *matRowDef="let row;
      columns: headerFields"></tr>
</table>
```

The preceding code contains three `data-cy` attributes, which you can find in the `td` element, and two `button` elements.

8. Next, we must edit the `anti-hero-command-bar.component.html` file using the following code:

```
<p>
  <mat-toolbar>
    <button mat-raised-button color="primary"
      (click)="emitAction(0)"data-cy="create">
      <mat-icon>fiber_new</mat-icon> Create
    </button>
     
    <button mat-raised-button color="warn"
      (click)="emitAction(1)"data-cy="delete-all">
      <mat-icon>delete</mat-icon> Delete All
    </button>
    <button mat-button color="danger"
      (click)="logOut()" data-cy="logout">
      <mat-icon>logout</mat-icon> logout
    </button>
  </mat-toolbar>
</p>
```

The preceding code contains three selectors, which you can find in the `button` elements.

9. The last file to update is `anti-hero-form.component.html`:

```
<mat-card class="form-card">
  <h2>{{ selectedAntiHero ? "Update/View Hero" :
    "Create Hero" }}</h2>
  <form class="anti-hero-form" [formGroup]="form">
    <mat-form-field class="example-full-width"
      appearance="fill"><mat-label>
      First Name</mat-label>
      <input matInput formControlName="firstName"
        placeholder="Ex. Tony" data-cy="firstName"/>
    </mat-form-field><mat-form-field
      class="example-full-width" appearance="fill">
      <mat-label>Last Name</mat-label>
```

```
        <input matInput formControlName="lastName"
          placeholder="Ex. Stark" data-cy="lastName"/>
      </mat-form-field>
      <mat-form-field class="example-full-width"
        appearance="fill"><mat-label>House</mat-label>
        <input matInput formControlName="house"
          placeholder="Ex. California" data-cy="house"/>
          </mat-form-field><mat-form-field
          class="example-full-width" appearance="fill">
          <mat-label>Known As</mat-label>
        <input matInput formControlName="knownAs"
          placeholder="Ex. Iron Man" data-cy="knownAs"
          /></mat-form-field><div class="button-group">
        <button mat-raised-button color="primary"
          (click)="emitAction()" data-cy="action"
        >{{ actionButtonLabel }}</button>
         
        <button mat-raised-button color="warn"
          (click)="clear()">Clear</button>
      </div>
    </form>
  </mat-card>
```

The preceding code contains five inputs, which you can find in the input elements and the button element.

With that, we have added the necessary test ID attributes to the HTML elements we are going to test later. We will need the mentioned data-cy test IDs when we start writing tests in the anti-heroes.cy.ts file.

10. Now, let's start writing tests in anti-heroes.cy.ts. Here is the new code:

```
/// <reference types="cypress"/>
describe("Login Page", () => {
  beforeEach(() => {
    cy.fixture("anti-heroes").then(function (data) {
      /* register custom commands. */
      cy.getCommand("/api/v1/anti-heroes", data);
      cy.deleteCommand("/api/v1/anti-heroes/*");
```

```
  });
  cy.visit("/");
  cy.fixture("user").then((data: { email: string;
    password: string }) => {
    cy.get("[data-cy=email]").type(data.email);
    cy.get("[data-cy=password]")
      .type(data.password);
    cy.get("[data-cy=submit-login]").click();
  });
});
afterEach(() => {
  cy.get("[data-cy=logout]").click();
});
it.skip("should display login page", () => {
  cy.visit("/");
  cy.url().should("include", "/login");
  cy.get("[data-cy=auth-title]").should("contain",
    "Login");
});
});
```

The preceding code shows a describe function that has two other functions inside it.

The first function inside the describe function is called beforeEach, which runs each time a test starts running. The beforeEach function keeps its state and uses it in the test. This function fits scenarios where the test has to do precisely the same thing that other tests will also have to do – for instance, going to a particular URL, logging in, and intercepting HTTP calls using custom chainable commands such as getCommand and deleteCommand.

The second function inside the describe function is called afterEach. The afterEach function runs every time a test ends. This function is suitable for cleaning up or logging out the user in the test. The beforeEach and afterEach functions save us a lot of repeatable code.

11. Now, let's add some tests to the anti-heroes.cy.ts file. Copy the following code and put it under the first test we wrote:

```
it("should display logo", () => { cy.get("[data-
cy=logo]")
.should("contain", "Angular CRUD");
});
it("should render anti-heroes", () => {
```

```
  cy.fixture("anti-heroes").then(function (data) {
    cy.get("[data-cy=row]").should("have.length", 24);
  });
});
it("should remove a card after clicking a delete button",
() => { const index = 1;
  cy.get("[data-cy=delete]").eq(index).click();
  cy.get("[data-cy=row]").should("have.length", 20);
});
it("should add a new hero", () => { const firstName =
"Bucky";
  const lastName = "Barnes";
  const house = "Marvel";
  const knownAs = "The Winter Soldier";
  cy.get("[data-cy=create]").click();
  cy.get("[data-cy=firstName]").type(firstName);
  cy.get("[data-cy=lastName]").type(lastName);
  cy.get("[data-cy=house]").type(house);
  cy.get("[data-cy=knownAs]").type(knownAs);
  cy.postCommand("/api/v1/anti-heroes", {
    firstName,lastName,house,knownAs,});
  cy.get("[data-cy=action]").click();
  cy.fixture("anti-heroes").then(function (data) {
    cy.get("[data-cy=row]").should("have.length", 24);
  });
});
```

The preceding code shows the tests we are going to use for Cypress. You can see that fixture needs a string, which is the name of the JSON file. The data from fixture is the parameter of the anonymous function.

We are asserting 24 because there are four elements for every object we use in data-cy=" row", which is how we built the HTML elements on the user interface. There are also six objects inside the array of the anti-heroes.json file.

The newly added tests show how we can pick a particular object from a list or array of rendered UIs using the eq keyword and an index number.

The newly added tests also show how to write text into an input field by calling the click and type functions. Then, you can use the postCommand custom chainable command to intercept HTTP POST requests.

12. Lastly, before running the test, make Cypress skip the simple test we wrote earlier by calling `skip`, like so:

```
it.skip("should display login page", () => {
```

The preceding code changed the simple test from *run* to *don't run*.

The entire code for the `anti-heroes.cy.ts` spec file can be found at `https://github.com/PacktPublishing/Spring-Boot-and-Angular/blob/main/Chapter-15/superheroes/cypress/e2e/anti-heroes.cy.ts`.

Now, we can run the `anti-heroes.cs.ts` spec file to see whether everything will pass, as shown in the following figure:

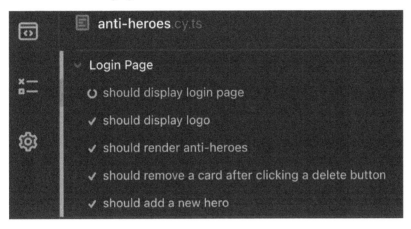

Figure 15.8 – Passing tests

Figure 15.8 shows that the **should display login page** test was skipped, while the rest of the tests passed.

You can see what is happening inside the `beforeEach` function, like so:

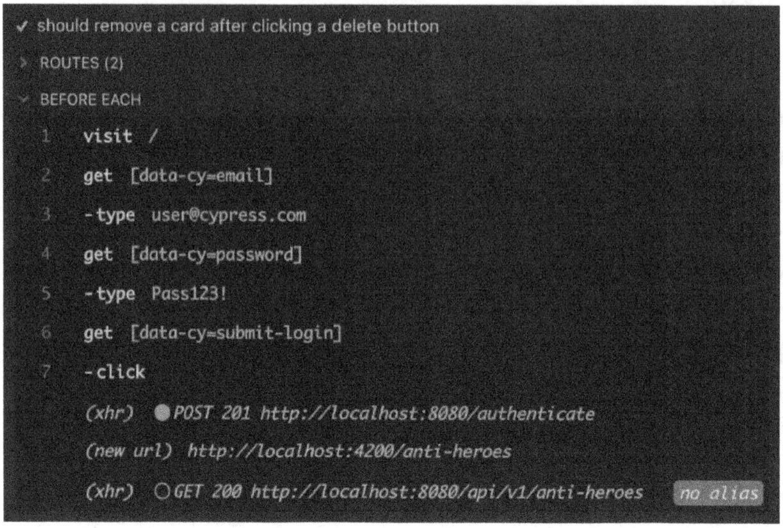

Figure 15.9 – BEFORE EACH DOM snapshot

Figure 15.9 shows the steps that were taken by the `beforeEach` function. The steps are DOM snapshots of the web application.

Let's also check the test body of the `anti-heroes.cy.ts` spec file. You should see the following information:

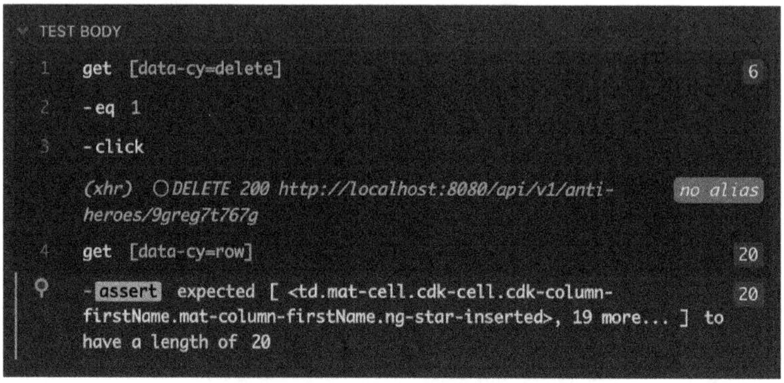

Figure 15.10 – TEST BODY DOM snapshot

Figure 15.10 shows the steps that were taken in the test body. These are the actions that you wrote in the `anti-heroes.cy.ts` file.

We can also see what happened inside the `afterEach` function. You should be able to see the following output:

```
AFTER EACH
1    get [data-cy=logout]
2    - click
     (new url) http://localhost:4200/login
```

Figure 15.11 – AFTER EACH DOM snapshot

Figure 15.11 shows the steps inside the `afterEach` function. Here, you can see that the `afterEach` function logged out and redirected the user to the application's login page.

And that's how you write Cypress tests. Now, let's summarize what was covered in this chapter.

Summary

With this, you have arrived at the end of this chapter. First, you learned what Cypress is and how easy it is to set up and write an end-to-end test. You also learned how to intercept HTTP requests and mock HTTP responses.

In the next chapter, you will learn how to package both frontend and backend applications into a single executable JAR file.

Part 4: Deployment

This part demonstrates the modern way of shipping backend and frontend applications. The following chapters are covered in this part:

16

Packaging Backend and Frontend with Maven

In the previous chapter, we learned what Cypress is and its benefits. We also learned how to write Cypress end-to-end tests and how to run them. Finally, we learned how to intercept HTTP requests to mock responses.

This chapter will teach you how to combine your Angular and Spring Boot applications and then run them on your local machine.

In this chapter, we will cover the following topics:

- What is frontend-maven-plugin?
- Adding configurations to Spring Boot and Angular's integration
- Packaging Spring Boot
- Running the JAR file

Technical requirements

The following link will take you to the finished version of code for this chapter: `https://github.com/PacktPublishing/Spring-Boot-and-Angular/tree/main/Chapter-16/superheroes`.

What is frontend-maven-plugin?

Okay – before I answer the question of what `frontend-maven-plugin` is, let's see how we can package our application. We can build Spring Boot to generate a JAR file and create a production build of Angular as well.

But what if we can create a JAR file for Spring Boot that will also contain the production build of Angular inside it? The approach of putting the frontend and the backend in a single JAR file will provide us with an easier way to deploy the application to test and production environments.

It will allow us to manage a single path for the API and the frontend application. To do this, we will require a Maven plugin called `frontend-maven-plugin` (`https://github.com/eirslett/frontend-maven-plugin`), which will help us create a JAR file that contains both our backend and frontend.

Some requirements ensure that our backend and frontend will work together. In the next section, we'll find out what configurations we need in our backend and frontend.

Adding configurations to Spring Boot and Angular's integration

In this section, we will write some configurations in the Spring Boot application and the Angular application to ensure that Spring Boot will run in production and that Angular will render the web application's user interface.

First, let's move the Angular app to the directory of our Spring Boot application.

Adding the Angular app to the Spring Boot project

In this section, we will move the Angular app to the Spring Boot project. By doing this, there will be an Angular project inside the Spring Boot project.

To start, create a new folder named `frontend` inside the Spring Boot project. Move all the files and folders of the Angular application inside the `frontend` folder, like so:

Figure 16.1 – The frontend folder inside the Spring Boot project

Figure 16.1 shows all the Angular files and folders inside the `frontend` folder, which is inside the Spring Boot project.

You can name the `frontend` folder whatever you want, so long as you map the path of the `frontend` folder to the `workingDirectory` property of **Frontend Mavin Plugin** and the `fileset` property of **Apache Maven AntRun Plugin**, which allows you to run Ant tasks from within Maven.

Let's use the two Maven plugins, `frontend-maven-plugin` and `maven-antrun-plugin`, which we need in the next section.

Using frontend-maven-plugin

In this section, we will use frontend-maven-plugin, which will install npm and Node.js locally. It will also run the npm build command in the frontend folder and copy the build files that npm build has generated.

So, let's start:

1. Go to your pom.xml file and insert the following code as one of the build plugins in your Maven pom file:

```
<plugin>
    <groupId>com.github.eirslett</groupId>
    <artifactId>frontend-maven-plugin</artifactId>
    <version>1.12.1</version>
    <configuration>
        <workingDirectory>frontend</workingDirectory>
        <installDirectory>target</installDirectory>
    </configuration>
    ...
    // See full code on https://github.com/PacktPublishing/
    Spring-Boot-and-Angular/tree/main/Chapter-16/superheroes
    <plugin>
```

The preceding markup shows that, while building the Spring Boot application, the plugin will install Node.js v16.17.0 and npm CLI 8.19.1 in the frontend working directory. It will also execute the npm install command to download all dependency packages of the Angular application.

After performing all the necessary installations, the next thing that the plugin will execute is the npm run build command, which will create a production build of the Angular application.

2. Next, we must edit the npm build script in the package.json file of the Angular application using the following code:

```
"build": "ng build --configuration production",
```

The preceding code tells Angular that npm run build is for a production build.

3. We also have to edit the `environment.prod.ts` file inside the environment folder of Angular. Change the code to this:

```
export const environment = {
  production: true,
  apiURL: "http://localhost:8080/api/v1",
  authURL: "http://localhost:8080"
};
```

apiURL and authURL are just temporary. We will change them and use the real API URL and Auth URL properties in the real deployment of the application. We need to add the preceding code because we are using apiURL and authURL in our app for development, but we are missing the values for the production environment.

When the app builds for the production environment, the Angular app will collect the values from environment.prod.ts instead of using the environment.ts file.

Now, let's learn about maven-antrun-plugin and configure our .pom file again.

Using maven-antrun-plugin

This section will use maven-antrun-plugin in the Spring Boot application. Open up your pom. xml file and insert the following code into one of the plugins in the build block of the markup. Put it below the markup of frontend-maven-plugin:

```
<plugin>
    <artifactId>maven-antrun-plugin</artifactId>
    <executions>
        <execution>
            <phase>generate-resources</phase>
            <configuration>
                <target>
                    <copy todir="${
                        project.build.directory}/classes/public">
                        <fileset dir="${project.basedir}/
                            frontend/dist/superheroes"/>
                    </copy>
                </target>
            </configuration>
            <goals>
                <goal>run</goal>
```

```
                </goals>
            </execution>
        </executions>
    </plugin>
```

Here, `maven-antrum-plugin` is a configuration that copies the files and folders of the `"${project.basedir}/frontend/dist/superheroes"` path and pastes them into the `todir="${project.build.directory}/classes/public"` path before running the task. This will copy the frontend app and put it in the root folder of the JAR file of Spring Boot.

Now, let's configure the Spring MVC configuration of our app.

Implementing WebMvcConfigurer

In this section, we will make the Spring Boot application a host for the Angular application by adding a configuration file. To do this, we must add a configuration class to the config directory of our Spring Boot application and name it `MvcConfig`.

After creating the `MvcConfig` class, add the `WebMvcConfigurer` interface to the file, like so:

```
@Configuration
public class MvcConfig implements WebMvcConfigurer {
    @Override
    public void addResourceHandlers(ResourceHandlerRegistry
      registry) {
… //See full code on https://github.com/PacktPublishing/Spring-
Boot-and-Angular/tree/main/Chapter-16/superheroes


    }
}
```

The preceding code can also be found in the GitHub repository for this chapter.

The `MvcConfig` class implements `WebMvcConfigurer` and overrides the `addResourceHandlers` method.

Pass the `"/**"` argument into `addResourceHandler`, like so:

```
addResourceHandler("/**")
```

This will make the configuration affect all project routes. This part belongs to the external-facing URI of the application.

Then, map the external-facing URI path to the directory where the resources are located, like so:

```
addResourceLocations("classpath:/public/")
```

Finally, add `new ClassPathResource("/public/index.html")`. This redirects requests that are not handled by the Spring Boot application that are going to the Angular application or the frontend application.

We are close to packaging both applications into one. We'll learn how to do this in the next section.

Packaging Spring Boot

In this section, we will package the Spring Boot application and the Angular application. The idea is to combine the two applications, giving you one single JAR file to deploy. Let's learn how to do this.

After all the configurations we did, now, it's a matter of running the following Maven commands in the same order:

```
mvn clean
mvn package
```

The `mvn clean` command cleans the Maven project by deleting the target directory, whereas the `mvn package` command builds the Maven project and creates an executable JAR file.

These two Maven commands are enough to create an executable JAR file with the Spring Boot and Angular packages inside it; see *Figure 16.2*:

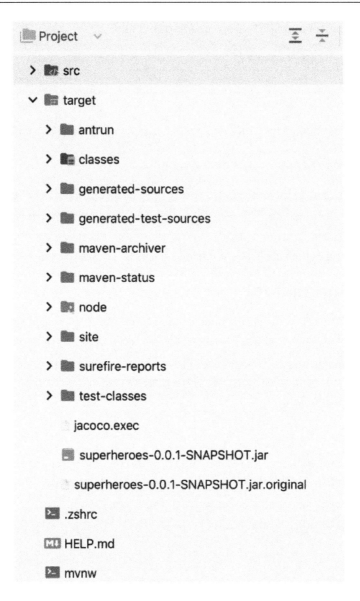

Figure 16.2 – Target folder with the JAR file inside

Packaging the applications is simple since we already did all the hard work configuring the Angular and Spring Boot applications.

Now, we have the JAR file. In the next section, we will run the JAR file using a Java command to see if everything is fine.

Running the JAR file

In this section, we will run the JAR file we have packaged and see that the Angular application communicates with the Spring Boot application. Follow these steps:

1. To run the application, you can either use the **Run** button via IntelliJ IDEA or use the following `java` command:

    ```
    java -jar superheroes-0.0.1-SNAPSHOT.jar
    ```

    The preceding Java CLI command will run an executable JAR file. In the CLI, you will see that the Tomcat web server has started on port `8080`.

2. Go to `http://localhost:8080`; you will be redirected to `http://localhost:8080/login`, which consists of a login form. *Figure 16.3* shows this login form:

Login

Username

Password

Login

Create account

Figure 16.3 – Login form

3. Try to log in and navigate to the anti-heroes page, where you can create new heroes or villains using the form:

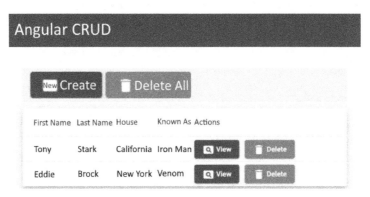

Figure 16.4 – Anti-heroes form

Figure 16.4 shows that everything is working on the anti-heroes form, from signing in to using CRUD operations.

With that, we have finished packaging the Spring Boot and Angular applications. Now, let's summarize what we have learned.

Summary

In this chapter, you learned that the `frontend-maven-plugin` and `antrun-maven-plugin` plugins can help you package your web client and Spring Boot application as one executable JAR file to make the deployment easy. You also learned how to run a JAR file on your local machine that helps you prepare your application for deployment.

In the next chapter, you will learn how to use GitHub Actions to prepare the applications for deployment. You will also learn how to use Heroku to create an instance of the database for the application and then deploy the application to Heroku.

17

Deploying Spring Boot and the Angular App

In the previous chapter, we learned what `frontend-maven-plugin` does and what we use it for. Then, we learned what configuration to write to run the Angular application within the Spring Boot application. After that, we learned how to package the two applications as one file. Lastly, we learned how to run the Spring Boot application with Angular.

This chapter will teach you the basics of GitHub Actions, the basics of Heroku, and how to deploy the app using Heroku.

In this chapter, we will cover the following topics:

- Understanding GitHub Actions
- Components of GitHub Actions
- Setting up Heroku
- Creating a CI workflow or pipeline

Technical requirements

The following link will take you to the finished version of this chapter: `https://github.com/PacktPublishing/Spring-Boot-and-Angular/tree/main/Chapter-17/superheroes`.

Understanding GitHub Actions

Let's start by defining **GitHub Actions**. This platform provides workflow automation for developers and operations for **continuous integration and continuous delivery (CI/CD)**. It can run a series of actions using scripts whenever someone creates a pull request, creates an issue, joins as a contributor, merges a pull request, and so on. In short, there are several events in your GitHub workflow that you can use to run a set of specific actions or scripts.

Now, let's review some of the components of GitHub Actions.

Components of GitHub Actions

Now that we've learned what GitHub Actions is, let's see the components of GitHub Actions that help us do DevOps and run workflows when events get triggered.

Here are the components of GitHub Actions:

- **Workflows**: This is a configurable YAML file in a repository's directory, such as `.github/workflows`, that runs jobs manually, automatically triggers an event, or does so by setting a schedule.

- **Events**: Events are activities in a repository that cause your workflow to start running. Common events you might see in a workflow file are `pull_request`, `push`, and `schedule`. However, other events can be useful, depending on your needs.

- **Jobs**: A job is a set or group of steps (script or action) in a workflow. A particular job executes in the same runner throughout the steps.

- **Actions**: An action performs the task at hand or anything you need, such as checking out your repository, building your application, testing your application, scanning your code for any vulnerabilities, or deploying your application.

- **Runners**: Runners are just servers. You can choose Ubuntu Linux, Microsoft Windows, or macOS runners in GitHub Actions. However, you are not limited to these three operating systems. You can also have self-hosted runners.

These are the components of GitHub Actions that we will use later in the *Creating a CI workflow or pipeline* section. But before that, we will set up Heroku, where we will deploy our full-stack application.

Setting up Heroku

In this section, we will use Heroku. It is a **Platform-as-a-Service (PaaS)** offering that lets us build and run applications in the cloud. Let's learn how to set up Heroku and our applications.

Creating GitHub and Heroku accounts

In this section, we will create an account for GitHub and then Heroku.

First, we must create a GitHub account by going to `https://github.com/`. We will use this as the repository for our project.

Then, we must create a Heroku account by going to `https://www.heroku.com/`. This is where we will deploy our application and create an instance of our database.

Creating a new app in Heroku

After signing in to Heroku, click the **New** button at the top-right corner of the page and click the **Create new app** button to create an app without a pipeline:

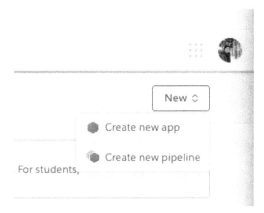

Figure 17.1 – Create new app

Figure 17.1 is where you create a new app for the full-stack application. Name the app anything you wish and choose a region, but don't add a pipeline.

Next, we will add a database for our full-stack application.

Adding a Postgres database

Now, let's add a Postgres database:

1. Go to the **Resources** tab and click the **Find more add-ons** button:

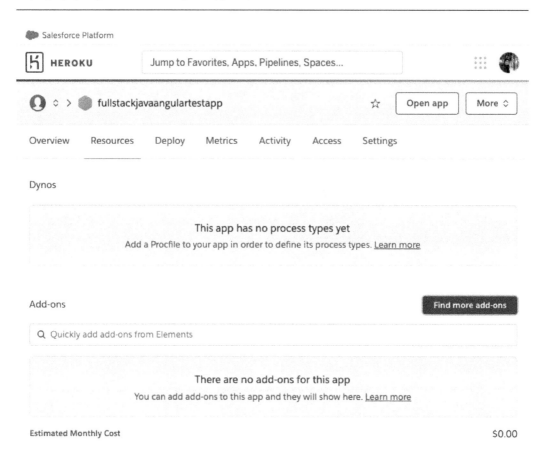

Figure 17.2 – Find more add-ons

Figure 17.2 shows where you can find the **Find more add-ons** button. This is where you can find Heroku add-ons and various tools and services for developing, extending, and operating your application. An example of this can be seen in *Figure 17.3*:

Figure 17.3 – Heroku Postgres

Figure 17.3 shows the Heroku Postgres add-on, which is a **Database-as-a-Service (DaaS)** offering based on PostgreSQL. Click it, install it, and then choose the free plan and provision the Heroku Postgres add-on to the full-stack application you created earlier. Then, click the **Submit Order Form** button.

2. Go back to the **Resources** tab of your app. You should see the Heroku Postgres add-on. Click the Heroku part of **Heroku Postgres**; a new tab will open.

    We have almost finished adding a database. We just need to add a Dataclip, which will let us create SQL queries for our database.

3. Go ahead and click the **Create Dataclip** button. Then, add the following SQL queries:

```
set transaction read write;


CREATE EXTENSION IF NOT EXISTS "uuid-ossp";


CREATE TABLE user_entity
(
    id   uuid PRIMARY KEY DEFAULT uuid_generate_v4(),
    username VARCHAR(50)  UNIQUE   NOT NULL,
    password VARCHAR(50)           NOT NULL,
    email    VARCHAR(255) UNIQUE NOT NULL
);


CREATE TABLE anti_hero_entity
(
    id   uuid PRIMARY KEY DEFAULT uuid_generate_v4(),
    firstName VARCHAR(50) UNIQUE NOT NULL,
    lastName  VARCHAR(50) UNIQUE NOT NULL,
    house     VARCHAR(50) NULL,
    knownAs   VARCHAR(50) NULL,
    createdAt TIMESTAMP NULL
);
```

4. Once you've added these SQL queries to the editor, click **Save & Run**.

With that, the database has been created. Now, let's create a `system.properties` file where we can declare the Java runtime version and Maven version.

Adding system properties

In this section, we will create a file that will specify a Java version and a Maven version using system.properties.

Go to the root directory of the Spring Boot application and create a file called system.properties. Then, add the following configurations:

```
java.runtime.version=17.0.1
maven.version=3.6.2
```

The preceding two configurations will be used in the deployment part of the full-stack application in Heroku.

In the next section, we will get the domain URL of our app and add it to the config variables.

Adding config variables

In this section, we are going to add config variables in Heroku. In our repository, we will add CLIENT_URL to Heroku's config vars section and the environment.prod.ts file for the frontend application. Follow these steps:

1. The first step is to get the application's domain name, which can be found by going to the **Settings** tab:

Figure 17.4 – Application URL

Figure 17.4 shows the application URL where the application will render.

2. Copy the URL of your full-stack application and go to the **Config Vars** area of the **Settings** tab. Click on the **Reveal Config Vars** button:

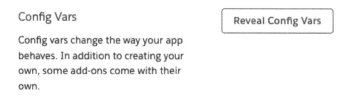

Figure 17.5 – Reveal Config Vars

3.   Add `CLIENT_URL` as a **Key** and add the URL of the application as a **Value**:

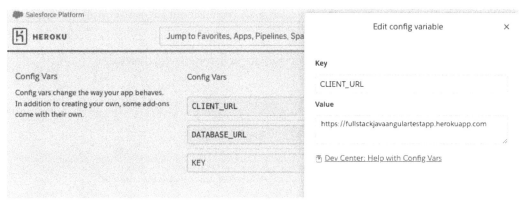

Figure 17.6 – Edit config variable

Figure 17.6 shows the form after adding environment variables or configuration variables.

Don't forget to add a value to your JWT secret. However, note that your development and production environments should differ.

4.   Now, open the `environment.prod.ts` file and add the following code:

```
export const environment = {
  production: true,
// your Spring API URL
  apiURL: "https://full stack
           javaangulartestapp.herokuapp.com/api/v1",
// your heroku URL
  authURL: "https://full stack
           javaangulartestapp.herokuapp.com"
};
```

The preceding code will replace the previous `localhost:8080` address of `apiURL` and `authURL` in the Angular application in production.

Next, we need to publish the full-stack application repository to GitHub since we will deploy the application through GitHub source control.

Manual deployment in Heroku

In this section, we are going to check if the application will run without any problems after we deploy it. Follow these steps:

1. To do that, go to the **Deploy** tab of your application in the Heroku dashboard:

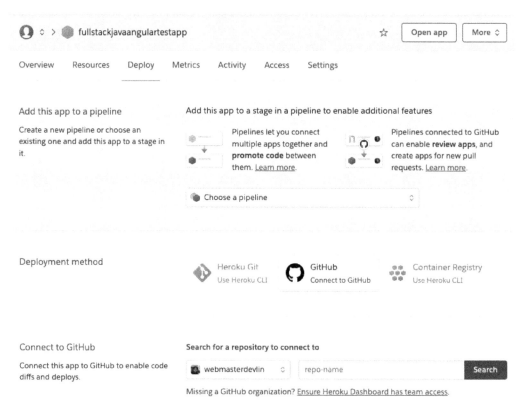

Figure 17.7 – Deploying the application

Figure 17.7 shows where to deploy an application via the Heroku dashboard manually. Use GitHub as the deployment method, then search your repository.

2. After choosing the repository of your full-stack application, go to the bottom of the page, where you will find the **Manual deploy** section. Then, press the **Deploy Branch** button to start deploying and running the application in Heroku:

Figure 17.8 – Manual deploy

Figure 17.8 shows the **Manual deploy** section of Heroku.

3. To check if everything is working, wait for the deployment to finish and then go to the URL of the application.

4. Register a new user and try to sign in. Make sure you open the **Network** tab of your browser; you will see that the requests are being sent via the application's URL. Note that the responses from the server have a **Status Code** of **200** or **201**:

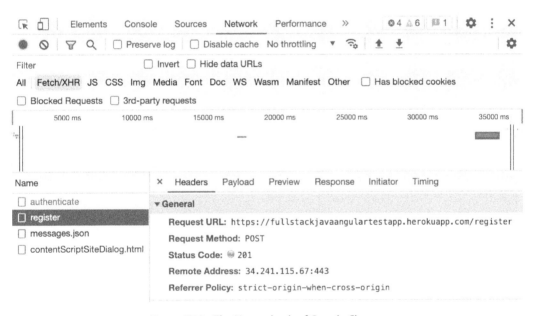

Figure 17.9 – The Network tab of Google Chrome

Figure 17.9 shows Google Chrome's **Network** tab in developer tools. Here, you can see that the **register** request returns **Status Code 201**. The Angular, Spring Boot, and Heroku Postgres database works perfectly.

Now that we've finished manually deploying our full-stack application, let's create an automated deployment using workflow in GitHub Actions.

Creating a CI workflow or pipeline

In this section, we will automate the deployment of our full-stack application by using a workflow in GitHub Actions. Follow these steps:

1. Go to the GitHub repository of your project, then click on the **Actions** tab. Search for `Publish Java Package` and pick the Maven workflow:

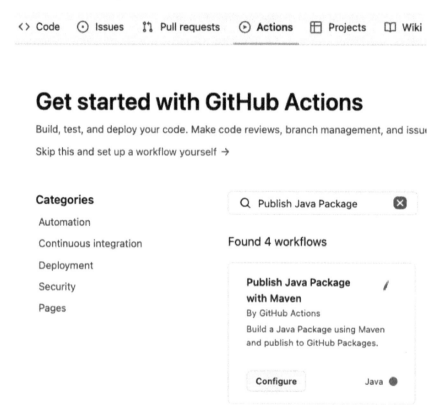

Figure 17.10 – Selecting a workflow

Figure 17.10 shows the basic and ready-made Maven workflow for building Maven projects.

2. Change the content of the YAML file in the editor by replacing it with the following YAML configuration:

```
name: CICD

on:
  push:
```

```
        branches:
          - master

    jobs:
      test:
        name: Build and Test
        runs-on: ubuntu-latest
        steps:
          - uses: actions/checkout@v2
          - name: Set up JDK 17
            uses: actions/setup-java@v2
            with:
              java-version: '17.0.*'
              distribution: 'temurin'
              cache: maven
          - name: test with Maven
            run: mvn test

      deploy:
        name: Deploy to Heroku
        runs-on: ubuntu-latest
        needs: test
        steps:
          - uses: actions/checkout@v2
            # This is the action
          - uses: akhileshns/heroku-deploy@v3.12.12
            with:
              heroku_api_key: ${{secrets.HEROKU_API_KEY}}
              heroku_app_name: "appname" #Must be unique
                                         #in Heroku
              heroku_email: "email"
```

The preceding code is the workflow for our full-stack application's CI/CD. It's called `CICD` because that's what this workflow is for.

The workflow has one event, `push`, which will cause the workflow to run if there's a push in the master branch.

The workflow also has two jobs: `test` and `deploy`. The `test` job's steps are to check out the code, build the application using Java 17, and run the test. On the other hand, the `deploy` job's steps are to check out the code and use the Heroku deploy action, which requires a Heroku API key, the application's name, and the Heroku account's email.

3. For the Heroku API key, you need to go to the **Account settings** menu of your profile on your Heroku dashboard:

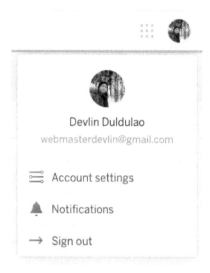

Figure 17.11 – Account settings

Figure 17.11 shows the **Account settings** menu under my profile on the Heroku dashboard.

4. Click **Account settings**, then go to **API Key** and generate an API key:

Figure 17.12 – API Key

Figure 17.12 shows where you can generate a Heroku API key.

Copy the Heroku API key since you will need to create a new Actions secret for GitHub Actions.

5. To do so, go to the GitHub repository of your application and open a new browser tab for the **Settings** tab so that you don't lose your workflow configuration.

6. Then, add the API key in the text area and name it HEROKU_API_KEY. This is the key you will be using in the deploy job of your workflow:

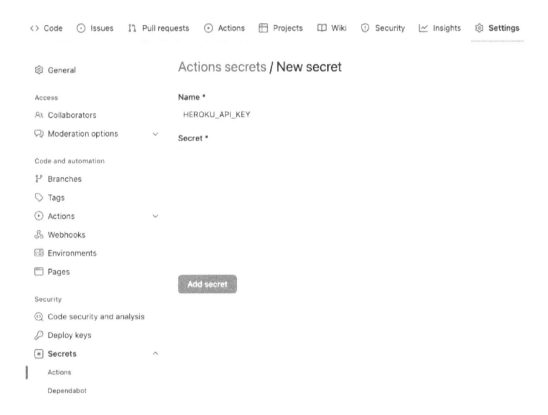

Figure 17.13 – The Actions secrets form

Figure 17.13 shows where you can add a new Actions secret to keep your sensitive values from being copied or read by anyone.

7. Once you've added a new secret, go back to your browser tab, where you start editing your workflow. Then, commit the file that you are editing:

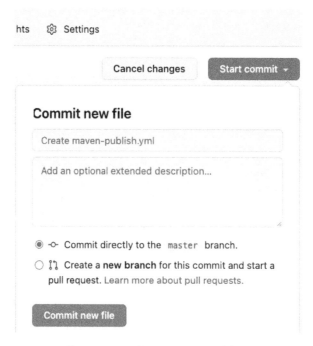

Figure 17.14 – Committing a workflow

Figure 17.14 shows the **Start commit** dropdown, where you can commit the new workflow. The new YAML file will be added to your repository, which means you can `git pull` it later so that it will be on your local machine.

8. CICD will kick in after you commit to your workflow. You can look at the progress of your CI/CD workflow by going to the **Actions** tab:

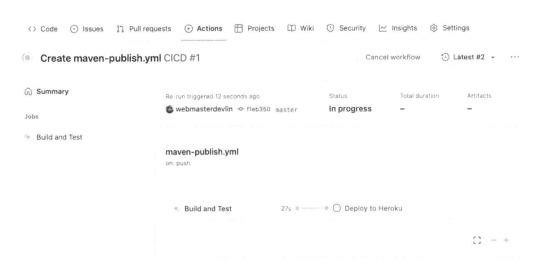

Figure 17.15 – Workflow status

Figure 17.15 shows the current status of the CI/CD workflow. You can see that it is running the **Build and Test** job.

9. You can also see what's happening in a particular job by clicking the name of the job via the left sidebar menu:

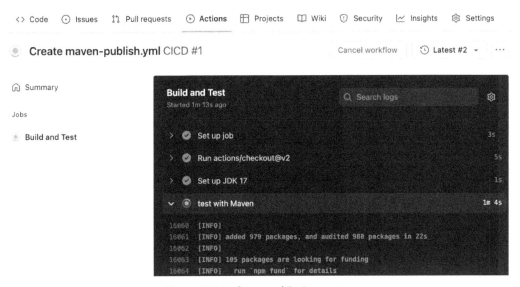

Figure 17.16 – Steps and Actions status

Figure 17.16 shows the output logs from each step in the **Build and Test** job. You can also use this part of GitHub Actions to debug errors that lead to the jobs and actions failing.

10. After running all the jobs in the CI/CD workflow you have created, you will see that the workflow has a green check icon next to it, meaning that the workflow has passed and everything is working:

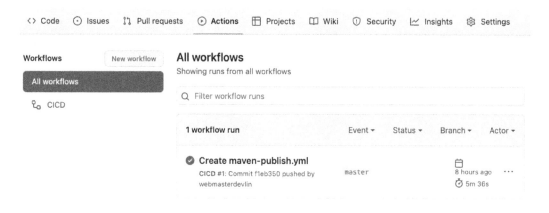

Figure 17.17 – Steps and Actions status

Figure 17.17 shows a passing GitHub workflow on the **Actions** tab of your repository.

11. Lastly, to check if the deployment automation has deployed our application in the Heroku cloud, we have to go back to the overview dashboard of Heroku and look for the latest activity:

Latest activity

webmasterdevlin@gmail.com: Deployed f1eb3508
Today at 8:33 AM · v11 · Compare diff

webmasterdevlin@gmail.com: Build succeeded
Today at 8:31 AM · View build log

Figure 17.18 – Build succeeded in the Latest activity area of an account in Heroku

Figure 17.18 shows that the build triggered by GitHub Actions succeeded. You can see that the application is running correctly.

With that, we have managed to automate our CI/CD workflow using GitHub Actions. Now, let's summarize what we have learned in this chapter.

Summary

With that, we have reached the last chapter of this book; let's recap the valuable things you have learned in this chapter.

First, you learned that GitHub Actions makes it easy to automate all your software workflows and perform CI/CD. You can build, test, and deploy your code right from GitHub. You also learned that Heroku is a PaaS that lets you build, run, and operate applications entirely in the cloud. Heroku Postgres is a managed SQL database service provided directly by Heroku that you can use for your applications.

So, you've made it this far. Thank you for finishing the book; I am proud of you and your enthusiasm for learning new tools and things. You can apply what you have learned here to a project, given that the requirements of your project match the problems and solutions you have learned about in this book.

This course has taught you how to build a Spring Boot 2 application and an Angular 13 application as a senior developer, bringing value to your companies, customers, and clients.

As a next step, my recommendation is that you get a new Packt book about standalone Spring Boot 2 or Spring Boot 3, or an Angular book to solidify what you have learned from this book.

On behalf of the Packt team and editors, we wish you all the best in all stages of your career and life.

Index

Other Books You May Enjoy

If you enjoyed this book, you may be interested in these other books by Packt:

Modern API Development with Spring and Spring Boot

Sourabh Sharma

ISBN: 978-1-80056-247-9

- Understand RESTful API development, its design paradigm, and its best practices
- Become well versed in Spring's core components for implementing RESTful web services
- Implement reactive APIs and explore async API development
- Apply Spring Security for authentication using JWT and authorization of requests
- Develop a React-based UI to consume APIs
- Implement gRPC inter-service communication
- Design GraphQL-based APIs by understanding workflows and tooling
- Gain insights into how you can secure, test, monitor, and deploy your APIs

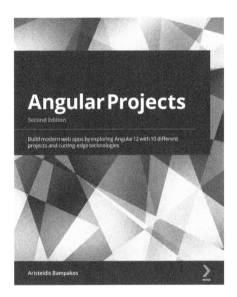

Angular Projects.– Second Edition

Aristeidis Bampakos

ISBN: 978-1-80020-526-0

- Set up Angular applications using Angular CLI and Nx Console
- Create a personal blog with Jamstack and SPA techniques
- Build desktop applications with Angular and Electron
- Enhance user experience (UX) in offline mode with PWA techniques
- Make web pages SEO-friendly with server-side rendering
- Create a monorepo application using Nx tools and NgRx for state management
- Focus on mobile application development using Ionic
- Develop custom schematics by extending Angular CLI

Packt is searching for authors like you

If you're interested in becoming an author for Packt, please visit authors.packtpub.com and apply today. We have worked with thousands of developers and tech professionals, just like you, to help them share their insight with the global tech community. You can make a general application, apply for a specific hot topic that we are recruiting an author for, or submit your own idea.

Share Your Thoughts

Now you've finished *Spring Boot and Angular*, we'd love to hear your thoughts! Scan the QR code below to go straight to the Amazon review page for this book and share your feedback or leave a review on the site that you purchased it from.

https://www.amazon.in/review/create-review/?asin=180324321X

Your review is important to us and the tech community and will help us make sure we're delivering excellent quality content.

Download a free PDF copy of this book

Thanks for purchasing this book!

Do you like to read on the go but are unable to carry your print books everywhere?

Is your eBook purchase not compatible with the device of your choice?

Don't worry, now with every Packt book you get a DRM-free PDF version of that book at no cost.

Read anywhere, any place, on any device. Search, copy, and paste code from your favorite technical books directly into your application.

The perks don't stop there, you can get exclusive access to discounts, newsletters, and great free content in your inbox daily

Follow these simple steps to get the benefits:

1. Scan the QR code or visit the link below

https://packt.link/free-ebook/9781803243214

2. Submit your proof of purchase
3. That's it! We'll send your free PDF and other benefits to your email directly